IMAGES
of America

SOUTH TACOMA

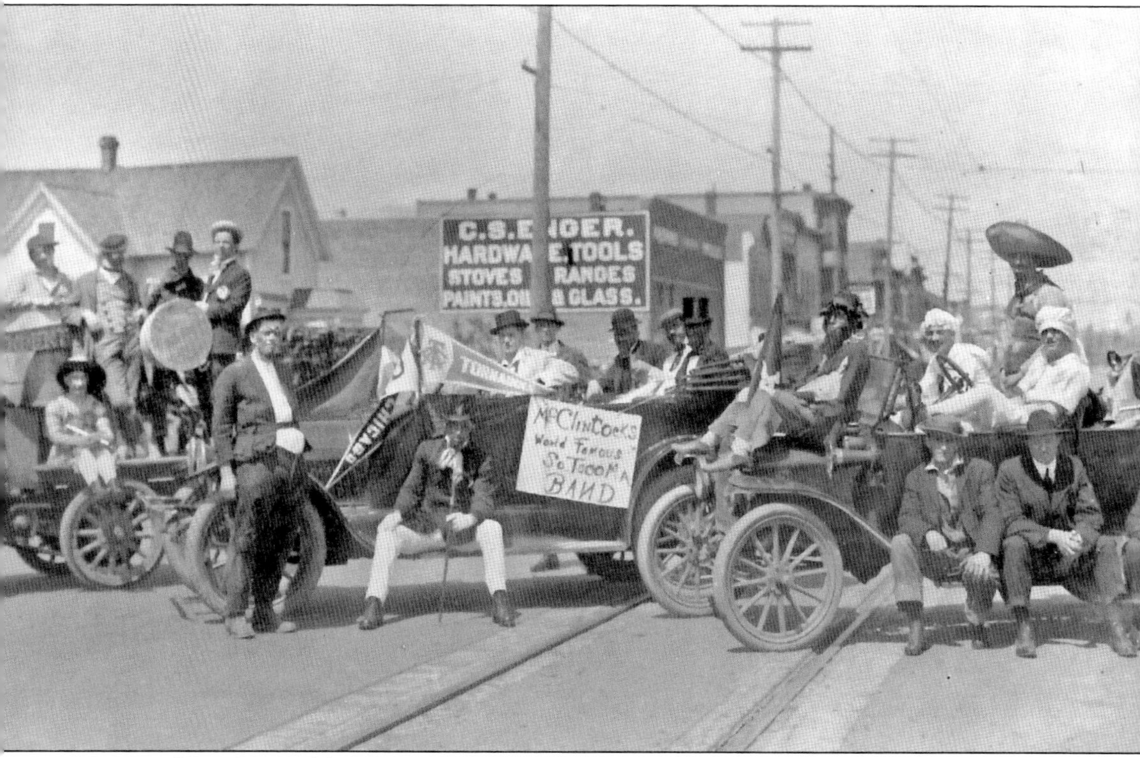

"McClintock's World Famous South Tacoma Band" poses on the trolley tracks in South Tacoma around 1908. The parade participants' costumes portray a variety of interests, and the prevailing theme is obviously fun for everyone. Many McClintock families lived and worked in the South Tacoma neighborhood. (Tacoma Public Library.)

ON THE COVER: Edison Elementary School opened in 1892 in the location for which it was named. In 1903, the school's first principal, William C. P. McGovern, takes the teachers for a sleigh ride. The ladies wear fashionable hats, and a few students hitch a ride. McGovern holds a drum and bugle to announce their adventure, while a student governs the reins. (Tacoma Public Schools.)

IMAGES
of America

SOUTH TACOMA

Darlyne A. Reiter

ARCADIA
PUBLISHING

ISBN 978-0-7385-4807-4

Published by Arcadia Publishing
Charleston, South Carolina

Printed in the United States of America

Library of Congress Catalog Card Number: 2007925810

For all general information contact Arcadia Publishing at:
Telephone 843-853-2070
Fax 843-853-0044
E-mail sales@arcadiapublishing.com
For customer service and orders:
Toll-Free 1-888-313-2665

Visit us on the Internet at www.arcadiapublishing.com

To my husband, Steve Romines, who encourages me to follow my dreams and savors them with me.

Contents

ACKNOWLEDGMENTS

The people of South Tacoma merit my utmost thanks for making this book possible. Individually, locked in their brains or a box in the attic, they have images, stories, and myths about their families, businesses, churches, schools, clubs, sports activities, public service, community events, and so on. Collectively they share a common bond of pride for their "town within a city," as historian Bob Tschida calls it. More than this page is needed to fully acknowledge all who contributed to this book. Each caption ends with a courtesy in parentheses to whoever shared the image and the story behind it. The unparalleled assistance from Brian Kamens, Bob Schuler, and Jody Gripp at Tacoma Public Library's Northwest Room deserve more than TPL, but they understand conciseness. Tacoma Historical Society (THS) gets a big thank you for providing a drop-off location for images. THS president Dale Wirsing, with patience and encouragement, always had the right answer that led to another question, which is what researching history is all about. When Caroline Gallacci mentioned at a THS meeting that South Tacoma's history should be written, without realizing it, she was talking to me. Elton Gatewood, City of Tacoma Neighborhood Council Office coordinator, gave me a jump start with an intern project about South Tacoma. To Julie Albright, my editor: thank you for patiently replying to my many questions. To friends and family who encouraged me to "go for it," my appreciation goes to every one of you. Thanks to Judy Johnson for editing text with skill and tough love. I won't pretend to know all the history of South Tacoma, but thanks to so many helpful South Tacoma folks I now know more. In the beginning, my only connection to South Tacoma was my father's burial plot in Calvary Cemetery. Nearly one year later, my connections include the entire South Tacoma neighborhood.

INTRODUCTION

In 1870, Mount Rainier peered majestically down at Hunt's Prairie as Irish immigrant John Rigney built one of Pierce County's first homes. In 1890, George W. Traver and the Excelsior Park Land Company purchased large parcels of land in the prairie south of Tacoma "and divided them into lots to sell for profit when the Northern Pacific Railway relocated its shops there," according to Herbert Hunt in his book *Tacoma: Its History and Its Builders*, Volume II. Thus the development of South Tacoma began.

On April 17, 1891, Ordinance No. 398 was approved to annex the South Tacoma area to the City of Tacoma. The special election was held in the City of Tacoma, Pierce County, State of Washington, and the territory was described in detail in the beginning of the ordinance. Each voter was asked to vote by placing either "For Annexation" or "Against Annexation" on his ballot. A notice was published in the *Tacoma Daily Ledger* for four weeks prior to the election. Inspectors, judges, and clerks were appointed for each precinct within the First Ward and the Second Ward. The approved annexation was inclusive to South Sixty-fourth Street. Additional ordinances passed in 1908 and 1909 extended the South Tacoma perimeter south to Eightieth Street to mark the southern boundary that remains today.

One hundred years later, the City of Tacoma Neighborhood Council Office established boundaries for the South Tacoma neighborhood as Center Street, Interstate 5, Eightieth Street, and Orchard Street, with multiple residential neighborhoods. In the early 1960s, Interstate 5 divided the community. Many homes were moved to construct the freeway, and many neighbors were no longer within yelling distance.

Although there are no people alive today who originally helped establish South Tacoma as a community, their descendants are here. Memories, images, family lore, and stories survive—albeit in somewhat varying narrations. This book voices their stories via their images.

The story begins with the establishment of the cemeteries in chapter one and continues with the arrival of the Northern Pacific Railway Shops in chapter two. Chapter three shows the need for an infrastructure in a fast-growing community. Chapter four embraces the importance of education. Chapter five demonstrates how a diverse population created a community and reveals how South Tacoma sustains their status as a respected neighborhood.

South Tacoma has thrived, survived, and arrived. From telegraph to the Internet, the community perseveres owing to a proud group of citizens committed to the South Tacoma way of life.

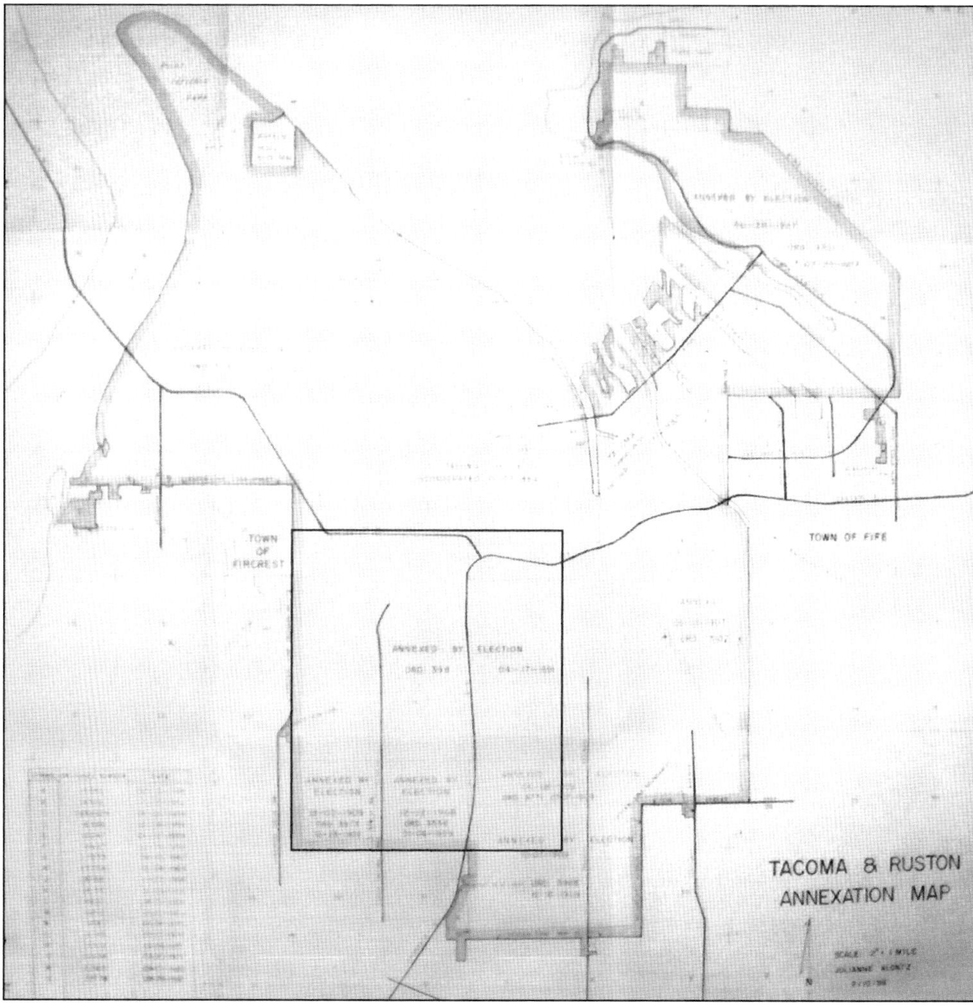

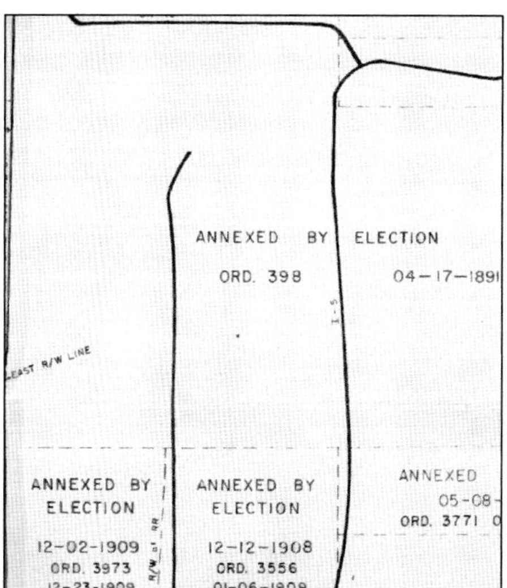

The town of Edison, as it was known at the time, was annexed to Tacoma April 17, 1891. By ordinance and a special election, the city limits was established at Sixty-fourth Street and, 18 years later, extended farther south to the present Eightieth Street. The area was officially named South Tacoma in 1895. (City of Tacoma Ordinance 398, TPL.)

One

A Grave Beginning

Stories gleaned in cemeteries contradict the belief that death concludes storytelling.

In 1873, pioneers John and Eliza Rigney sold four acres of family land for $1 to A. M. A. Blanchet, bishop of Nisqually, for a place to bury Tacoma's Catholics. By 1905, the old cemetery, Pioneer Catholic Cemetery, was full. An adjacent 35 acres were purchased, and Calvary Cemetery Association was incorporated.

In 1874, Tacoma Land Company deeded 60 acres of prairie land south of Tacoma to establish a cemetery for all Tacomans. Reminiscent of the land it occupied, the 60-acre parcel was named Prairie Cemetery, now known as Oakwood Hill Cemetery. The main entrance was on Edison Avenue, where today South Park Community Center on South Tacoma Way is located. The land remained in the hands of the city for nine years, when it was turned over to the families who owned cemetery property or had a loved one buried there.

When ownership transferred, the acreage was amicably divided into three sections: Oakwood Hill Cemetery's entrance moved to the south side of the property; Tacoma Cemetery's entrance was a short distance north and up the hill from the original entrance; and the Pauper Cemetery was tucked behind the two without its own entrance.

In 1910, Tacoma Mausoleum Association opened its first building next to Oakwood Hill Cemetery to offer an alternative means for burials.

By then, trolley cars were being used to carry funeral groups from the mortuary in the city to the cemeteries to the south. According to *South Tacoma History*, compiled for the City of Tacoma in 1985, "Often a casket would ride in the vestibule of the trolley car."

With the Northern Pacific Railway Shops soon to be built, coupled with water and electricity lines extending south, South Tacoma was shaping up to be a lively community as the new century peeked around the corner.

Tales are shouted from the famous, the infamous, and the families of Tacoma who rest with the flowering tulips planted beside their graves to those who stroll under the huge trees and past the markers.

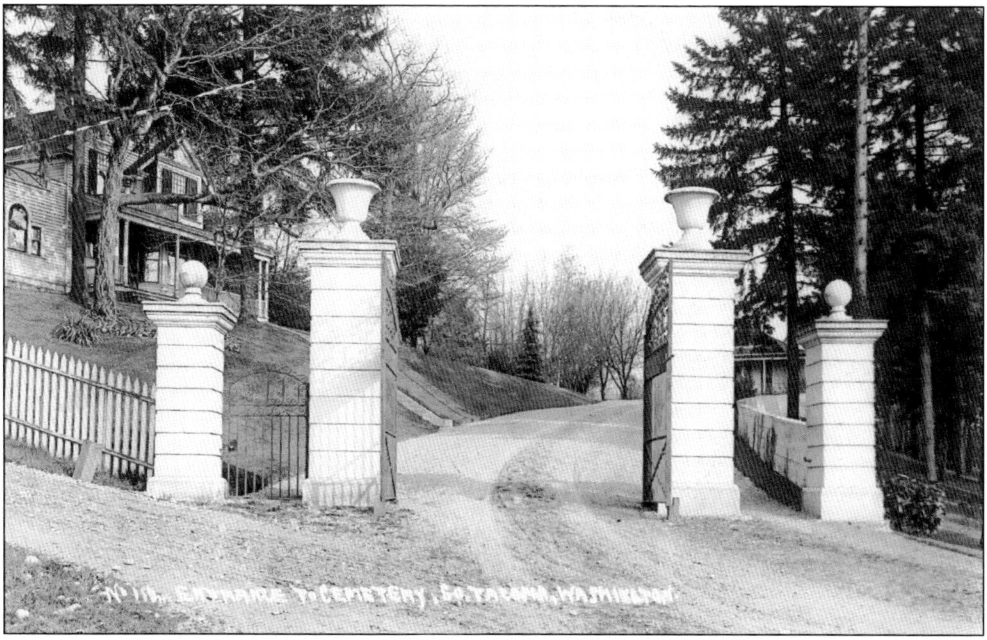

The entrance to Old Tacoma Cemetery was moved to this spot c. 1885. The caretaker's house on the left was moved across the street and later demolished. The two inside gate pillars were eliminated to make a wider entrance to allow two-way traffic in and out of the cemetery. (Thomas R. Stenger collection.)

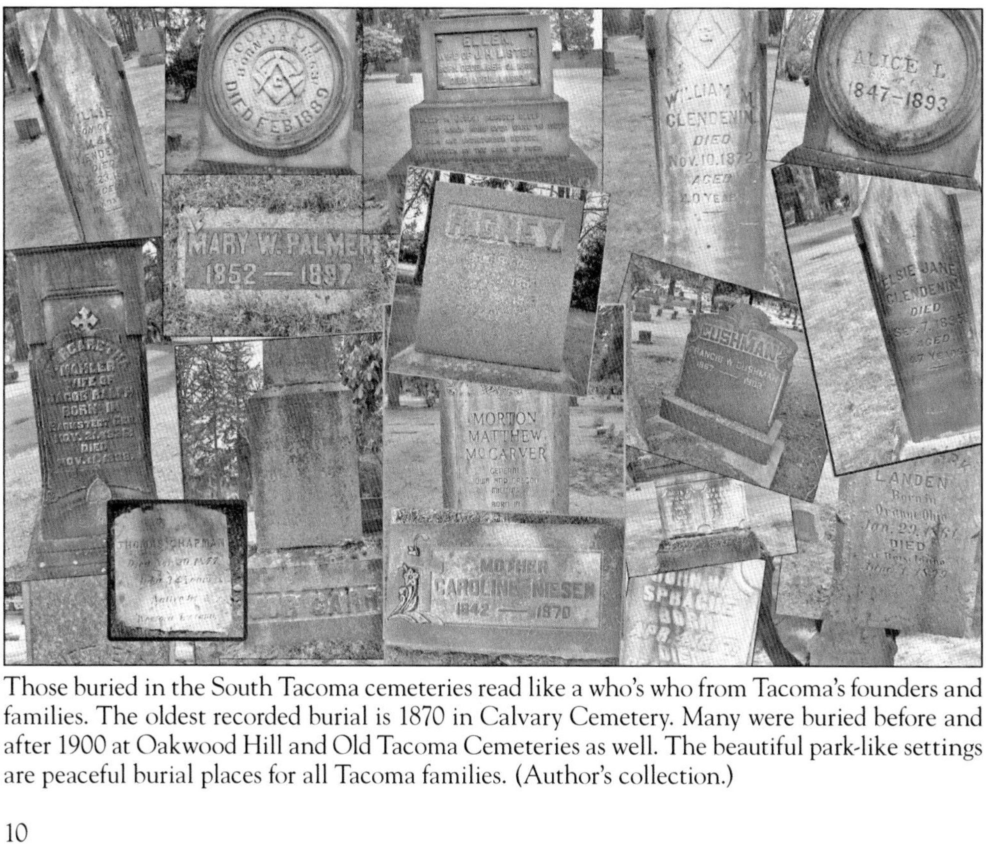

Those buried in the South Tacoma cemeteries read like a who's who from Tacoma's founders and families. The oldest recorded burial is 1870 in Calvary Cemetery. Many were buried before and after 1900 at Oakwood Hill and Old Tacoma Cemeteries as well. The beautiful park-like settings are peaceful burial places for all Tacoma families. (Author's collection.)

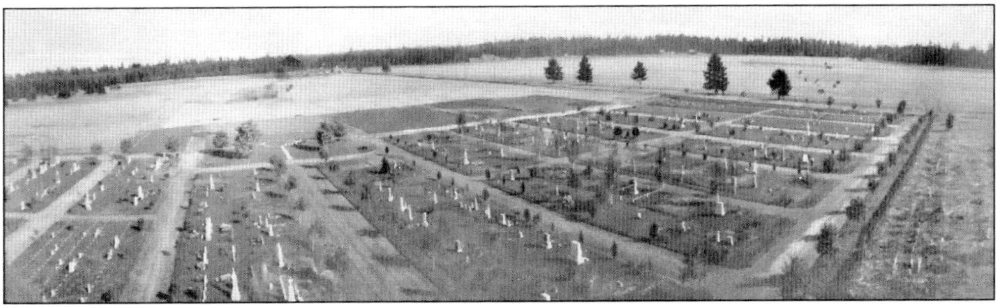

In 1873, John and Eliza Rigney sold four acres of dairy land to form the beginning of Calvary Cemetery. This 1914–1915 image shows what Calvary Cemetery looked like in its infancy as a final resting place for Tacoma's Catholics, which included Rigney family burials, looking south toward today's Seventy-fourth Street. (Calvary Cemetery.)

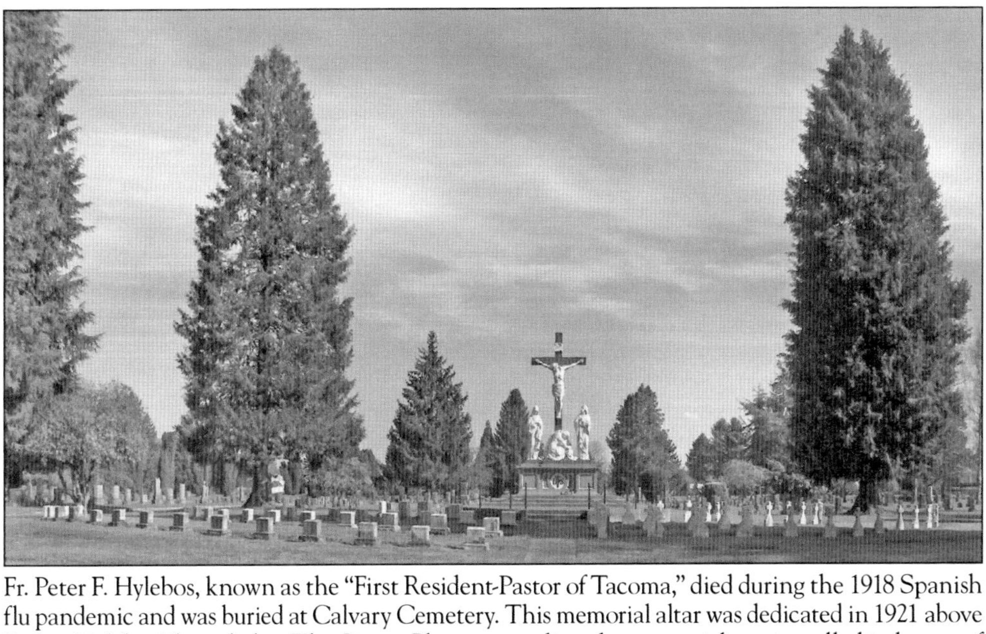

Fr. Peter F. Hylebos, known as the "First Resident-Pastor of Tacoma," died during the 1918 Spanish flu pandemic and was buried at Calvary Cemetery. This memorial altar was dedicated in 1921 above Father Hylebos's burial plot. The Sisters Plot surrounding the memorial was installed in honor of Father Hylebos's efforts to bring various orders of nuns to Tacoma. (Calvary Cemetery.)

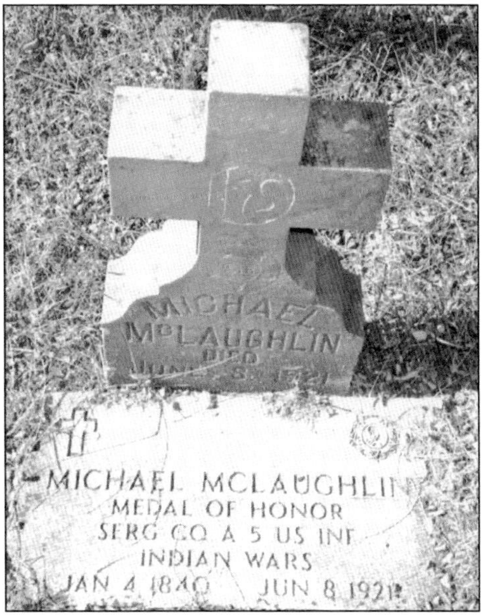

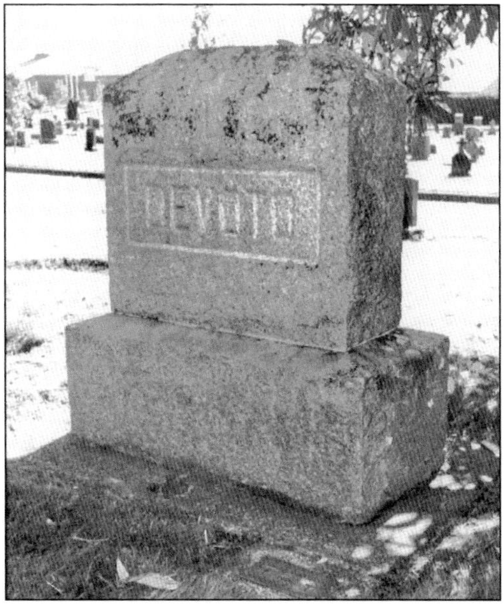

Many who served their country with honor are buried in South Tacoma cemeteries. Michael McLaughlin showed courage during the battle between the U.S. Army and the Lakota Sioux at Cedar Creek, Montana, in 1876–1877. Augusto Devoto served with Gen. George Custer at the Little Big Horn Battle in June 1876. Both soldiers are buried in Calvary Cemetery. (Calvary Cemetery.)

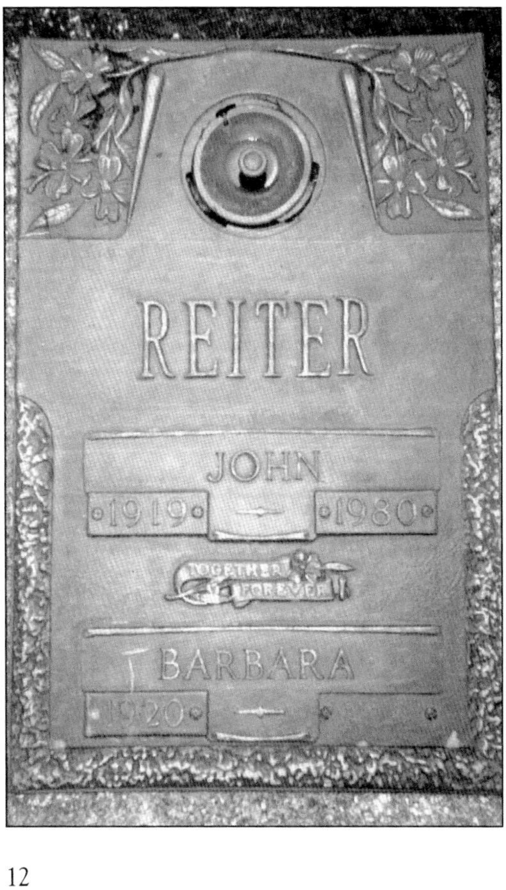

Although it was established around 1850, no written records exist for the pioneer section of Calvary Cemetery. When the original four acres were full, additional land was purchased so burials could continue for many years. The final resting place for the author's father, John Reiter, who died 130 years later, is among thousands of others for Catholics buried in Calvary Cemetery's newer addition. (Author's collection.)

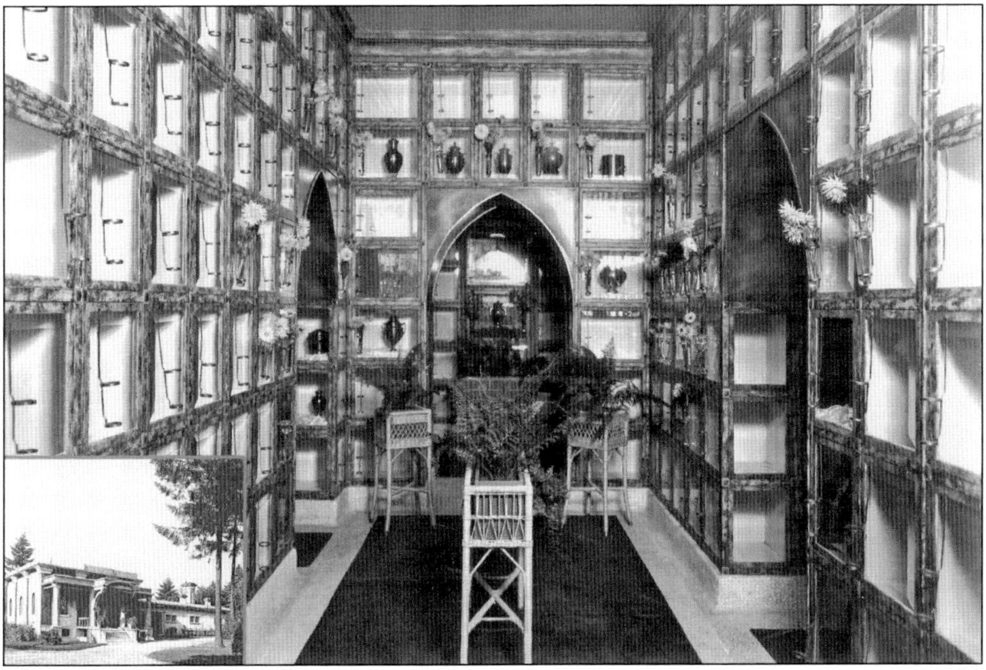

This 1922 image shows Oakwood Cemetery's columbarium one year after it was built next to the 1908-constructed crematory (inset). The concrete-and-steel structure contains 979 glass-and-steel niches with a total capacity of more than 3,000 urns. A stained-glass dome above casts a colorful glow over niches and visitors. (Oakwood Hill Cemetery.)

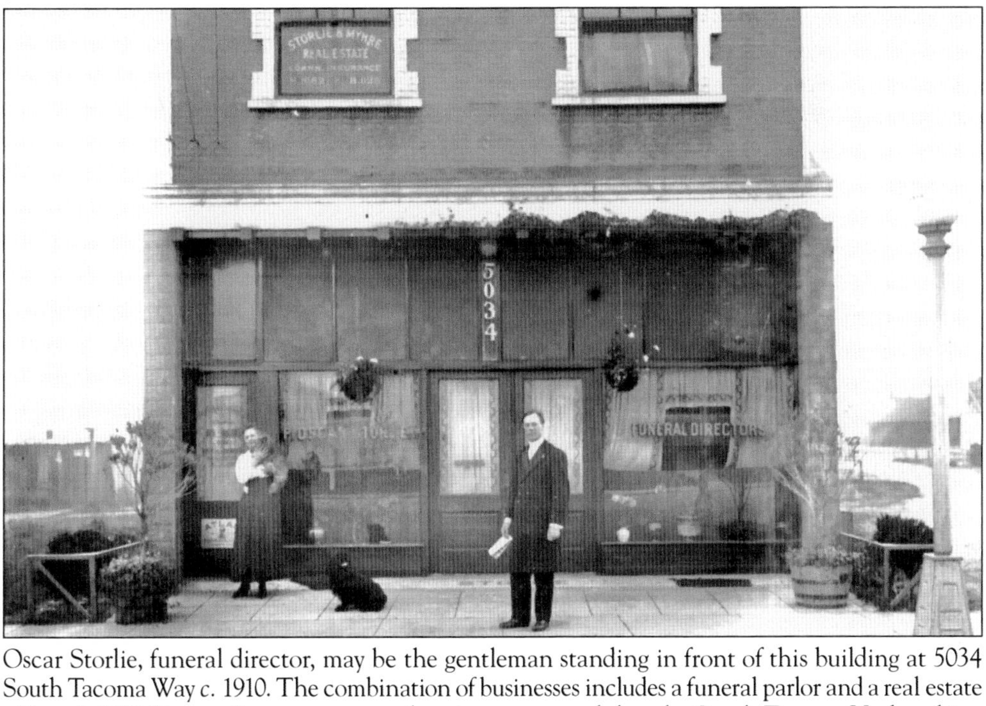

Oscar Storlie, funeral director, may be the gentleman standing in front of this building at 5034 South Tacoma Way *c.* 1910. The combination of businesses includes a funeral parlor and a real estate office. A 1956 *Tacoma Star* newspaper advertisement stated that the South Tacoma Undertaking Company, owned by Storlie, had been in business since 1908. (TPL/Bill Habermann.)

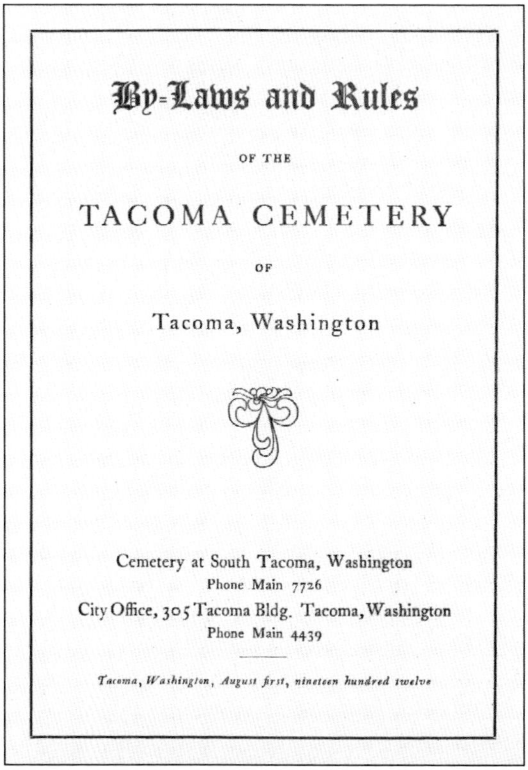

By-Laws and Rules

OF THE

TACOMA CEMETERY

OF

Tacoma, Washington

Cemetery at South Tacoma, Washington
Phone Main 7726
City Office, 305 Tacoma Bldg. Tacoma, Washington
Phone Main 4439

Tacoma, Washington, August first, nineteen hundred twelve

The 1912 booklet *Tacoma Cemetery Bylaws and Rules* begins this way: "There is nothing else so deeply interesting to the living as the disposal of those whom they have loved and lost." The Rules and Regulations for Visitors chapter ends by stating, "Touch Nothing in the Cemetery That Does Not Belong To You, where the temptation to pick flowers is so great." (Tacoma Cemetery.)

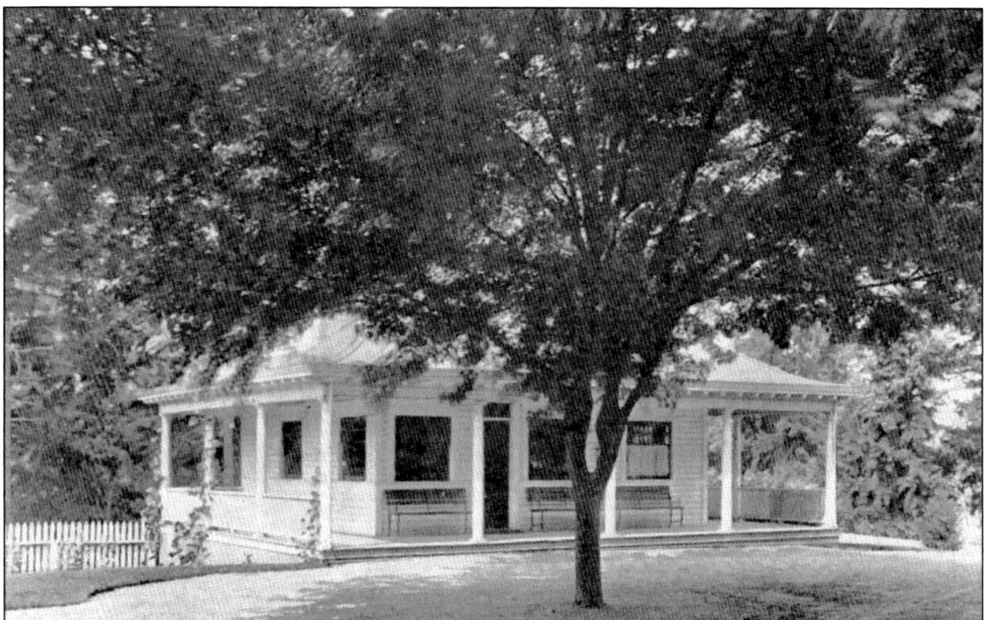

Tacoma Cemetery's original office was constructed around 1884 by the Tacoma Cemetery Association. The office, a caretaker's house, and a grand, gated cemetery entrance were built by and for the people who owned cemetery lots. The office building was used for 110 years before it was demolished and replaced. (Tacoma Cemetery.)

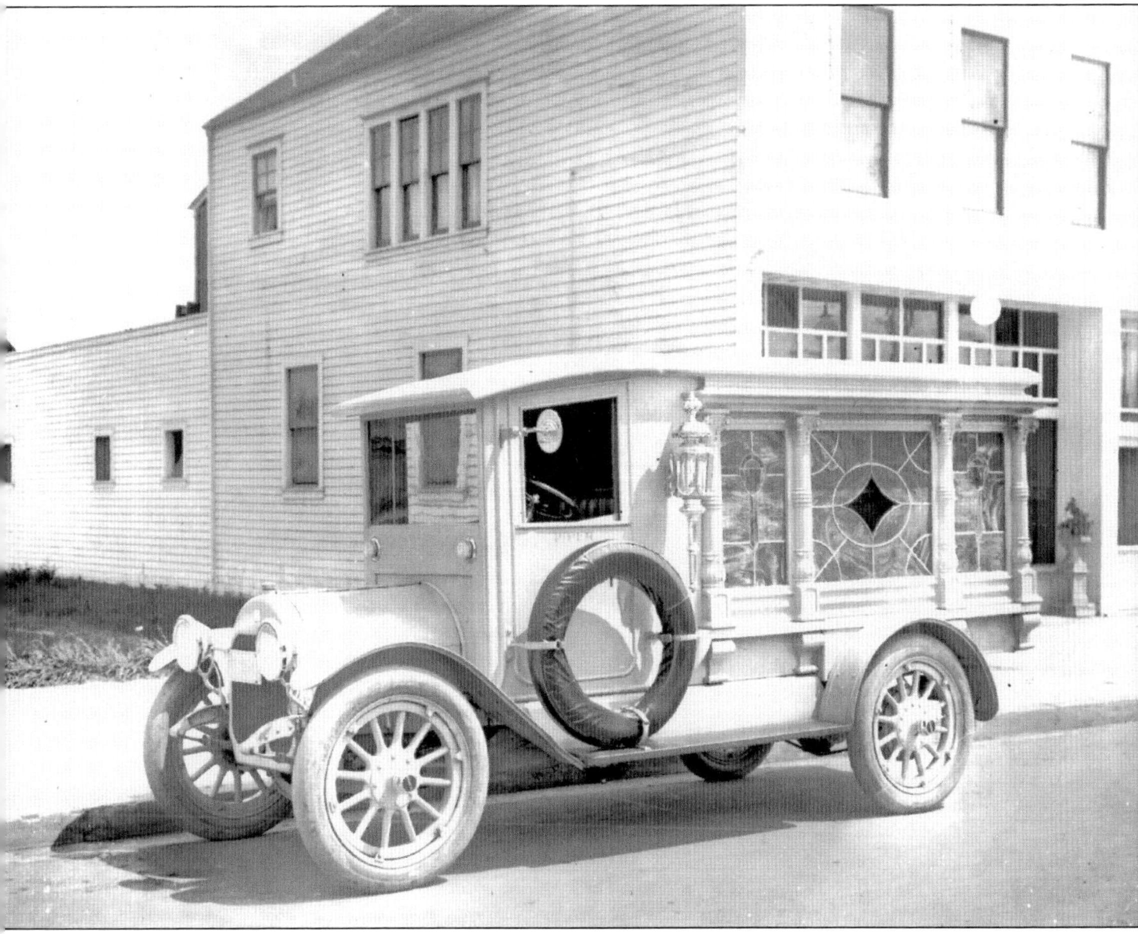

In 1910, Maude and George Piper opened Piper Funeral Home in South Tacoma. Piper Undertaking was listed in the 1910 Tacoma City Directory with George W. Piper as proprietor. When the building was gutted by fire in 1914, George Piper temporarily moved the business to a garage next door until the present location was built at 5436 South Puget Sound Avenue. Many South Tacoma residents recall Maude Piper's tradition of opening her home for neighborhood children on Halloween and giving the biggest candy bars in town. In 1984, Fred Morley purchased Piper Funeral Home and merged it with Morley-Mellinger to create Piper-Morley-Mellinger Funeral Home. George Piper's original hearse, parked in front of the original building, has decorative, stained-glass windows, a lantern near the driver's door, spoke wheels, and the name "PIPER" above the spare wheel mounted on the door. (Piper-Morley-Mellinger Funeral Home.)

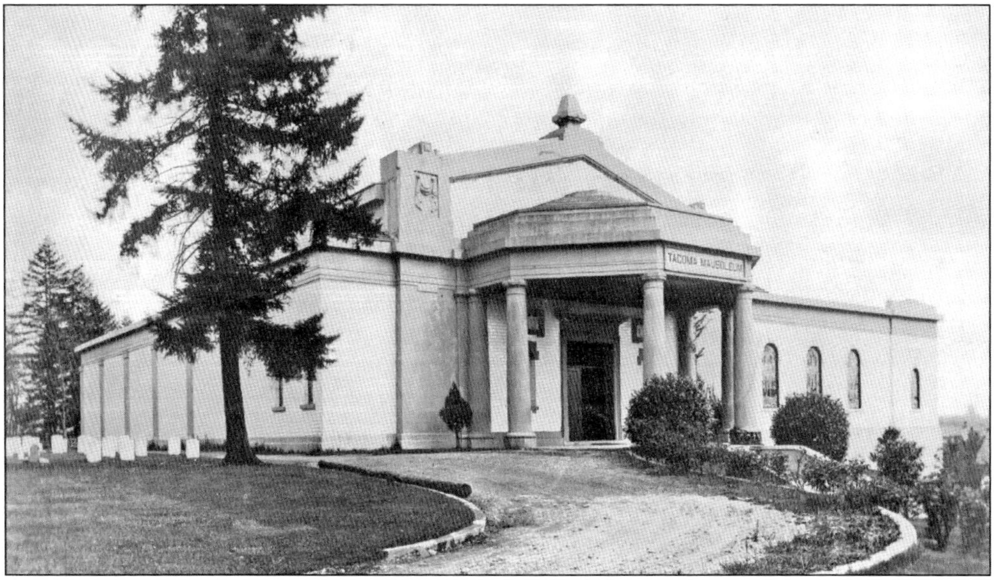

When approached by the National Mausoleum Association about building a community mausoleum, a group of Tacoma businessmen purchased the patent right for Pierce County. The first unit, shown seven years after it opened as the first mausoleum west of the Mississippi, was completed in 1910, and five other units have been added since. The pet crematory on the far right opened in 2006. (Tacoma Mausoleum and Mortuary.)

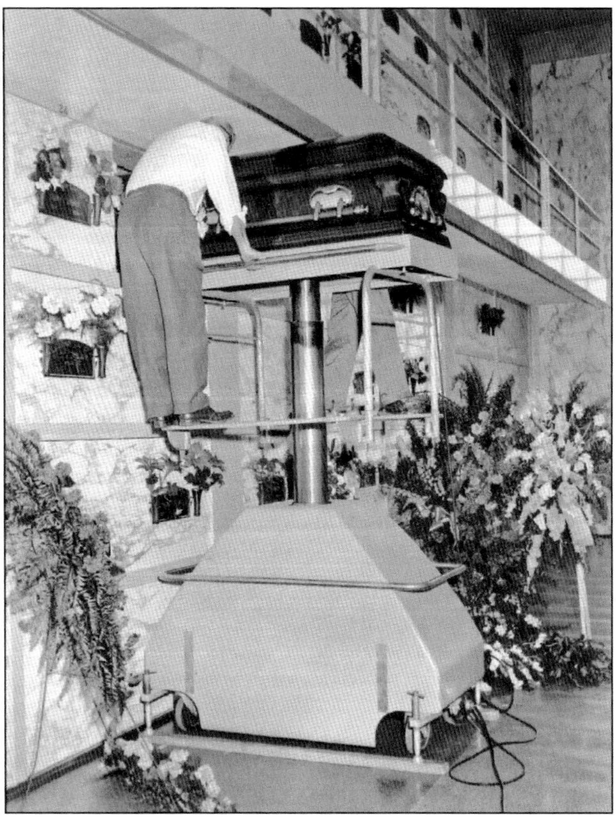

A casket is raised to the proper height and partially placed in an unsealed crypt in the Tacoma Mausoleum. Around 1955, an unidentified gentleman stands on a hydraulic casket lift, which allows him rise to the proper height and slide the casket into the burial chamber. The presence of flowers tells us the committal service for the deceased person has concluded. (Tacoma Mausoleum and Mortuary.)

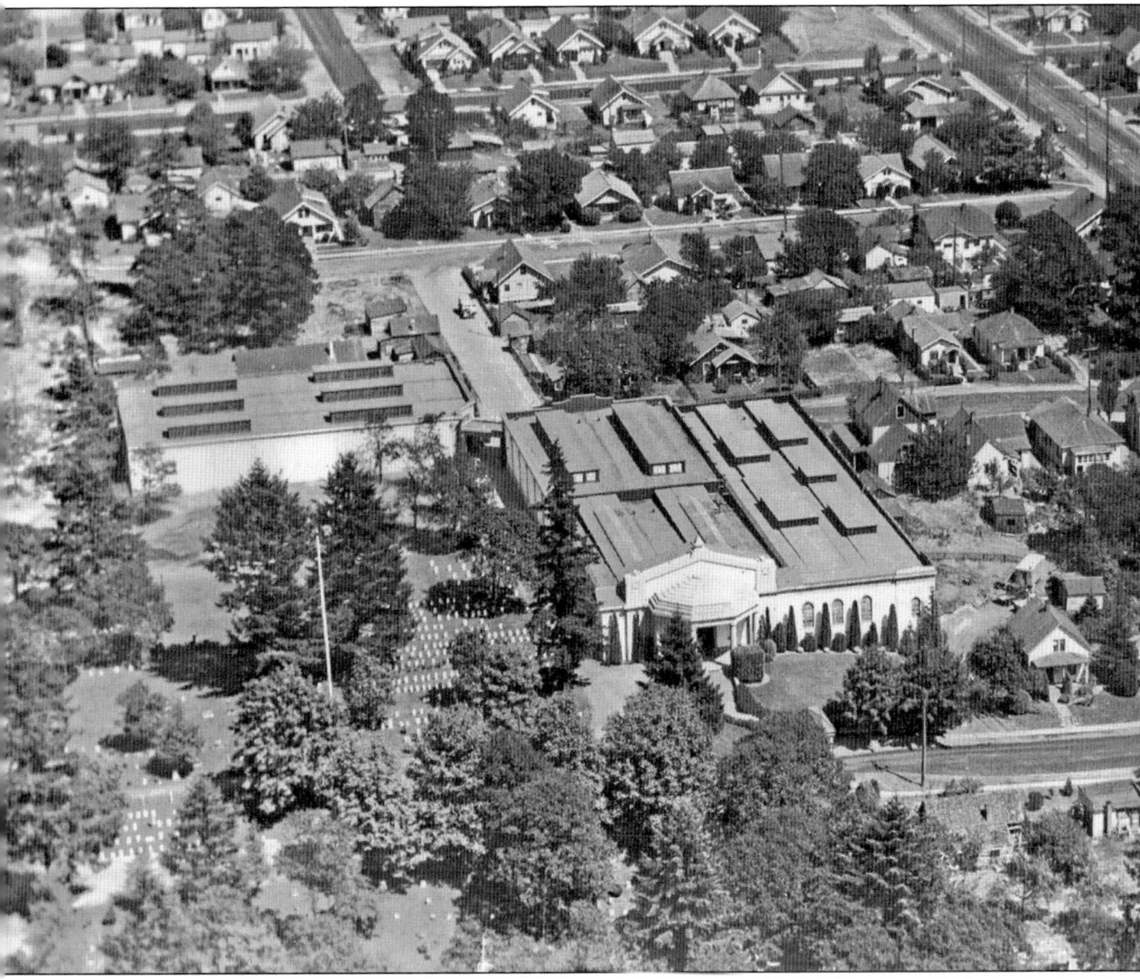

Tacoma Mausoleum is bordered by a South Tacoma neighborhood's Craftsman-style homes in 1938. In the lower left, a portion of Oakwood Hill Cemetery displays rows of white markers honoring Civil War veterans. The Grand Army of the Republic (GAR) was founded in 1866 to support veterans in the aftermath of a devastating time in their lives. GAR was responsible for setting aside a day to remember fallen comrades—Memorial Day. In early 1893, GAR's local group, Custer Post No. 6, purchased this section of land at Oakwood Hill to honor Civil War veterans who came home to live or relocated here after the war ended. Many widows are also buried in the section, and additional veterans chose burial in existing family plots elsewhere in the cemetery. Veterans are still buried in the GAR section. (Tacoma Mausoleum and Mortuary and Oakwood Hill Cemetery.)

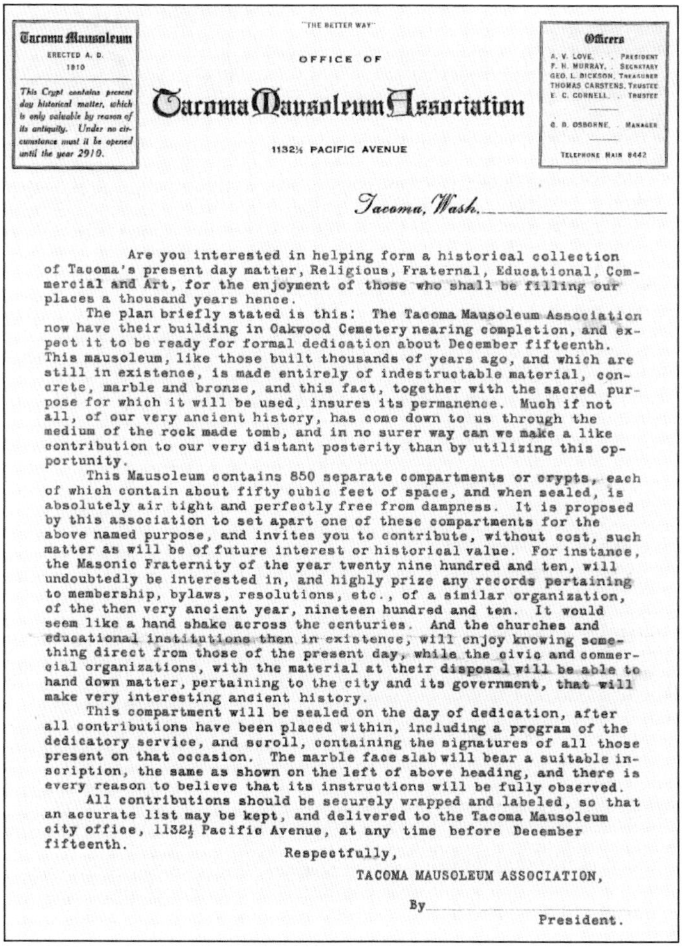

Tacoma Mausoleum
ERECTED A. D.
1910

This Crypt contains present day historical matter, which is only valuable by reason of its antiquity. Under no circumstance must it be opened until the year 2910.

"THE BETTER WAY"

OFFICE OF

Tacoma Mausoleum Association

1132½ PACIFIC AVENUE

Officers
A. V. LOVE . . . PRESIDENT
F. H. MURRAY . . SECRETARY
GEO. L. DICKSON, TREASURER
THOMAS CARSTENS, TRUSTEE
E. C. CORNELL . . TRUSTEE

G. D. OSBORNE . . MANAGER

TELEPHONE MAIN 8442

*Tacoma, Wash.*__________

Are you interested in helping form a historical collection of Tacoma's present day matter, Religious, Fraternal, Educational, Commercial and Art, for the enjoyment of those who shall be filling our places a thousand years hence.

The plan briefly stated is this: The Tacoma Mausoleum Association now have their building in Oakwood Cemetery nearing completion, and expect it to be ready for formal dedication about December fifteenth. This mausoleum, like those built thousands of years ago, and which are still in existence, is made entirely of indestructable material, concrete, marble and bronze, and this fact, together with the sacred purpose for which it will be used, insures its permanence. Much if not all, of our very ancient history, has come down to us through the medium of the rock made tomb, and in no surer way can we make a like contribution to our very distant posterity than by utilizing this opportunity.

This Mausoleum contains 850 separate compartments or crypts, each of which contain about fifty cubic feet of space, and when sealed, is absolutely air tight and perfectly free from dampness. It is proposed by this association to set apart one of these compartments for the above named purpose, and invites you to contribute, without cost, such matter as will be of future interest or historical value. For instance, the Masonic Fraternity of the year twenty nine hundred and ten, will undoubtedly be interested in, and highly prize any records pertaining to membership, bylaws, resolutions, etc., of a similar organization, of the then very ancient year, nineteen hundred and ten. It would seem like a hand shake across the centuries. And the churches and educational institutions then in existence, will enjoy knowing something direct from those of the present day, while the civic and commercial organizations, with the material at their disposal will be able to hand down matter, pertaining to the city and its government, that will make very interesting ancient history.

This compartment will be sealed on the day of dedication, after all contributions have been placed within, including a program of the dedicatory service, and scroll, containing the signatures of all those present on that occasion. The marble face slab will bear a suitable inscription, the same as shown on the left of above heading, and there is every reason to believe that its instructions will be fully observed.

All contributions should be securely wrapped and labeled, so that an accurate list may be kept, and delivered to the Tacoma Mausoleum city office, 1132½ Pacific Avenue, at any time before December fifteenth.

Respectfully,

TACOMA MAUSOLEUM ASSOCIATION,

By__________
President.

While Tacoma Mausoleum was nearing completion in 1909, the Tacoma Mausoleum Association was busy marketing a new way of burial. To alleviate concerns and involve people in this new venture, the association proposed forming a historical collection and sealing items in a crypt for 1,000 years. The handbill details the specifics and encourages participation. It states, "It would seem like a hand shake across the centuries." The drawing shows what the crypt may look like next to a fictitious crypt with a death date prior to the mausoleum opening. The photograph shows what was actually engraved on the crypt and what it looks like today. There is no record or written account of what was placed inside. (Tacoma Mausoleum and Mortuary.)

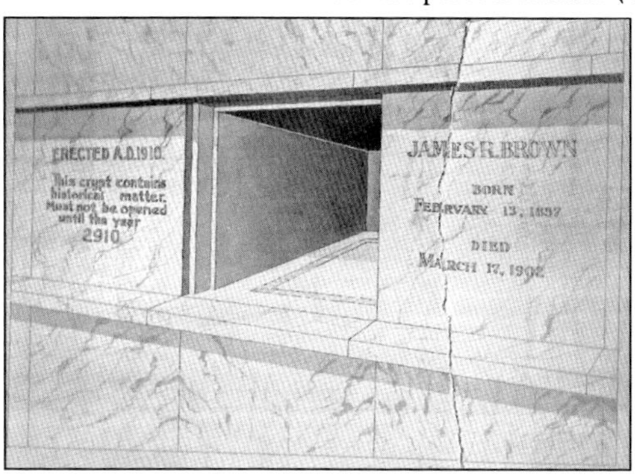

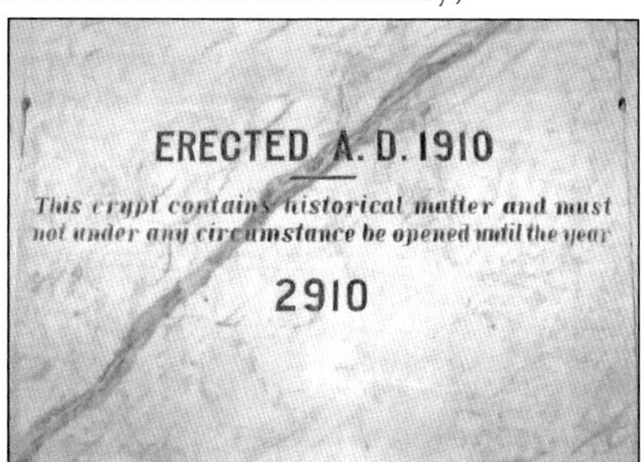

Two

The Railroad Shops Entice

Transportation has long been a fundamental component of South Tacoma.

In the mid-1800s, Oregon and Washington Territories' pioneers, in their need to connect with others, passed through South Tacoma. Travel from Seattle to Portland, as well as between most southern Washington towns, was routed through South Tacoma's flat plains. The first passenger train passed through South Tacoma in 1873.

Prior to trolley cars as an early commuter option for the railroad workers, horse-drawn tallyho wagons transported people to outlying areas. Between the 1890s and early 1900s, bicycles were a common mode of transportation. The main north-south highway in Washington State made its way through South Tacoma and became part of Highway 99 in 1926. By the 1950s, South Tacoma Way had gained fame as the Auto Row of the Northwest. Each year in August, a stretch of South Tacoma Way is closed for those who journey there for the annual Classic Car Show.

Consequently, is it any wonder the Northern Pacific Railway made a monumental decision in 1890 to move the railroad shops from downtown Tacoma to the prime prairie land south of the city? The "Shops," as they were known, encompassed 131 acres, were 6,400 feet long and 700 feet wide beside the railroad tracks, and stretched from Fifty-sixth Street to Union Avenue. The complex opened in 1891 and included machine shops, a cooling plant, power plant, water tank, well, compressor room, dry kiln, air storage tanks, new and old car sheds, reclaiming plant, welding plant, and 141 fire hydrants. In the glory days of this major industry, the shops employed more than 1,000 skilled workers who kept the rolling stock running by repairing and painting on a regular schedule, as well as providing complete overhauls every four years. The shops closed and were demolished in 1974, when Northern Pacific merged into the Burlington Northern system.

The South Tacoma community was built around the Shops and thus began the changes that make it the community it is today.

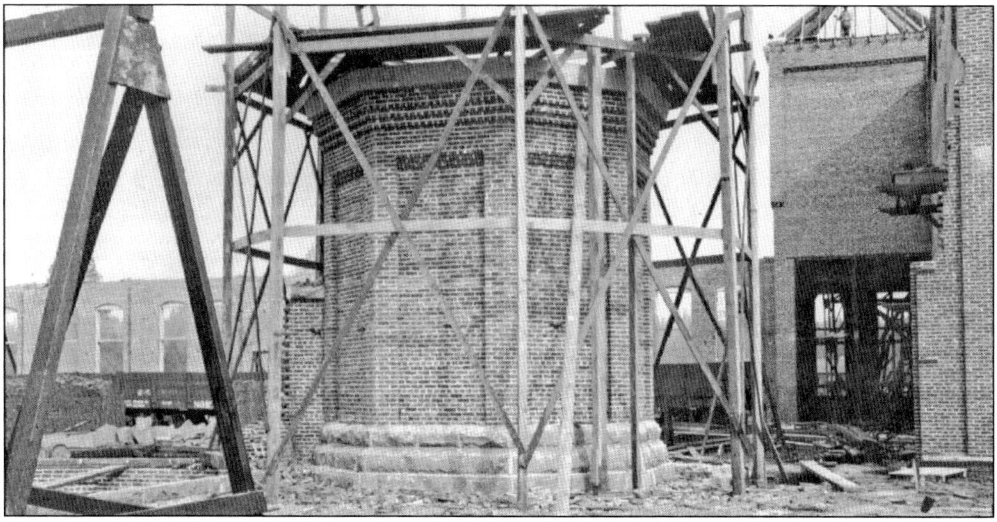

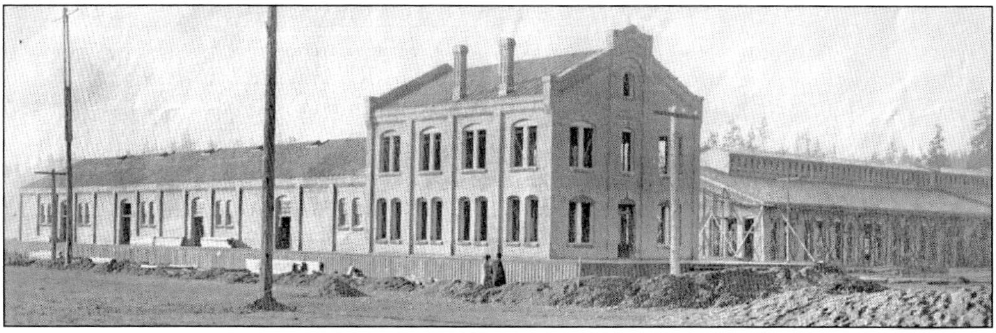

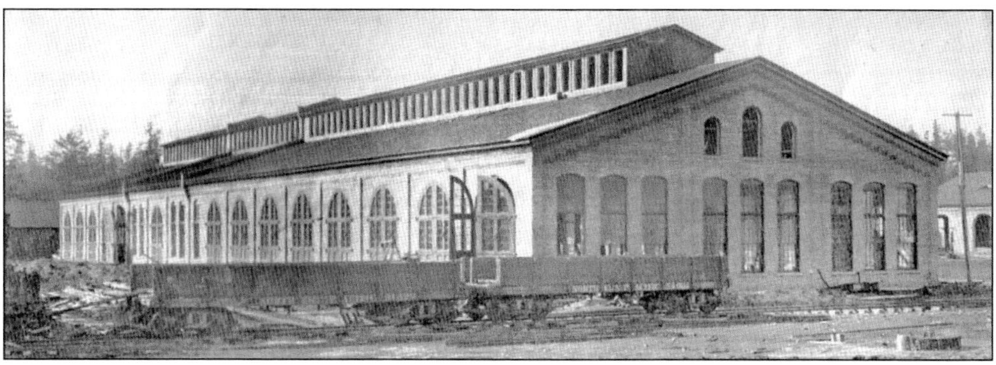

Once the decision was made to locate the Northern Pacific Shops in South Tacoma, the company moved quickly to construct buildings needed to repair and maintain Northern Pacific locomotives for the western segment of the system. Under construction by October 1890, the Smoke Stack (top) is a fraction of its final height of 150 feet. With the completion of the office and storeroom (middle) in January 1891, the southwest corner was ready for occupancy. The Boiler and Copper Shop (bottom) in the northwest corner was completed by March 1891. The plant consisted of 13 brick buildings, and 11 more were built of wood. In case of fire, the complex had a pump pit, fire hydrants, and three hose-carts on the property. The company's water tank had a 100,000-gallon capacity. The Shops contributed to the local economy by spending thousands of dollars a month on materials from local businesses, as well as an annual payroll in the hundreds of thousands dollars. (Jim Fredrickson collection.)

Realty Loan and Investment Company's business venture lured prospective buyers to property near the new Northern Pacific Railway Shops. Lots adjacent to Hunt's Prairie were sold for $200–250. The 1890 sales advertisement enticed with "on the qui vive," and seduced with promised inflationary gains within 90 days in an area surrounded by booming South Tacoma. (Tacoma Railcar Preservation Society and David Burns collection.)

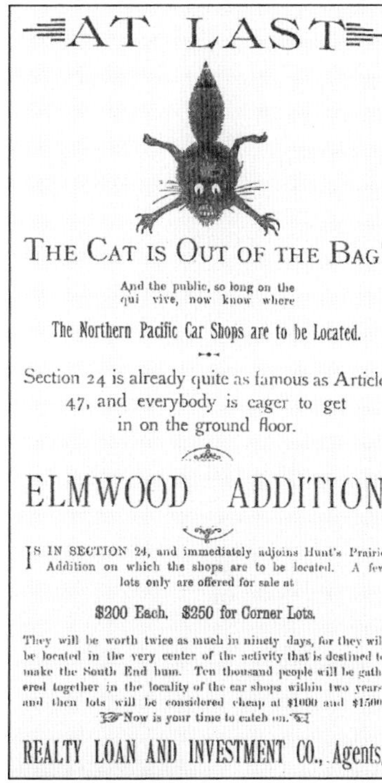

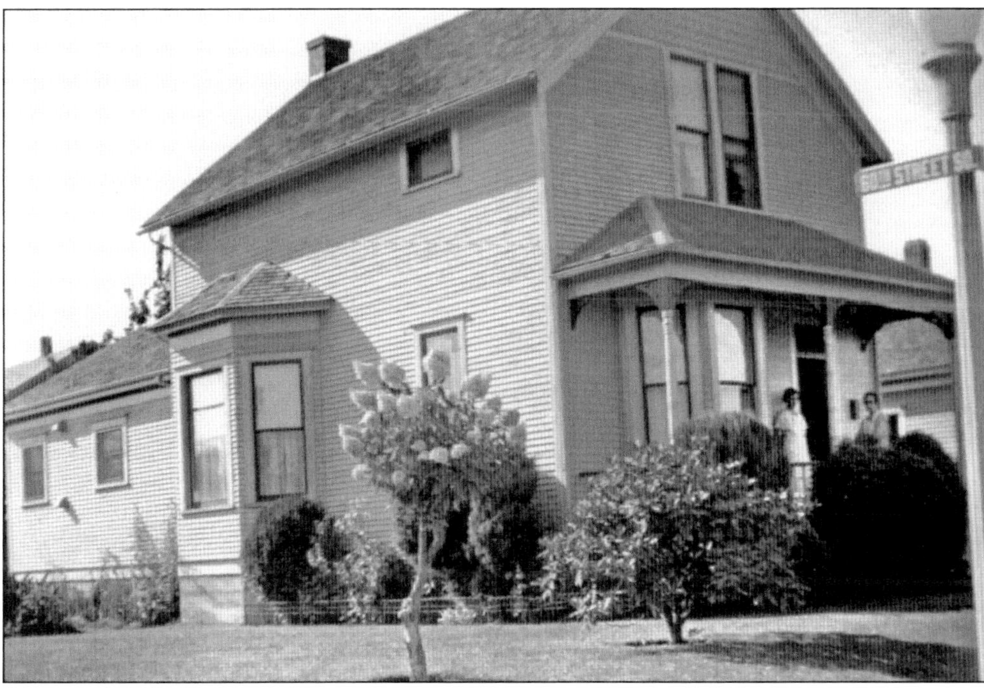

Swedish immigrants Harold and Elizabeth Gustafson built their South Tacoma home in 1894. Four of their five children were born in the home during the 59 years the family lived there. Elizabeth's sisters, Christine Erickson (left) and Mary Nelson, stand in front of the home c. 1933. The house remains occupied 113 years later at its original corner lot at 5834 South Puget Sound Avenue. (Bruce Petersen family collection.)

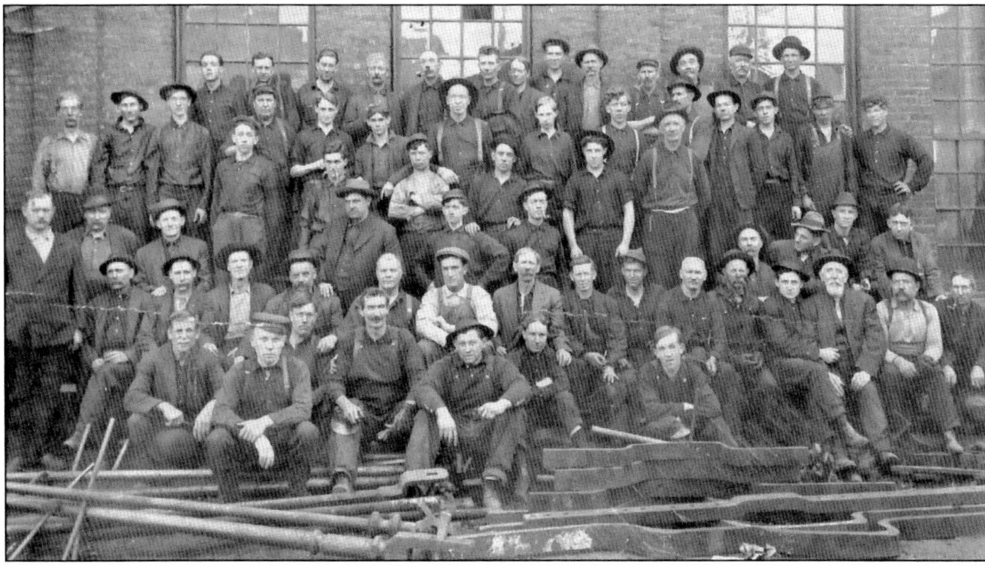

Thomas Delaney, third from right, seventh row, began his career at the Northern Pacific Railway Shops before the beginning of the 20th century. Born November 11, 1855, thirty-four years to the day before Washington became a state, Delaney died on his 91st birthday in 1946. Delaney is shown with other workers around 1900 posing with locomotive parts they used to repair trains in the shops. (Josephine Delaney Sleet Estate.)

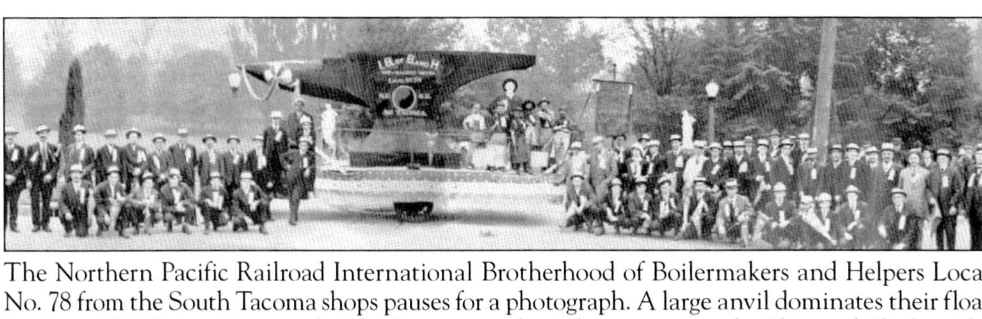

The Northern Pacific Railroad International Brotherhood of Boilermakers and Helpers Local No. 78 from the South Tacoma shops pauses for a photograph. A large anvil dominates their float for the c. 1916 Labor Day parade. The banner on the right announces the Ship and Blacksmiths Local No. 78 Ship and Machine Blacksmiths of Tacoma. Thomas Delaney stands to the right of the telephone pole. (Josephine Delaney Sleet Estate.)

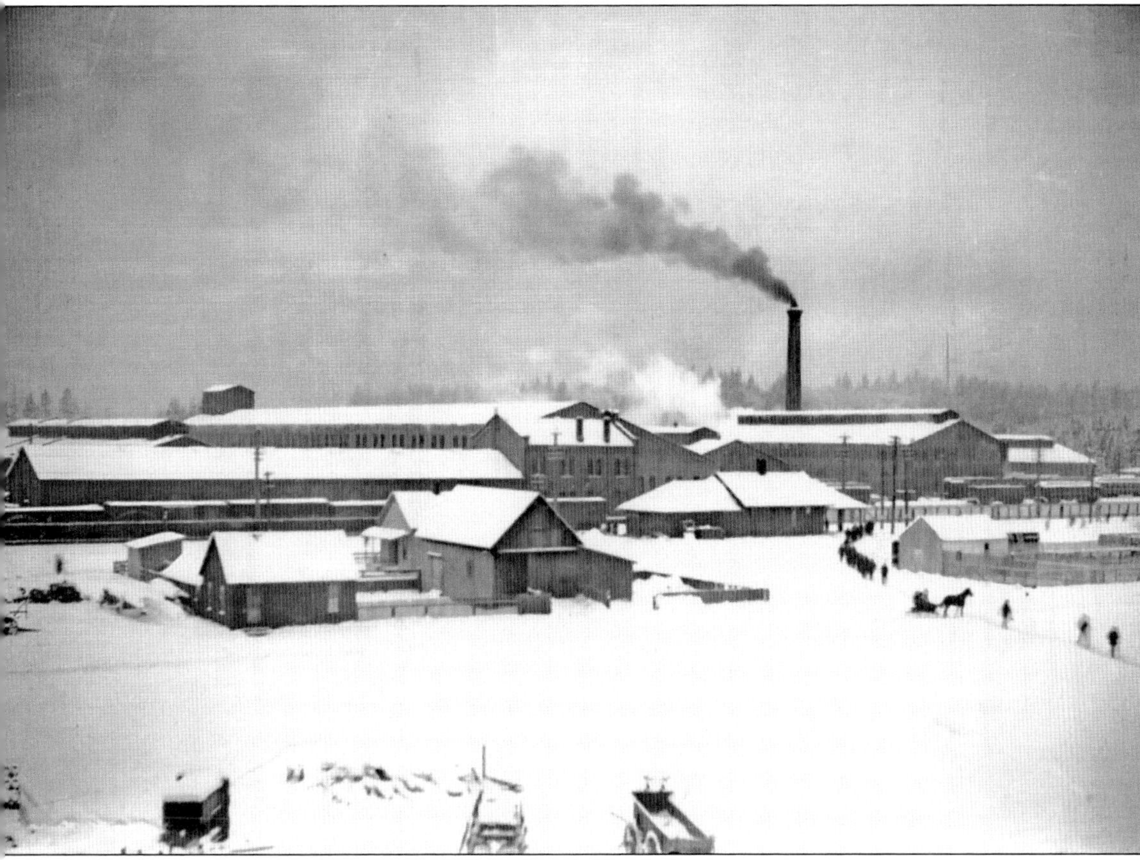

The Northern Pacific Railway Shops, still in the infancy stage of their 83-year presence, had been maintaining and repairing railroad cars and locomotives for about 16 years when this winter storm dumped a cover of snow on the area around 1908. The 150-foot smokestack, sending out an imposing amount of dark smoke above the snow-covered buildings, indicates there is work going on within the maintenance shops. A horse-drawn sleigh outside the entrance waits to give a ride to someone from the line of railroad workers making a path through the snow as they leave the complex at the end of the daily shift. The residence in the center of the image, with no smoke coming from the chimney, may be waiting for someone to start the fire. The serene, untouched blanket of white gives South Tacoma a winter-wonderland appearance. (TPL.)

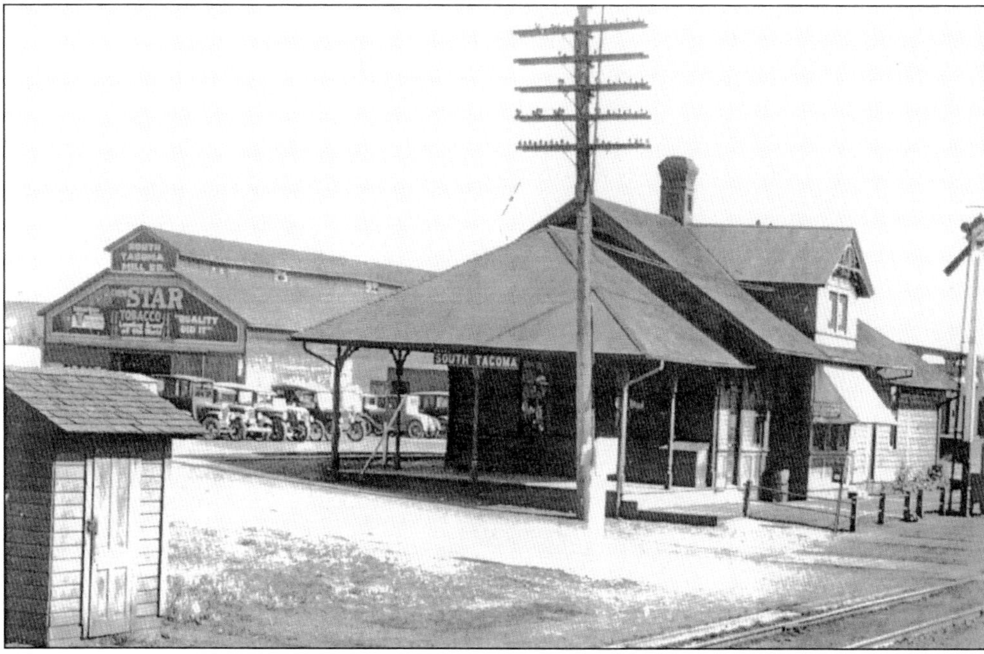

Although the first passenger train passed through South Tacoma in 1873, this station was built after the Northern Pacific Railway Shops opened in 1892. The station remained open at 3709 South Fifty-first Street until end of business on December 31, 1965, and was later demolished. The last agent-telegrapher was Robert F. Hall. (Jim Fredrickson collection.)

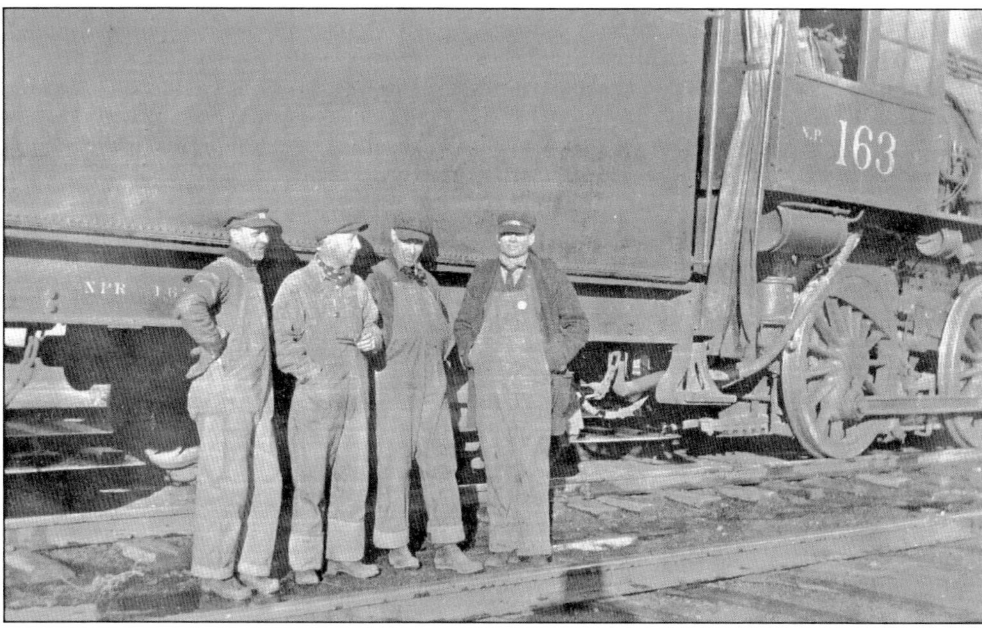

Engine No. 163 was built in the Schenectady, New York, Locomotive Works factory in 1898. The Class-S, Type 4-6-0 engine was scrapped at the Northern Pacific Shops in 1928. The four unidentified men are, from left to right, a fireman who shoveled coal into the fire bin, an engineer wearing a kerchief for protection from flying cinders, a brakeman, and a conductor. (Thomas R. Stenger collection.)

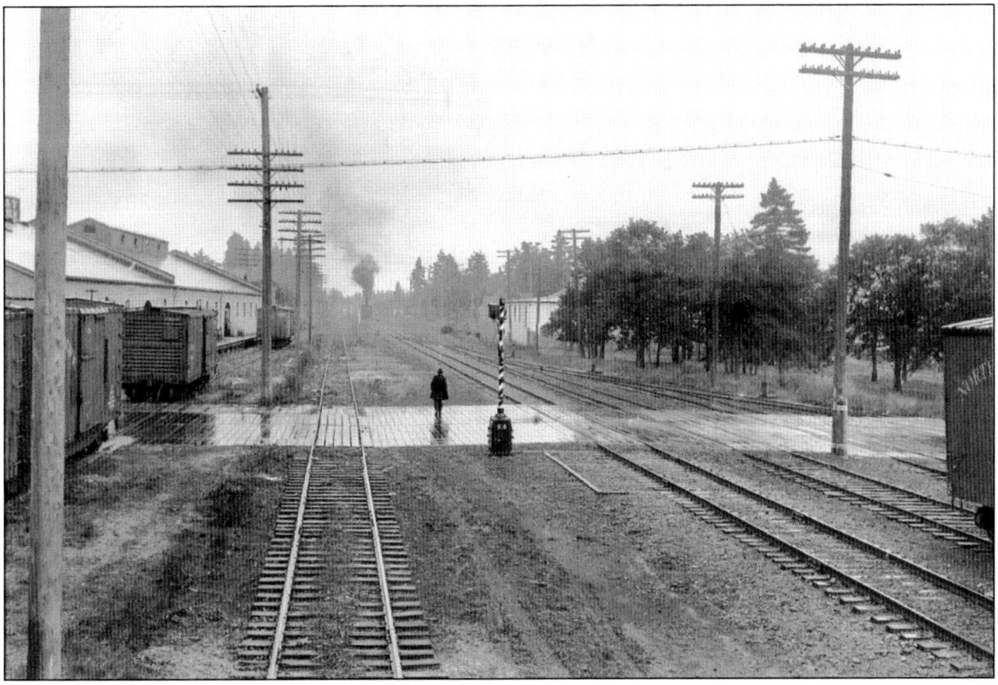

An unidentified man standing beside the tracks at Fifty-sixth Street in 1927 waits for an approaching train. The battery-operated wigwag signal and crossing alarm were installed by the railroad to protect the operation of the main line. The Northern Pacific Right-of-Way Department agreed to allow the street open to its full width across the right-of-way. (Jim Fredrickson collection.)

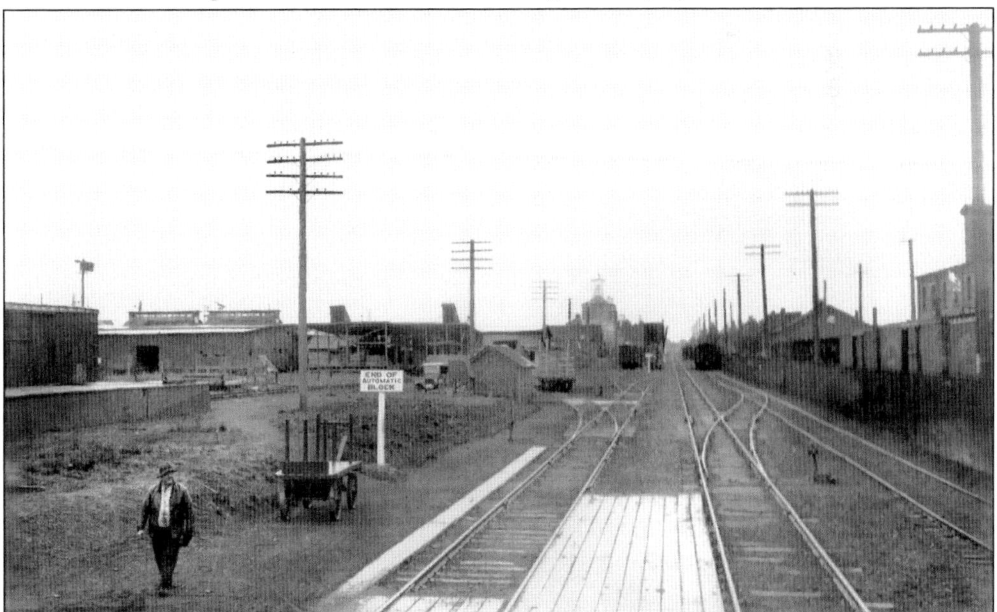

Looking south from the Northern Pacific South Tacoma Station at Fifty-first Street, an unidentified man walks along the tracks in 1927. The sign behind him indicates the end of the automatic block signaling, which conveyed to trains the occupancy and/or condition of the track ahead of them. The fence on the right surrounds the railroad shops. (Jim Fredrickson collection.)

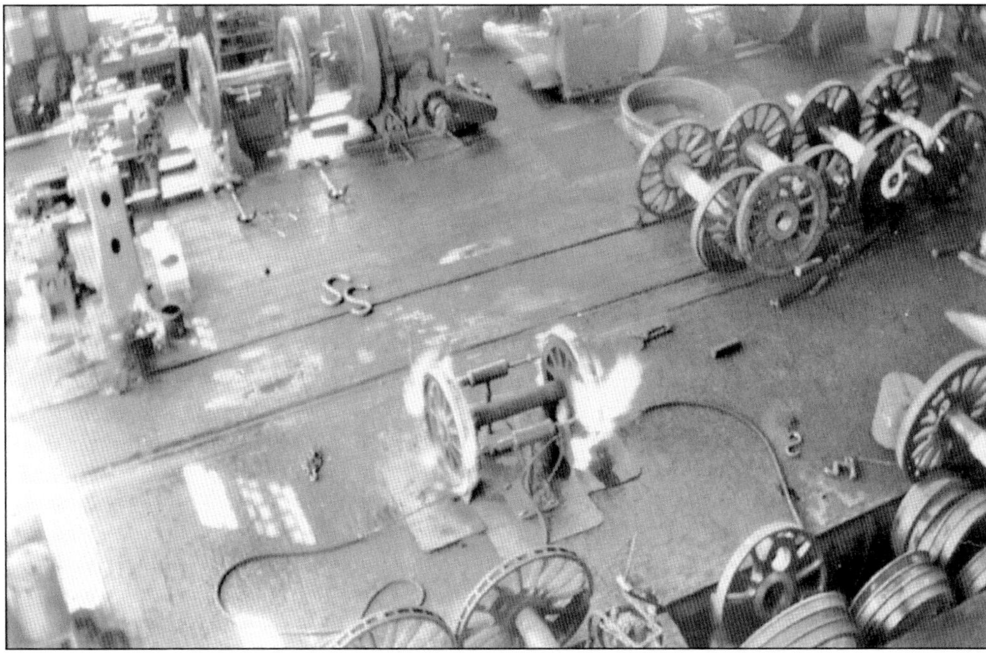

As many as 40 pairs of wheels a day were removed, checked, repaired, or replaced in the Northern Pacific machine shops. A new tire (above) is being heated in 1949 to expand enough to slide over the wheel. The drive wheels for steam engine 1529 (below) are being inspected or repaired. (Jim Fredrickson collection.)

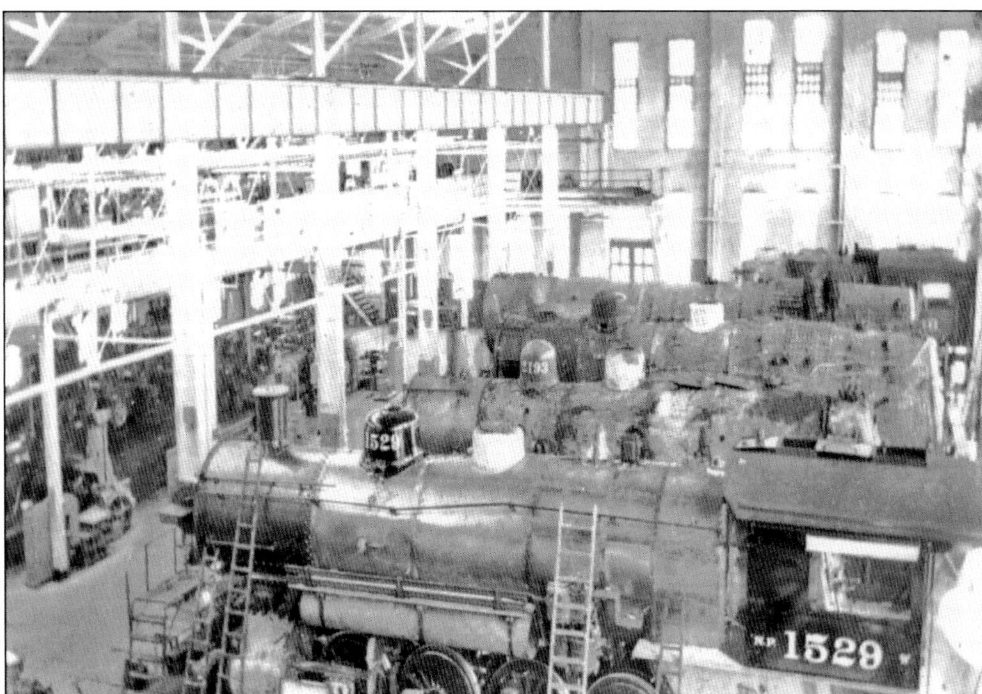

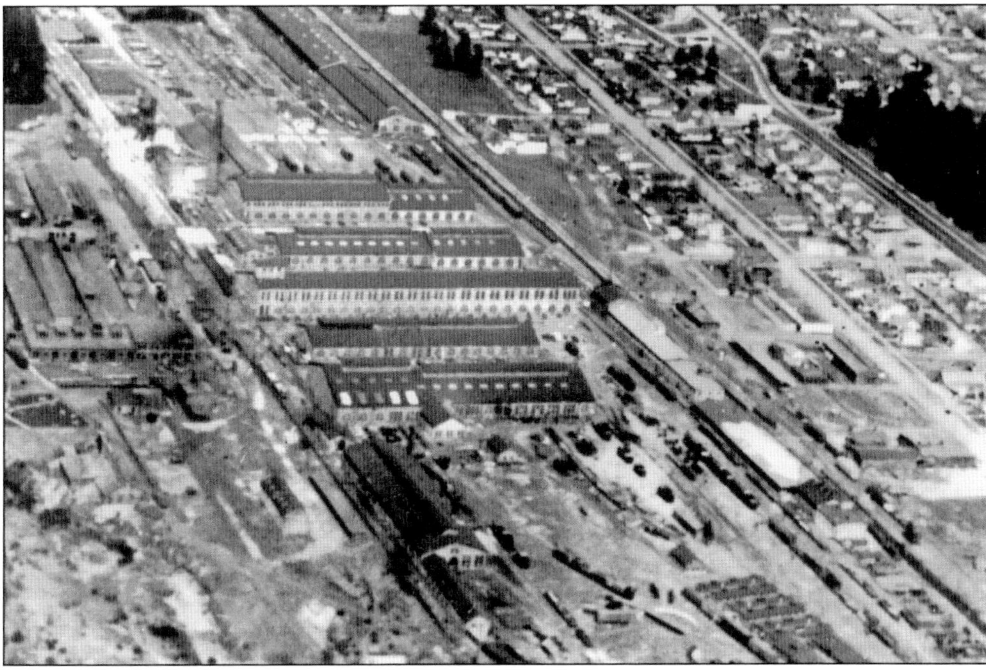

Two aerial images show Northern Pacific Shops as they reached their peak in the 1940s and just before their decline and demise in the 1970s. The upper image shows the shops in full capacity as the workers maintained and repaired the railroad cars and locomotives. As the merger with Burlington Northern neared, the shops began to shut down. The amalgamation was finalized March 3, 1970. The South Tacoma passenger station is gone from the lower image, which places the date past December 31, 1965, when the station closed and was demolished. The South Tacoma Airport, hangars, and airplanes are visible on the upper left. A portion of South Fifty-Sixth Street shows in the lower left and the elevator of X-Cel Feeds, Inc., originally Kenworthy Grain and Milling Company, is visible in the lower right. (Jim Fredrickson collection.)

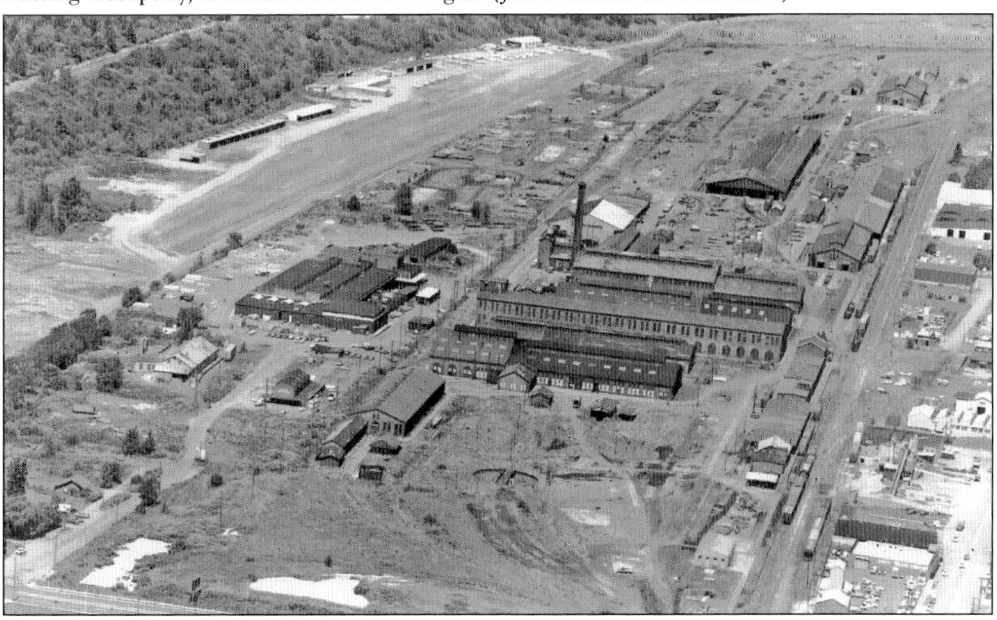

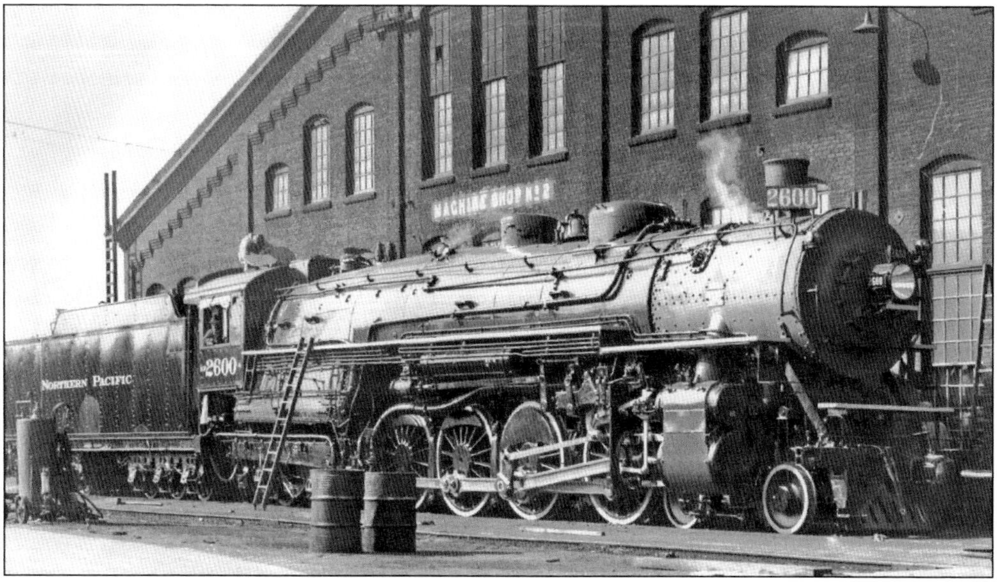

The Class-A passenger locomotive No. 2600, standing stately on the tracks alongside Northern Pacific Machine Shop No. 2 in 1946, was the first 4-8-4 built. The design was adopted by most major railroads and labeled "Northern" due to its origin on the Northern Pacific Line. It was built by Alco-Schenectady in 1926 and dismantled at the South Tacoma Railroad Shops in 1956. (Jim Fredrickson photograph.)

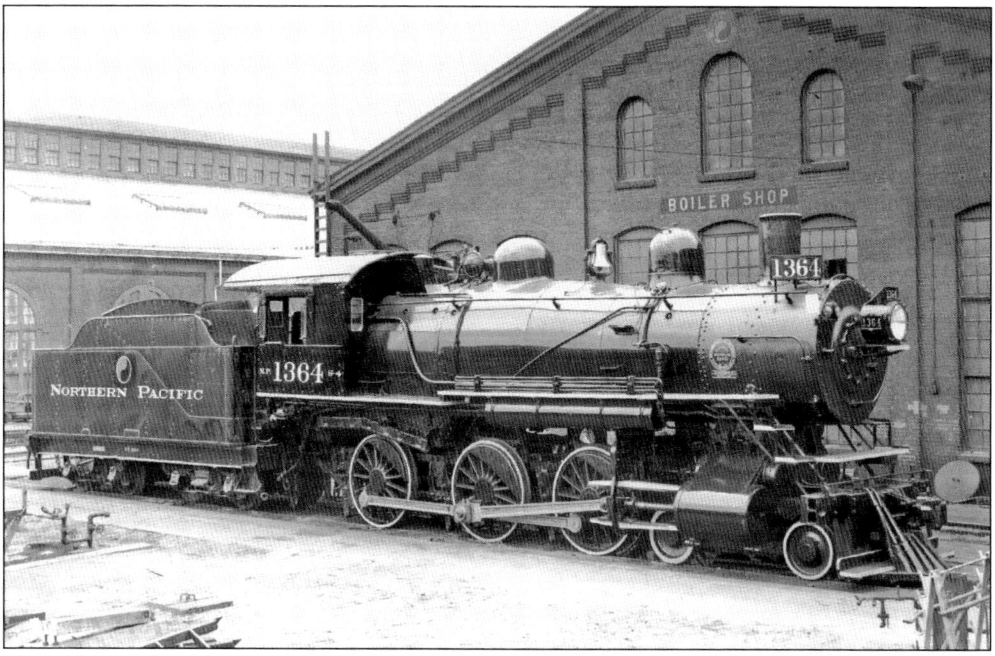

The 1954 Northern Pacific steam locomotive No. 1364 S-4 waits by the boiler shop in the Northern Pacific Railway Shops compound. All locomotives were given a complete overhaul every four years as part of a regular railroad maintenance program. The 1364 was eventually put on display at Point Defiance Park in Tacoma and is currently being restored at a museum in Toppenish, Washington. (Jim Fredrickson photograph.)

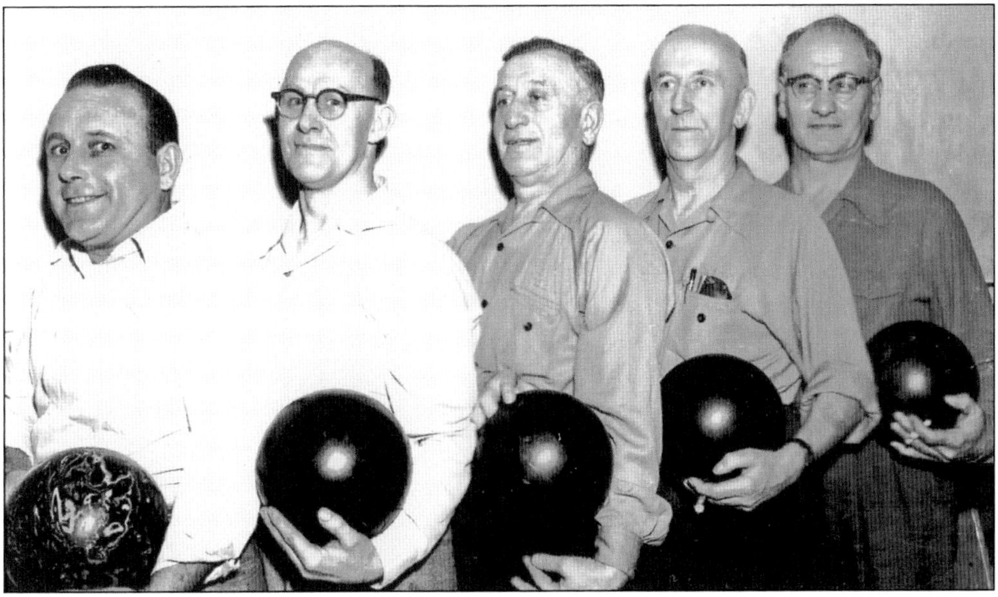

In 1953, these five mill workers bowled in one of the many leagues composed of employees from various railroad shops. The rivalry was intense but fun among the teams. This team includes, from left to right, Ted Kercher, Del Miller, Peter Lanz, Birger Johnson, and Gregory Lantz. (Jim Fredrickson collection.)

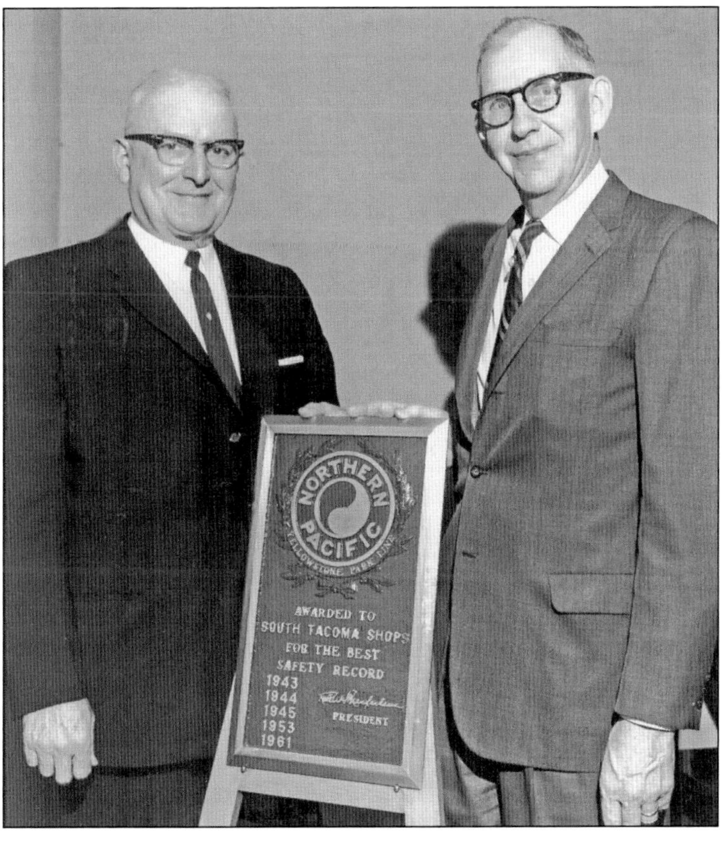

South Tacoma Shops general mechanical superintendent J. A. Cannon (left) and shop superintendent R. H. Spellmeyer proudly represent the Shops in 1961 to accept an award at the annual Temple Theatre Banquet. This was the fifth year the railway Shops had received the award for the best safety record. (Jim Fredrickson collection.)

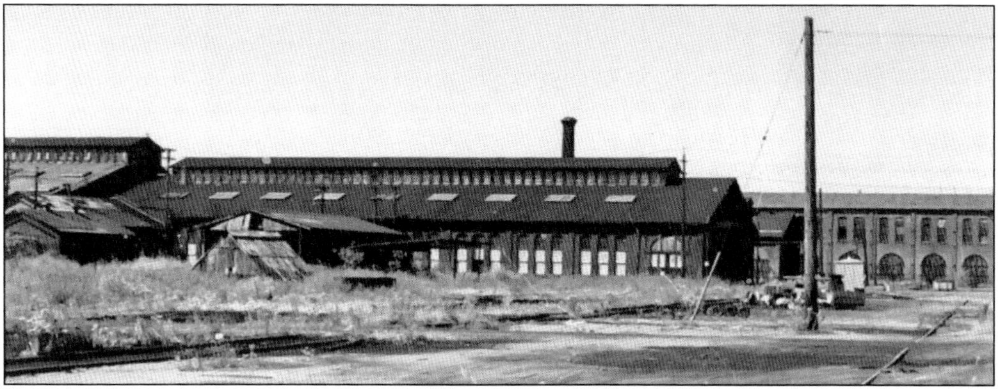

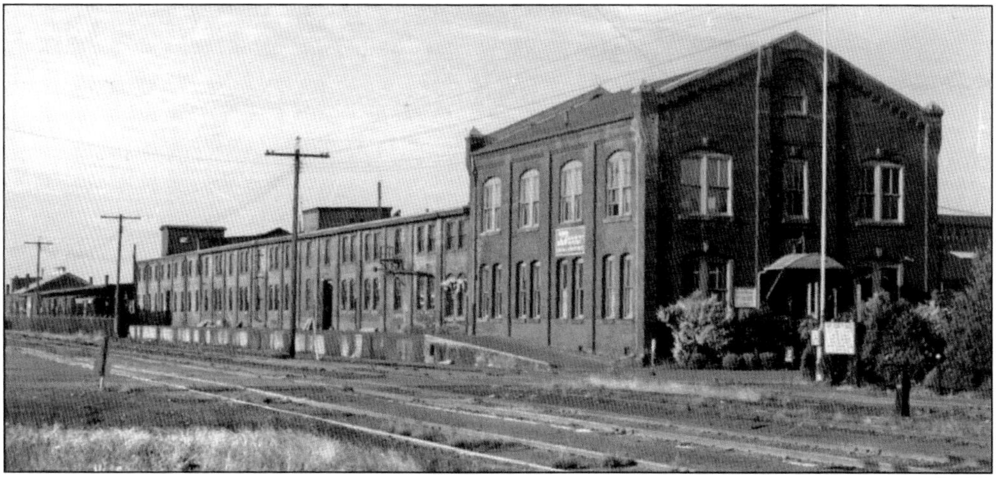

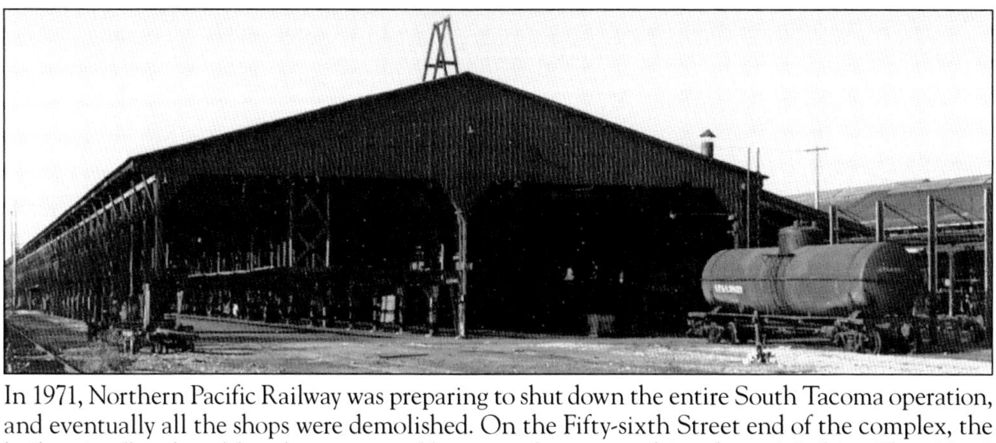

In 1971, Northern Pacific Railway was preparing to shut down the entire South Tacoma operation, and eventually all the shops were demolished. On the Fifty-sixth Street end of the complex, the boiler-pipe-flue shop (above) was situated between the two machine shops. Machine Shop No. 1 was home to 22 pits and two 10-ton Whiting overhead cranes. The oil house, store department, and office buildings (middle) show a Burlington Northern sign, evidence of the previous year's merger. The store department operated a reclamation plant for locomotives, cars, and old machinery, which were dismantled and salvaged for other uses. The new car shed (bottom) measured 106 feet wide and 854.5 feet long. A busy shop in its heyday prior to World War II, the car shed was known to turn out 10 boxcars, 6 refrigerator cars, and 19 flat cars during an eight-hour shift. (Jim Fredrickson collection.)

Three

AN INFRASTRUCTURE DEVELOPS

As the South Tacoma community grew along the tracks and spread in all directions, the need for a public infrastructure became apparent.

In 1904, a prominent South Tacoma citizen spouted in the *Tacoma Daily Ledger*, "It is an outrage. Here is the city's leading cemetery and to reach it in the winter it is necessary to zigzag around stumps and drive through mud almost hub deep."

People wanted electricity in their homes, business owners needed power, and everyone wanted healthy drinking water. Transportation to South Tacoma for workers as well as for social activities called for streetcars and better roads.

Houses and shops were built of wood; the need for a local fire station became crucial. Occasionally a rowdy situation called for police intervention and jail accommodations.

New residents wanted to keep in touch with family and friends left behind. According to a 1985 South Tacoma History report prepared for the City of Tacoma, the first post office, known as Excelsior, was established at South Fifty-eighth and Orchard Streets in 1891. Later the post office was known as Edison—the name was chosen when Thomas Edison promised to equip an experimental laboratory in the Northern Pacific Shops. In 1895, since there was already an Edison Post Office in Skagit County, and since Thomas Edison never honored his promise, the name was changed to South Tacoma.

As neighborhoods grew, so did the parks—complete with picnic areas for large and small neighborhood gatherings and wading pools for the young and old. A library with a reading room provided a gathering place for the more tranquil population.

The humane society was established to protect horses and cows from abusive treatment and as a shelter for domestic animals with no home.

The infrastructure took shape, and the people settled into a community-building mode. South Tacoma was becoming an urban destination.

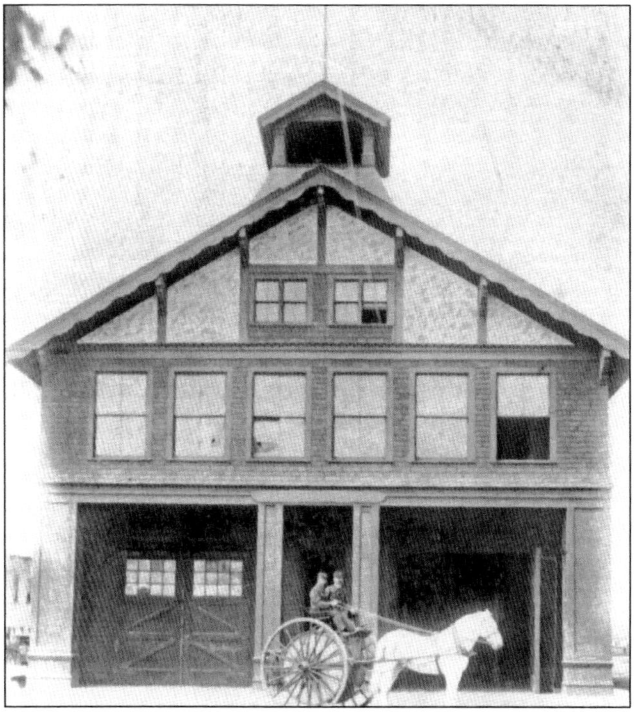

A. Dougherty sits proudly holding the reins in front of South Tacoma's first fire station the day it opened, February 19, 1892. Hose Company No. 1, at 5048 South Puget Sound Avenue, provided service for 28 years until closed in 1920. Dougherty's passenger is Capt. Fred Bowers. The two-wheeled hosecart, with 800 feet of hose wound between the wheels, was pulled by one horse. (Ralph Decker.)

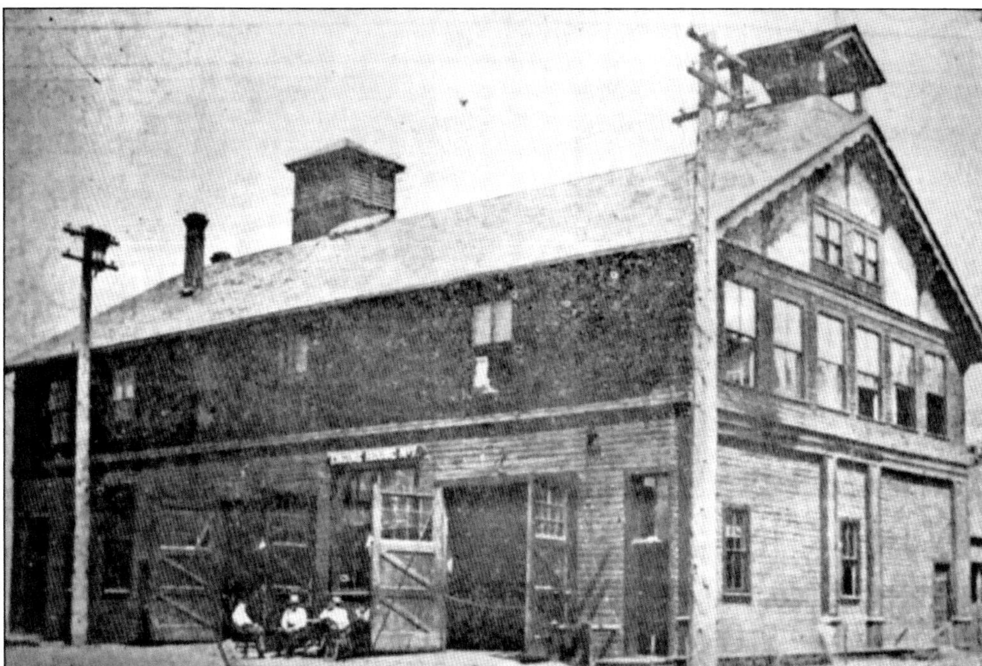

According to a 1956 special edition of the *Tacoma Star*, a popular pastime for local folks was to assemble at the South Tacoma fire station at 6:00 p.m. to watch the firemen slide down the brass pole for their daily practice alarm. The cupola on the left contained a bell. The other tower was used to dry the company's hoses after putting out a blaze. (Larry Kilen Barbershop.)

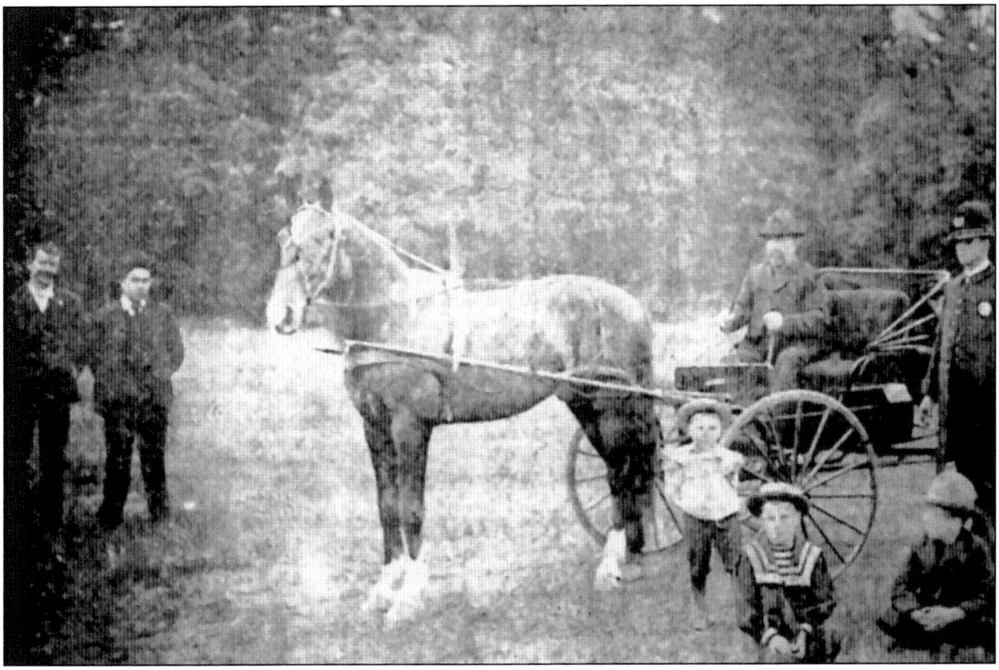

The 1956 *Tacoma Star* "South Tacoma Progress Edition" noted it had been quite some time since a horse had been seen in South Park. In c. 1905, the tyke standing next to the buggy wheel is future South Tacoma car dealer Tommy Mallon. Others are, from left to right (on the left) B. Desmond and Frank Doane; driver H. Doane; policeman E. Webb; (seated) Fred Doane and Floyd Dougherty; and Look Out, the horse. (Larry Kilen Barbershop.)

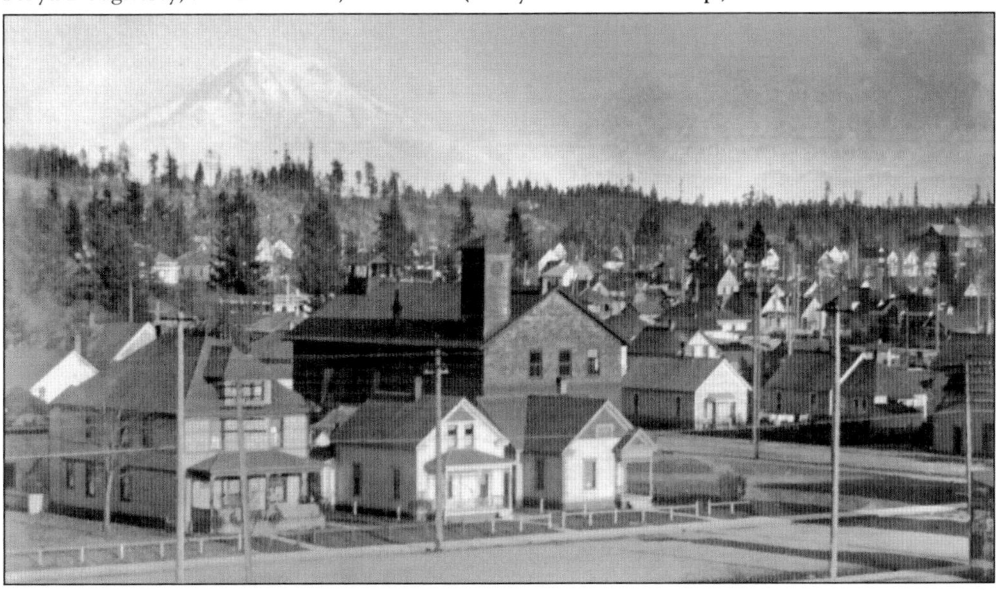

In 1908, South Tacoma's first fire station towers above the neighborhood homes at 5048 South Puget Sound Avenue. Built in 1892, Hose Company No. 1 later changed to Engine Company No. 7. The building closed in 1920 when the new station opened on South Fifty-Sixth Street. Mount Rainier looms above, and Edison Elementary School nestles near the horizon on the far right. (Thomas R. Stenger collection.)

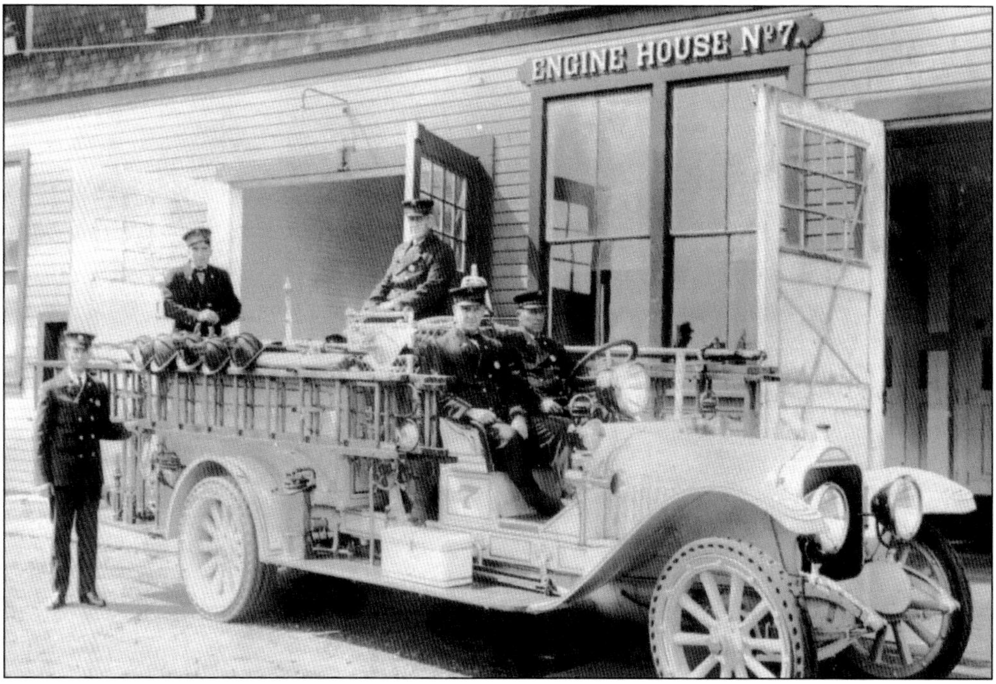

Five firefighters pose with a 1915 White combination hose and chemical engine in front of Engine House No. 7. The only White ever owned by the South Tacoma fire department, it was purchased from the White Motor Company and was in service from 1915 to 1929. The firefighters are, from left to right, Dave Carstens, Howard Sayres, Charles Armson, Emory Whitaker, and Art Ludden. (Ralph Decker.)

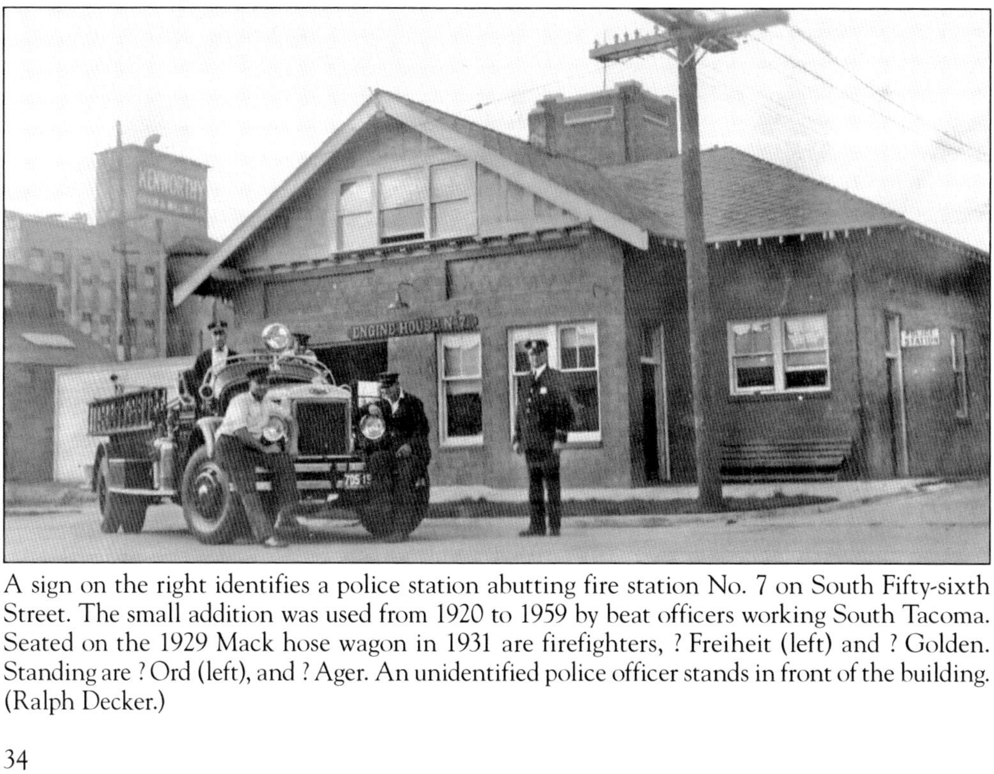

A sign on the right identifies a police station abutting fire station No. 7 on South Fifty-sixth Street. The small addition was used from 1920 to 1959 by beat officers working South Tacoma. Seated on the 1929 Mack hose wagon in 1931 are firefighters, ? Freiheit (left) and ? Golden. Standing are ? Ord (left), and ? Ager. An unidentified police officer stands in front of the building. (Ralph Decker.)

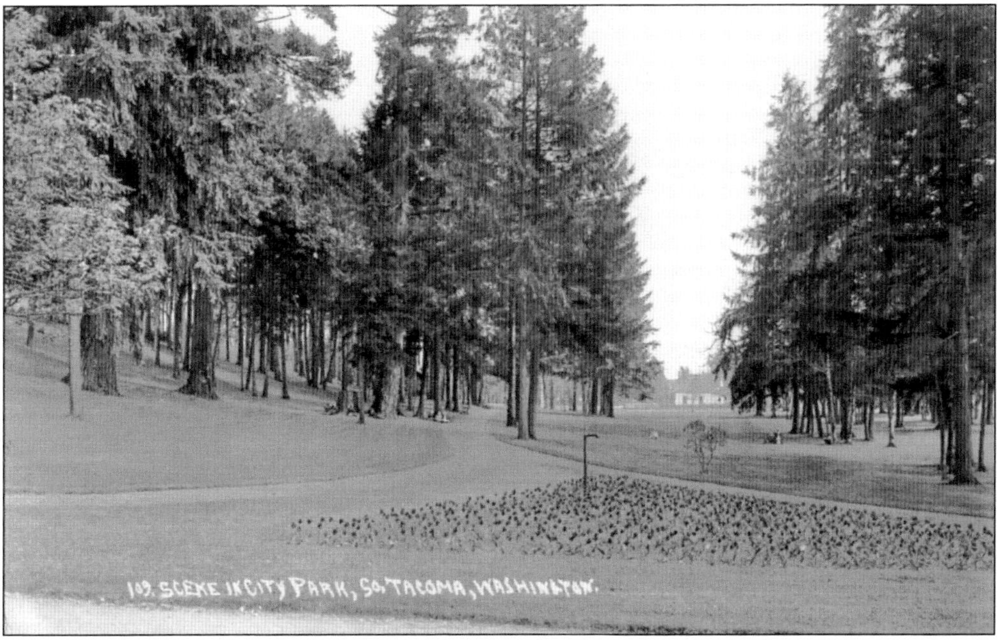

In 1905, land that was originally part of a water right-of-way was reserved to create South Park. These two views show the park at different periods of time. Above, spring brings blooming tulips with a water spigot standing by to keep the park's flowers beautiful. People lounge in the grassy area enjoying a day in the park. The lower image displays tall trees shading the pathway, while a bench beckons any passerby who appreciates the serenity of the park. The play apparatus across the path awaits an energetic child. South Tacoma boasts six city parks spread throughout the neighborhoods, including Oakland/Madrona Park, Oak Tree Park, Manitou Park, South End Recreation Area (SERA), South Park Community Center, and Wapato Hills Park. (Above, Thomas R. Stenger collection; below, Hazen family.)

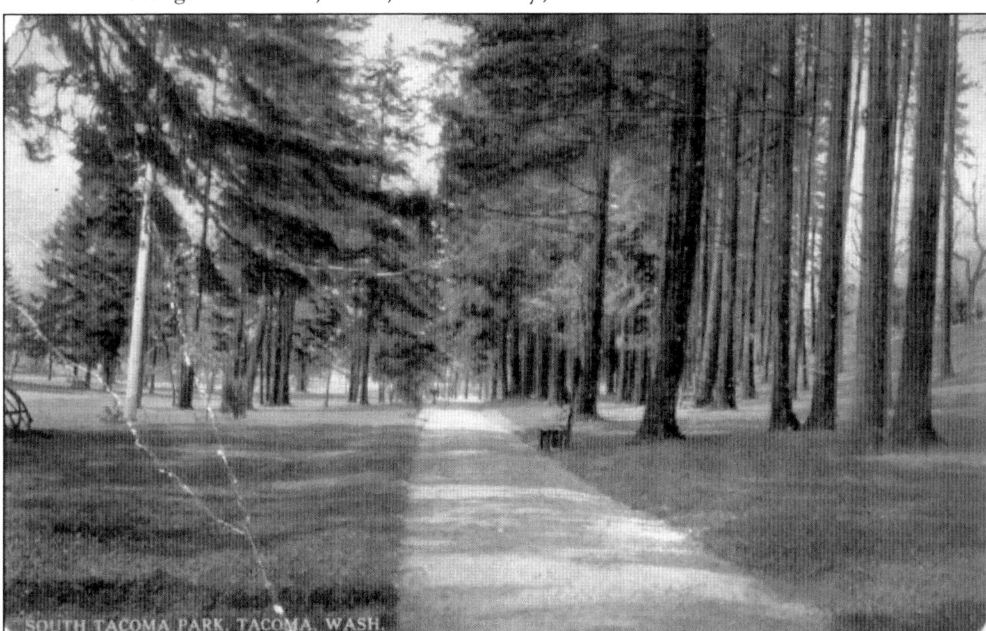

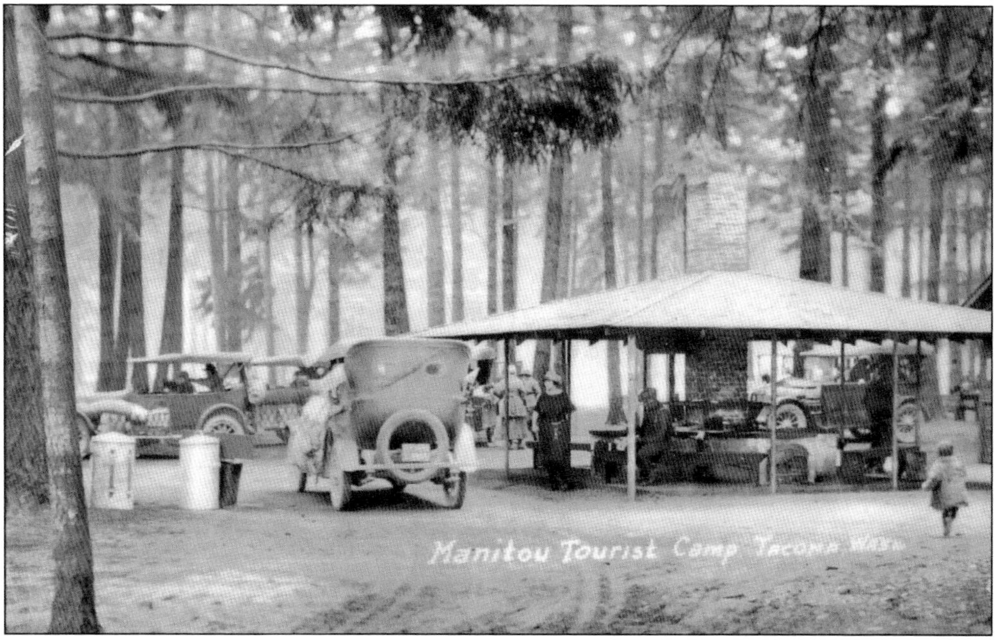

Tacoma's Park District purchased land in the southeastern corner of the city to create Manitou Park in 1915. Originally divided by the trolley car route, the park later acquired the right-of-way and created a popular tourist camp. The predecessor to motels, tourist camps enticed travelers with a relatively safe, inexpensive place to spend the night in the early part of the 20th century. One such park thrived in South Tacoma's Manitou Park. An automobile with a 1922 license plate from Ohio (above) belongs to travelers using the ovens and tables under the shelter on their journey through Tacoma. The lower image shows a tent behind a tree and numerous automobiles as travelers stop to enjoy the accommodations—such as water, lights, and basic comforts. (Manitou Park Presbyterian Church.)

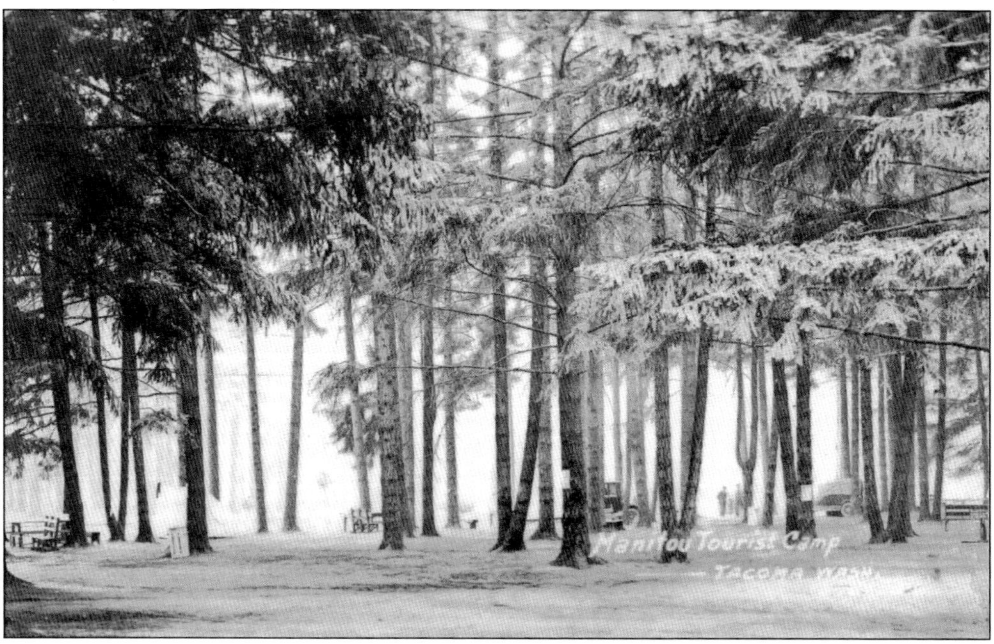

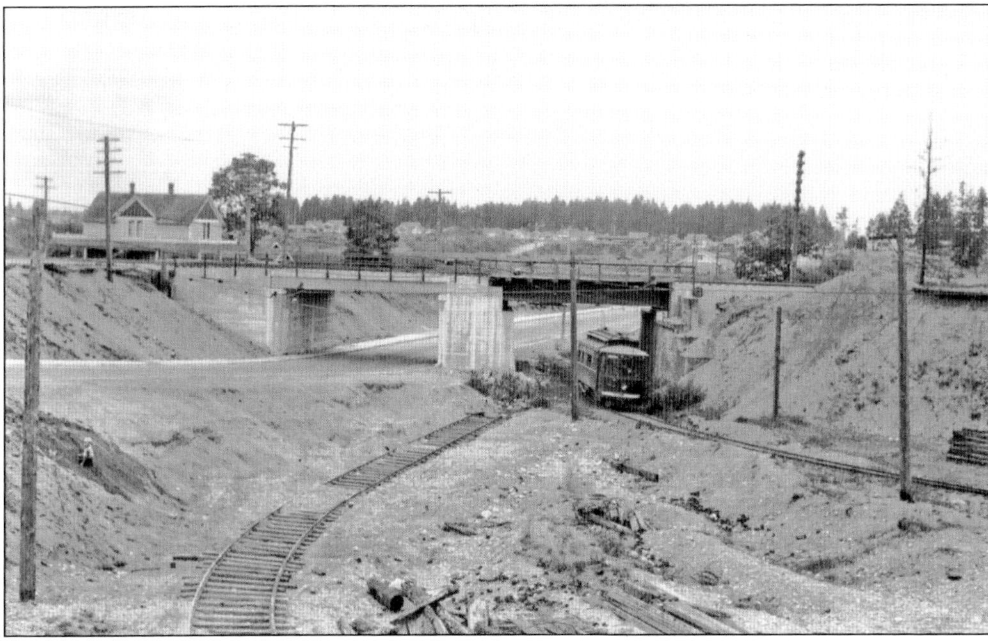

In 1927, Northern Pacific Railway visually documented its bridge over South Sixty-sixth Street and the streetcar track below to show it was compliant with a 1908 Pacific Traction Company contract. The streetcar line ran from downtown to Manitou via South Tacoma Way, making a curve at this spot. The young lad to the left playing in the sandy hillside seems oblivious to the streetcar returning to town. (Jim Fredrickson collection.)

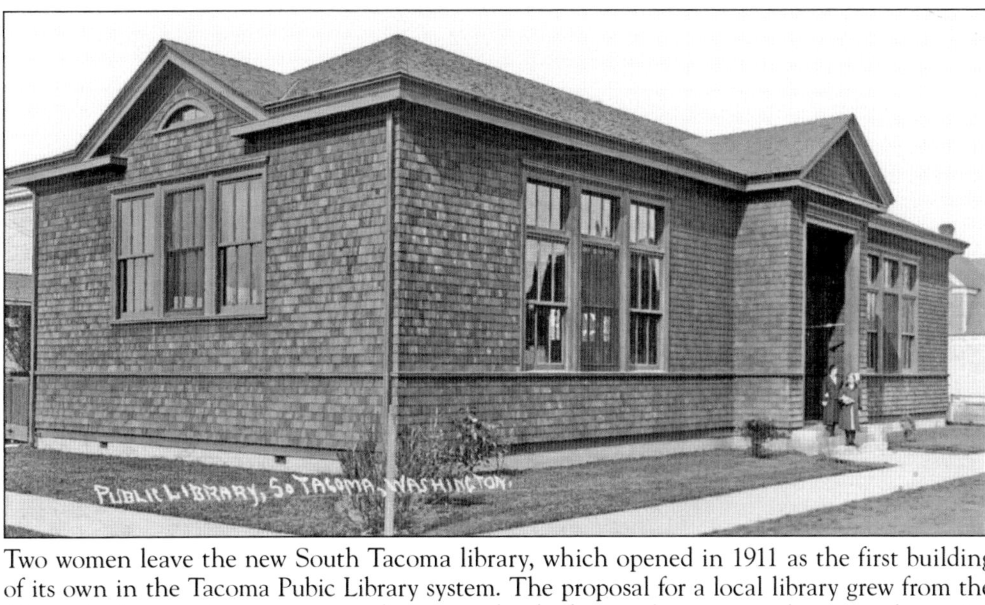

Two women leave the new South Tacoma library, which opened in 1911 as the first building of its own in the Tacoma Pubic Library system. The proposal for a local library grew from the Women's Christian Temperance reading room that had opened six years earlier as an alternative to South Tacoma saloons. The library was designed by architect George Gove and built at a cost of $3,620. (Eric Swanson collection.)

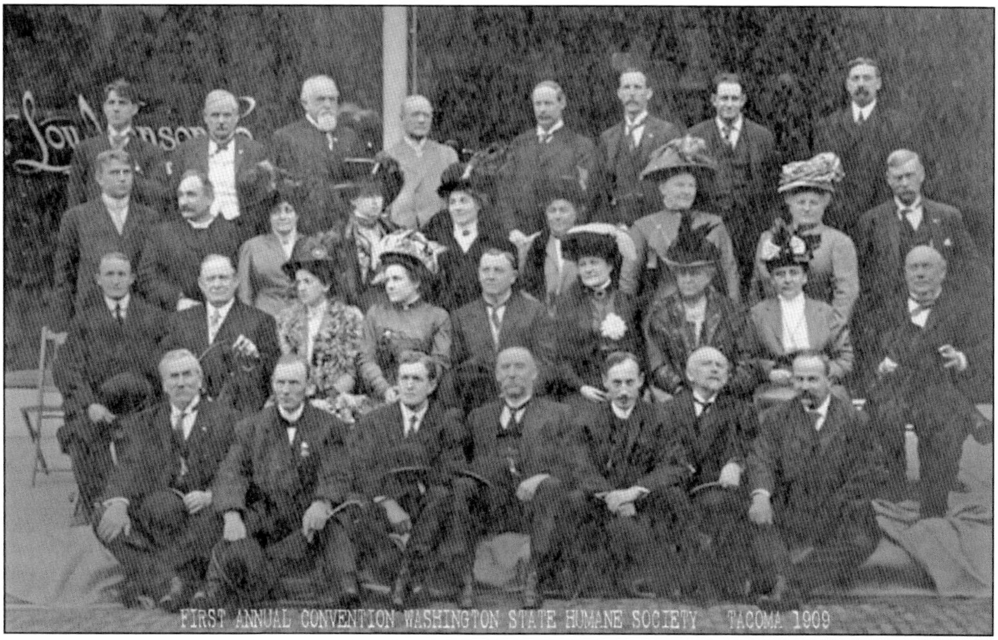

Tacoma residents formed the first local humane society in 1888. Attending the first Washington State Humane Society Convention, the founders pose in 1909 in front of Lou Johnson Clothing Store in Tacoma. Identified are J. S. Isted (fourth row, fourth from left), W. J. Thompson (first row, second from right), and H. S. Griggs (second row, left). In the absence of child welfare services, the humane society protected abused children and also improved the treatment of workhorses and cows. By the 1920s, responsibilities expanded to include all animals when the humane society moved to South Tacoma and operated an animal shelter in the Oakland area. In 1943, it moved to 2608 Center Street (below) to assume animal control duties for the city. The building has been replaced; however, the society remains at that location. (The Humane Society for Tacoma and Pierce County.)

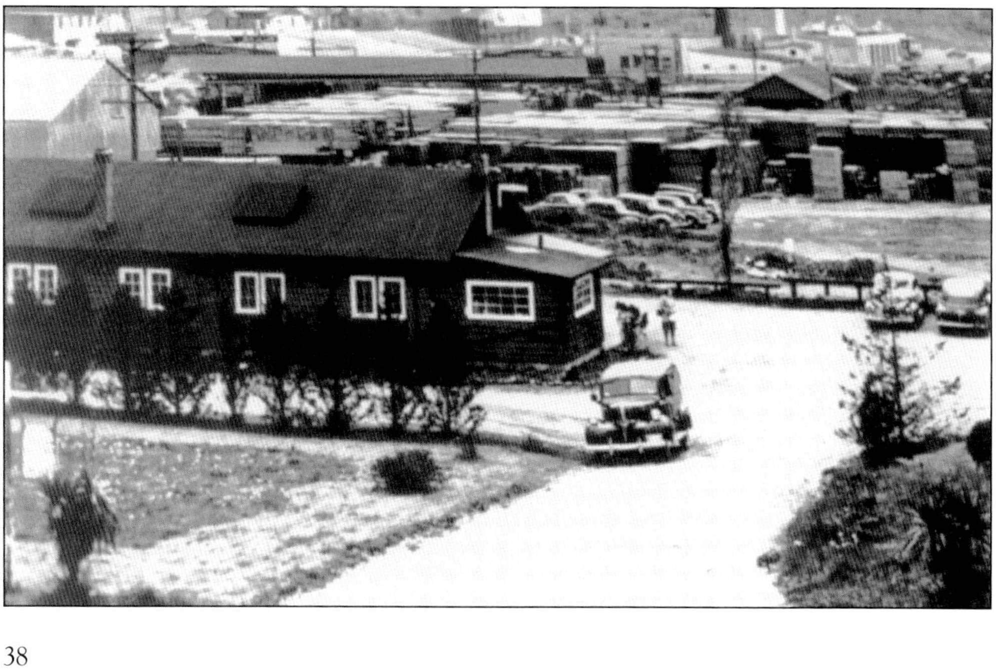

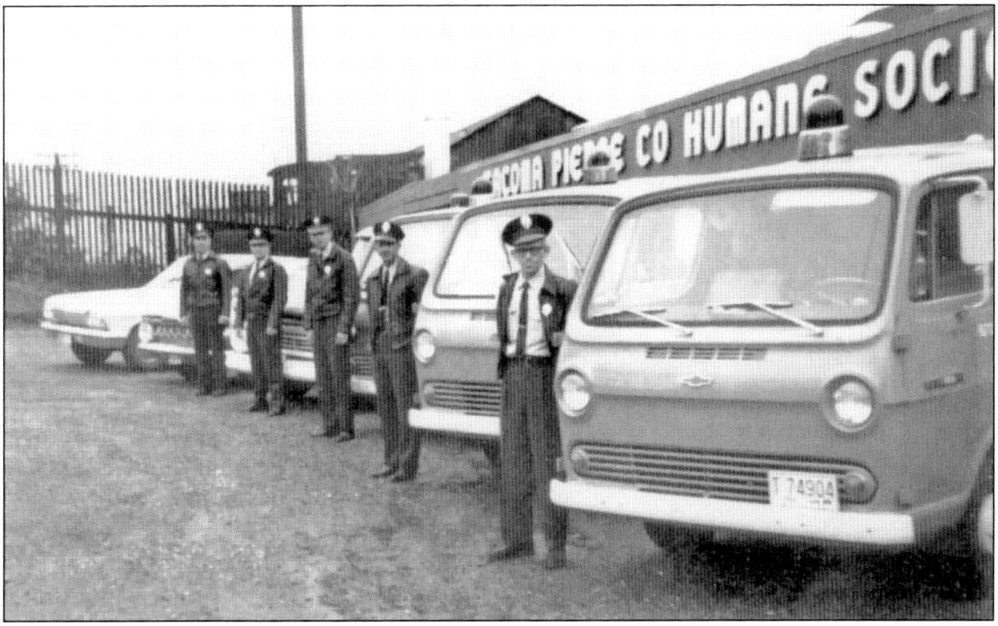

The year 1964 was for "Animal Control Officers," as they were called then. From left to right, Floyd Herron, Phil Jacobson, Phil Walsh, unidentified, and Earl Jorgenson take time to pose beside four recently purchased humane society vans. It was the same year the society reported 4,000 complaints, 7,000 truck trips, and 43,000 telephone calls for a small staff, crowded conditions, and a limited budget. (The Humane Society for Tacoma and Pierce County.)

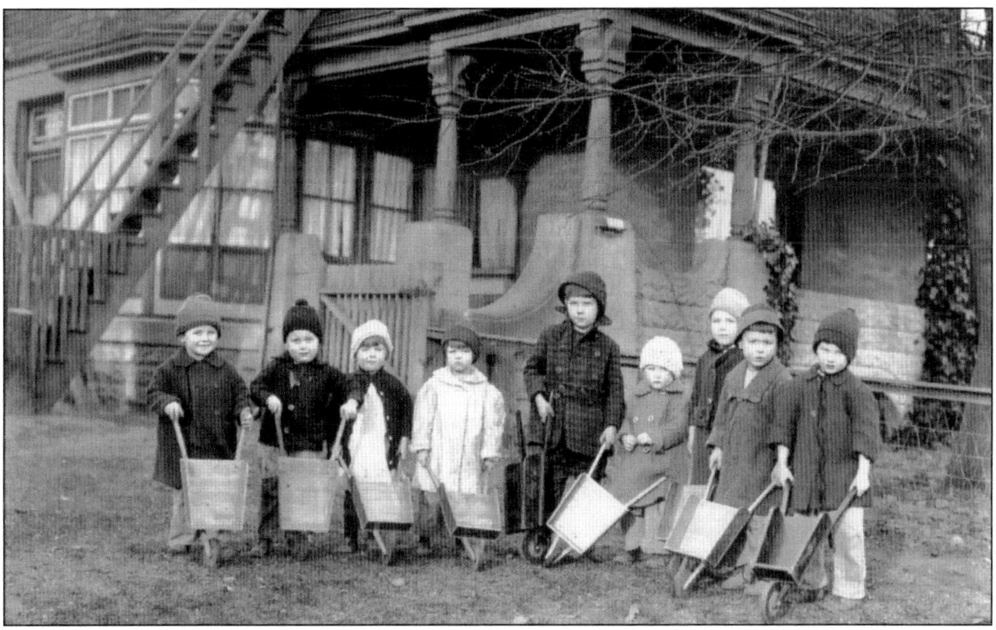

An orphanage opened in South Tacoma at 3000 South Washington Street in 1890. It was named Children's Industrial Home because it taught children to establish habits of the industries. Nine unidentified children, posing with wheelbarrows in front of their home in 1925, may be going to work in the garden. Children's protective services were formed in the 1920s and took over the responsibility of neglected children from the humane society. (TPL.)

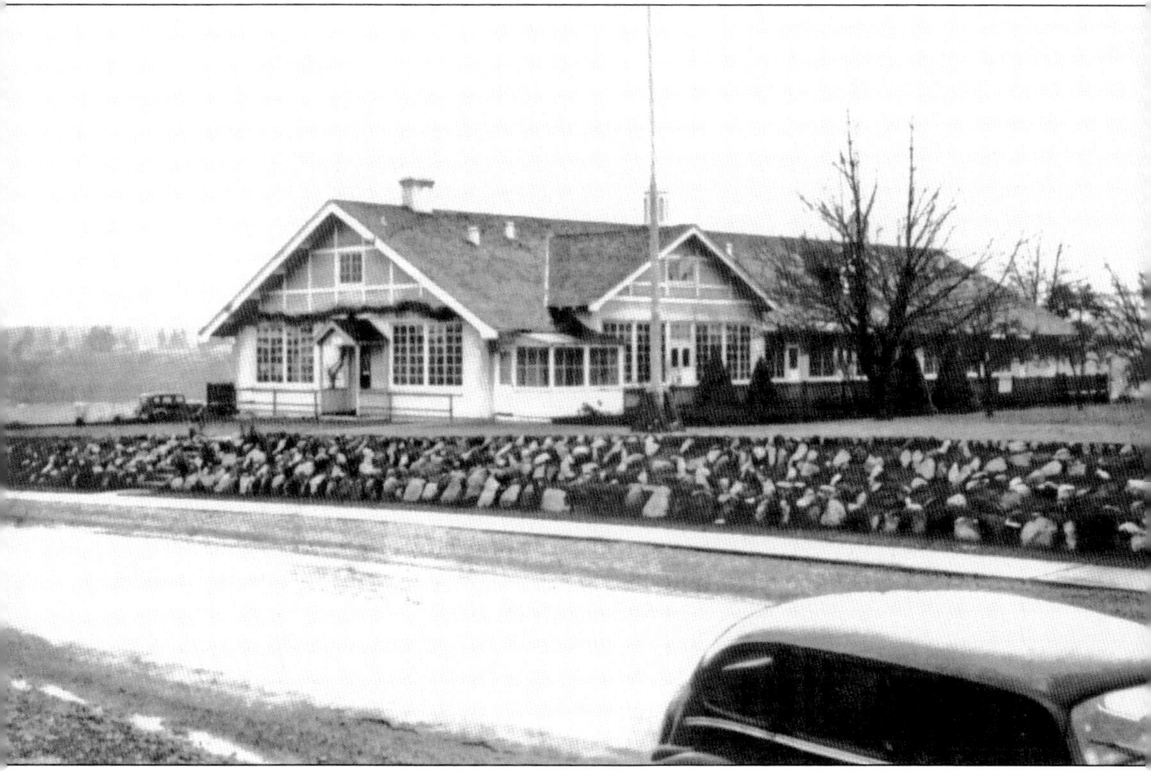

In July 1912, the city building inspector granted permission to build the first unit of the new City Contagious Hospital. According to the *Tacoma Daily Ledger*, "work began immediately at a cost of $10,000 and would be ready before the rains begin. When completed, the complex will have four separate buildings on the four corners of the grounds, and each building will be used for different diseases." The "pest house" (pestilence), as it was called, would include an engine room and kitchen in the basement, with dumb-waiters to the wards. Also included would be visitors' and nurses' rooms, a dining room, and a physician's office. Constructed by public works, the South Tacoma hospital would be one of the most modern and sanitary contagious hospitals in the Northwest, with no corners for dust and dirt to lodge. In 1927, facilities opened for treatment of diseased women. The hospital closed in 1937. During the Depression, it was a Works Progress Administration headquarters and housed defense workers during World War II. The building at 3333 South Thirty-eighth Street has been occupied by Coca-Cola since 1948. (TPL.)

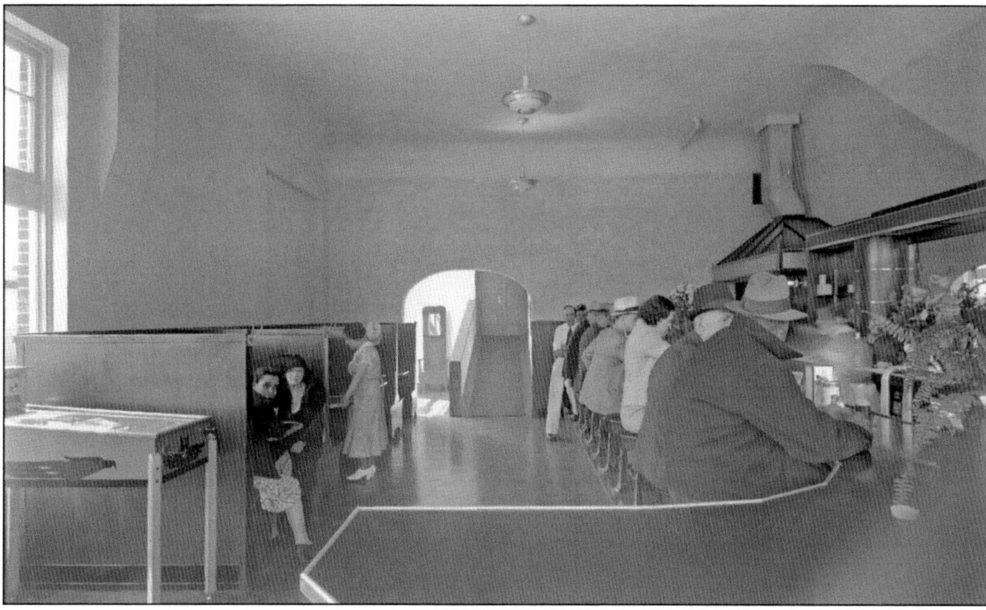

In 1937, the newly opened 50-50 Café at 5046 South Tacoma Way hosted customers enjoying the building's new conversion to electricity. The building was originally built around 1891 as Edison Hardware. The building was remodeled in 1926 for the Knights of Pythias Ladies Auxiliary Annex before it became the 50-50 Café. Gas installation also proved popular in 1938. (Tacoma Public Utilities.)

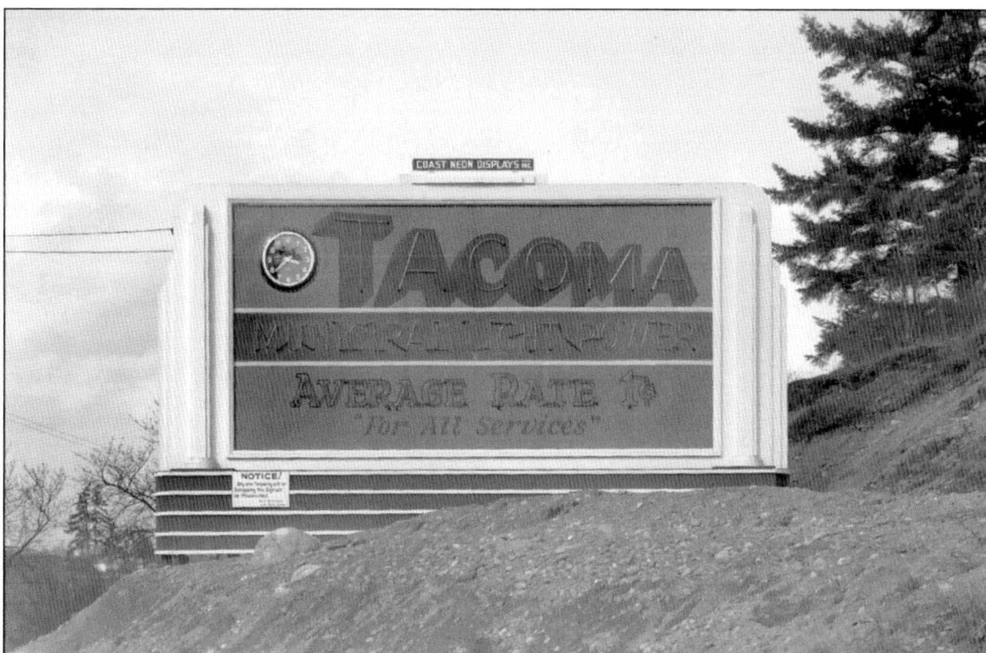

High on a hill near the South Tacoma utilities plant, a Tacoma Municipal Light and Power neon sign states the average rate for all services was 1¢ in 1939. The small sign below gives notice that "Any one Tampering with or Damageing [sic] this Sign will be Prosecuted" and is signed by Ira S. Davisson, commissioner of public utilities. (Tacoma Public Utilities.)

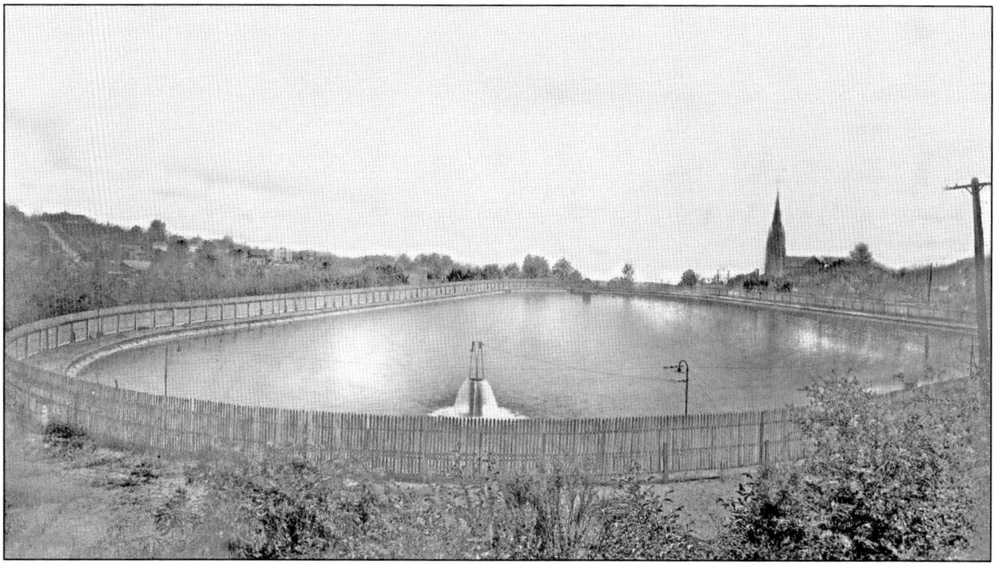

Hood Street Reservoir was built to serve, by gravity, the low-lying districts of Tacoma, including South Tacoma. The water was to be conveyed through an open-topped box-flume and emptied into the reservoir. In the foreground, an aerator is putting oxygen into the water to help prevent the growth of anaerobic bacteria in 1926. The reservoir is now capped. In the distance is Holy Rosary Catholic Church steeple. (Tacoma Public Utilities.)

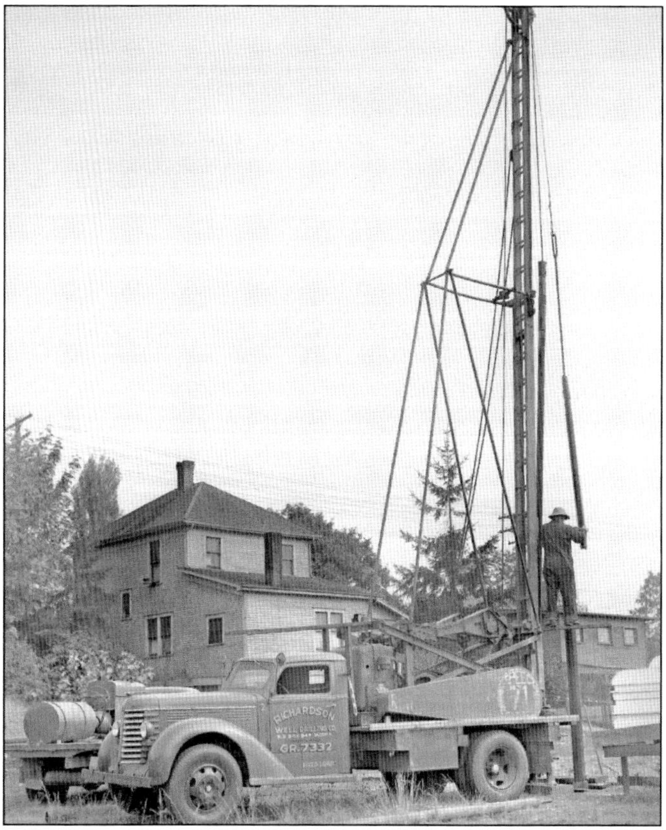

Tacoma Public Utilities Water Division contracted in 1947 with Richardson Well Drilling to determine if an adequate amount of water was available at this location for a main well. The driller is retrieving a sand pump bailer from the well, which removes the cuttings the drill bit has ground up so the drilling process can continue near Forty-fifth Street and South Tacoma Way. (Tacoma Public Utilities.)

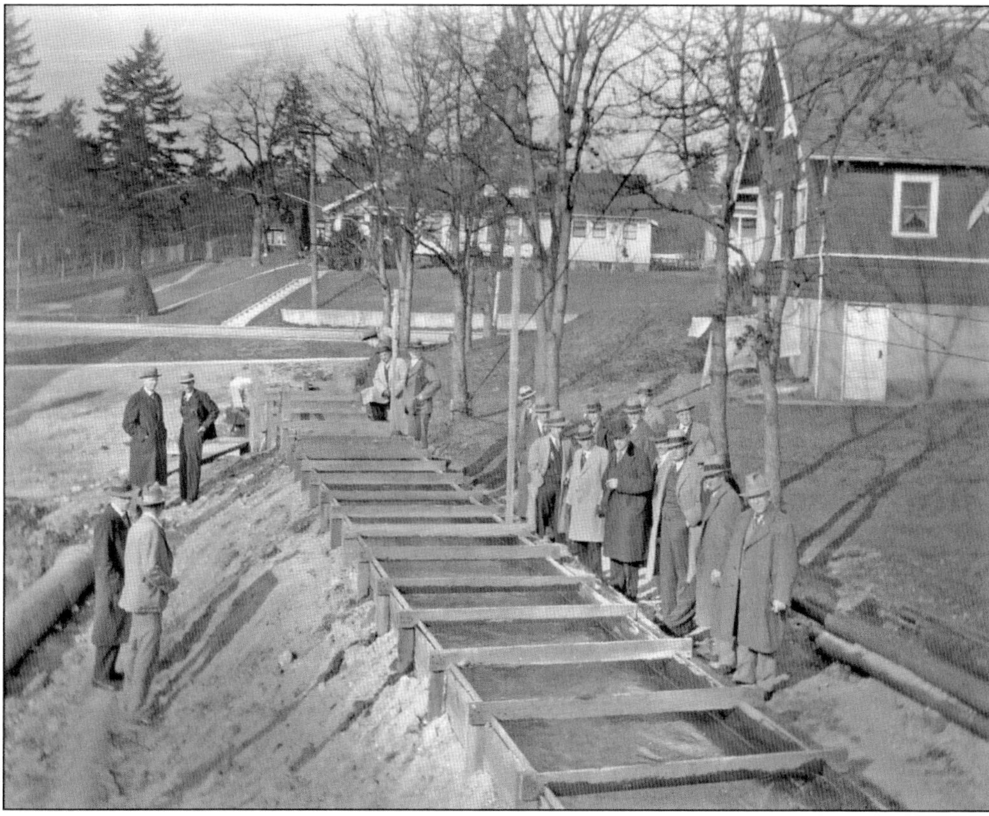

Ira S. Davisson, public utilities commissioner, center of the group at the right of the flume, has gathered men to test the output of well No. 5, one of the many wells in South Tacoma. Conferring with unidentified engineers and managers, they watch a flow test in February 1931 after contracting to drill additional wells in South Tacoma. (Tacoma Public Utilities.)

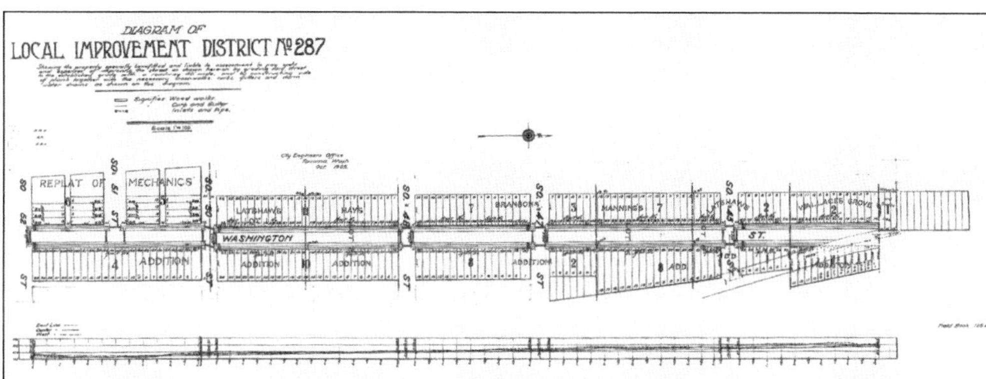

South Tacoma's population grew rapidly, and the city quickly responded to requests for improvements. This 1905 diagram from the city engineer's office states that the property that benefited would be assessed for grading five blocks of Washington Street and adding curbs, gutters, wooden sidewalks, and storm-water drains. Additional diagrams illustrate improvements such as 1906 sewer, 1914 concrete sidewalks, 1949 paving, 1957 street lighting, and many others. (Tacoma Public Works Department.)

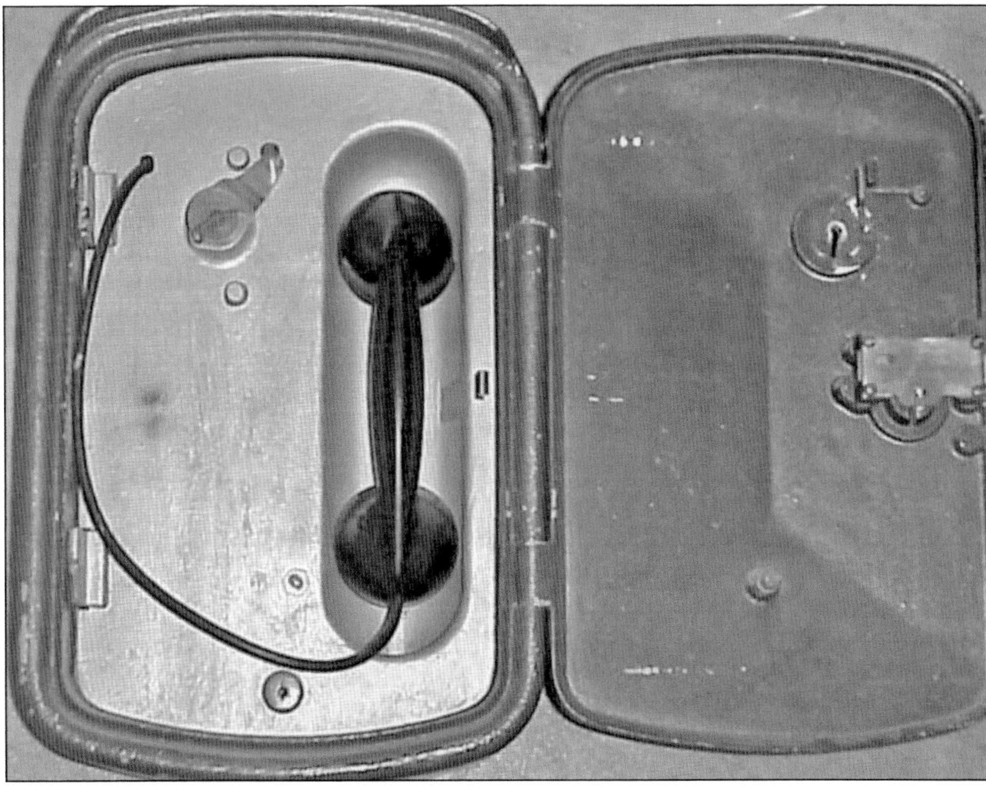

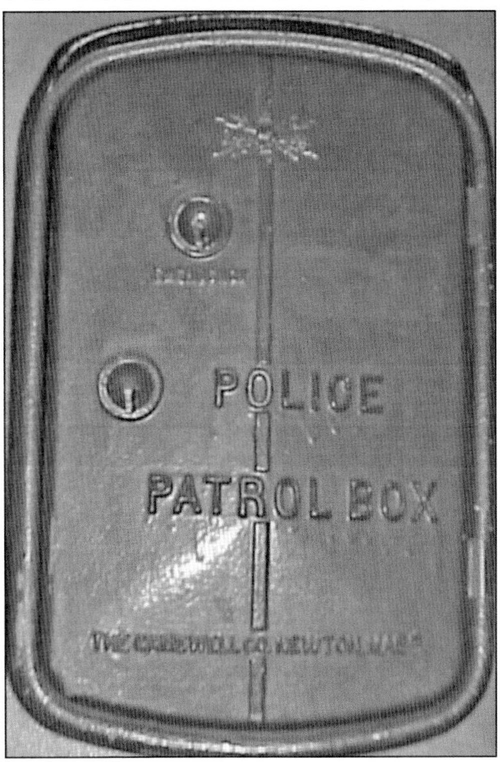

The Call Box Communication System, used by police in South Tacoma to transmit messages, was in service throughout the city from 1891 to 1973. Cast-iron boxes, mounted on poles, contained a telegraph, telephone, an emergency slot, and a light that flashed. Beat officers were required to report to the desk sergeant every hour using the call box. Officers unlocked the box with a large brass key and pulled a lever inside to send a signal to the sergeant's desk. The register made a rapping sound as it punched holes in a paper tape corresponding to the number of the call box. When needed, patrolmen turned a key in a slot marked "Emergency" to alert the desk sergeant to dispatch a wagon. "Call Lights" were used to contact officers. If a patrolman was assigned number four, the desk sergeant flashed call lights in his assigned area four times and continued until the officer called in. If the officer failed to respond, the sergeant sent the wagon to look for him. (Erik Timothy.)

Four

EMBRACING EDUCATION

The cry for public schools was heard by the school board when Junett Homestead School opened at 3319 South Adams Street in 1889. Two years later, with annexation to the Tacoma School District, the school was renamed Oakland School to identify the South Tacoma neighborhood where it was located. In 1907, after 18 years of pumping water and drinking from a single tin cup, water lines were extended to the school where students had been using two outhouses separated by a woodshed.

This was only the beginning for public and parochial schools in South Tacoma. Between 1891 and 1926, seven new public and two parochial schools opened to educate youth.

While waiting to build Edison School, anxious parents arranged for classes to begin in temporary classrooms over Scott's Feed Store at Fifty-eighth Street and Edison Avenue. The following year, 1892, Edison School opened at Fifty-eighth and Cedar Streets. South Tacoma students attended public Oakland, Edison, Manitou, Arlington, or Madison Elementary Schools and continued their education at the Barlow Annex until Lincoln Park High School opened in 1914 ("Park" was deleted from the name in 1917). After Gray Intermediate School opened in 1926, public school students attended Gray before going to Lincoln. Representing the connection to Native Americans who once hunted on the South Tacoma plains, Mount Tahoma High School opened in 1961.

The German Catholics at Holy Rosary Parish opened the first parochial school in South Tacoma in the fall of 1891. Originating in the church choir loft, 30 pupils were taught by J. Stellbring, the church organist. A three-story building was ready for the students by September 1892. By 1908, 350 students attended Holy Rosary School. Amid resistance to additional parochial schools in the Northwest in 1925, Visitation Catholic School opened with 170 pupils and a faculty of four Benedictine Sisters. By 1957, Visitation School had an enrollment of 567 students.

Whether parochial or public, many generations of families have attended the same schools in South Tacoma for the past 120 years and continue to embrace the educational needs of their community.

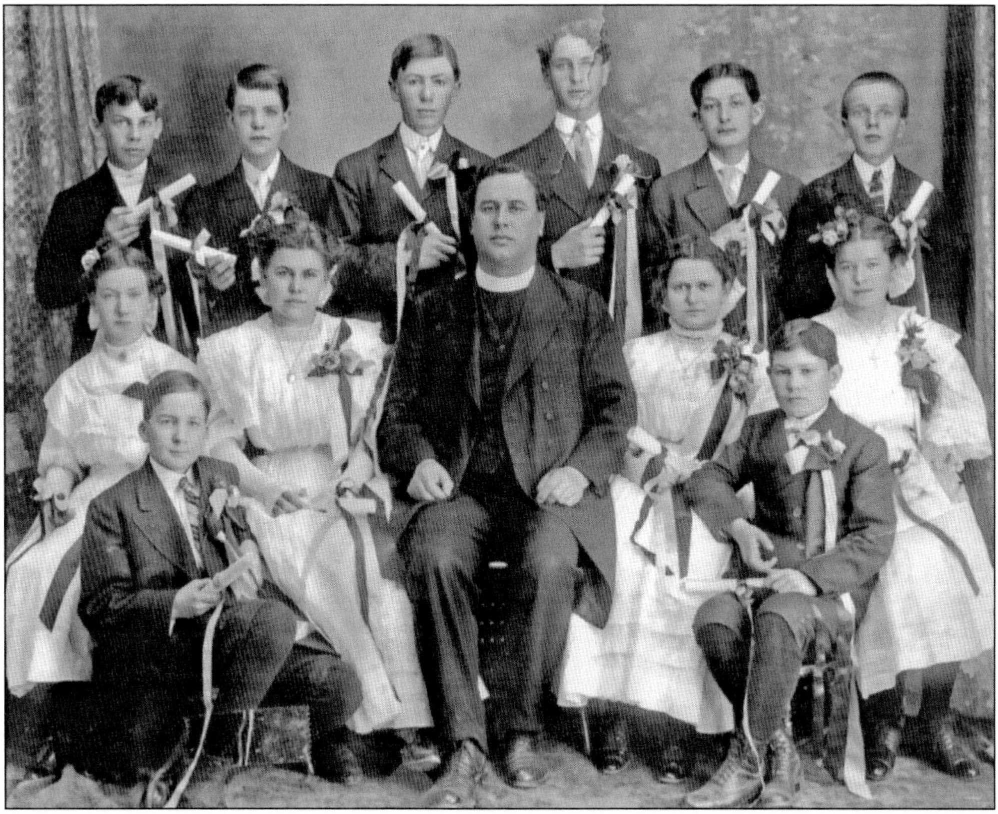

In September 1891, Holy Rosary School opened at 512 South Thirtieth Street with a dozen pupils attending the first parochial school in Tacoma. This 1905 graduation class surrounding Father Oswald includes, from left to right, (first row) ? Monaghan and ? Baglay; (second row) Mary Cleary, ? Reuter, ? Lorenzo, and ? Graisy; (third row) ? Maloney, ? Wuest, George Bader, Frank Auer, ? Devoto, and ? Traut. (Art and Loretta Boyle.)

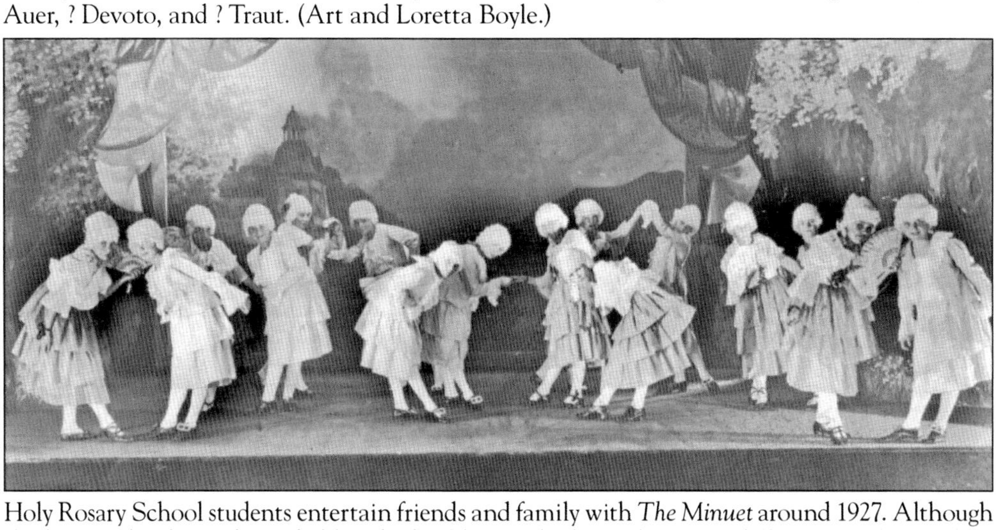

Holy Rosary School students entertain friends and family with *The Minuet* around 1927. Although the boys and girls are dressed alike, the buckles on the boys' shoes can differentiate them, while the girls' shoes have straps. This may have been a benefit performance to raise money for the newly built church. Julie Sousa, second from right, holds a fan. (Art and Loretta Boyle.)

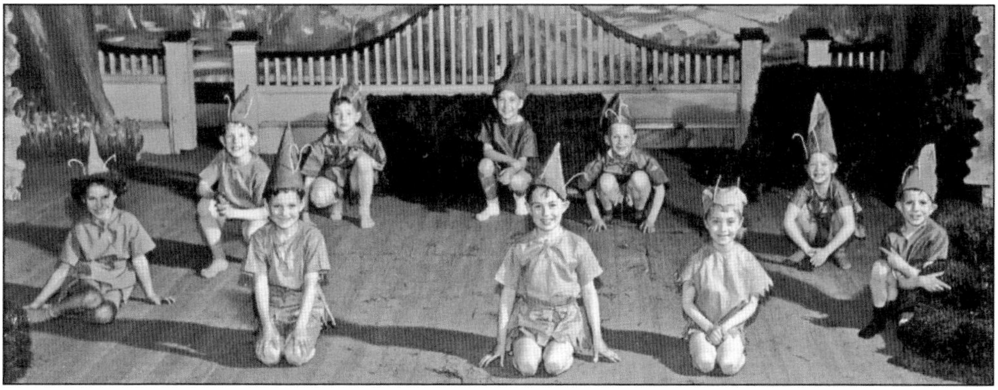

Holy Rosary School students innovatively entertained guests in 1948, fifty-seven years after the first children attended the Catholic school. The mixed-grade elves (top) on the school stage are, from left to right, (first row) Jean Weller, Gary Sabol, Eddie Hazuka, Cathy Sleet, and Jerry Morris; (second row) Eddie ?, Mike Failor, Beatrice Zemanek, Ted Fick, and Judy Nygaard. The second-grade nursery rhyme characters (bottom) are (left group) Norris Thompson (Gingerbread Boy), Judy Hanson (Bo Peep), Kenneth Miller (Jack), Darlene Barney (Jill), Karen Rawlings (Miss Muffet), Richard Schwarz (Black Sambo), Cynthia Reese (left Cinderella), and Beatrice Reese (Cinderella); (middle group) David Warnke (Pinocchio), Sammy Allotta (Guido), and Bill Bryon, John Vargo, Bobby ?, and Serge Grant (soldiers, from left to right); (right group) Sharon Hartman (Raggedy Ann), Duane Weaver (Raggedy Andy), Janet Horace (Floretta), Bobby Schneider (Peter Rabbit), Joan Theriault (Red Riding Hood), Gary Flannigan (Little Boy Blue), and Doreen Spadafore (Snow White). (Cathy Bunger family collection.)

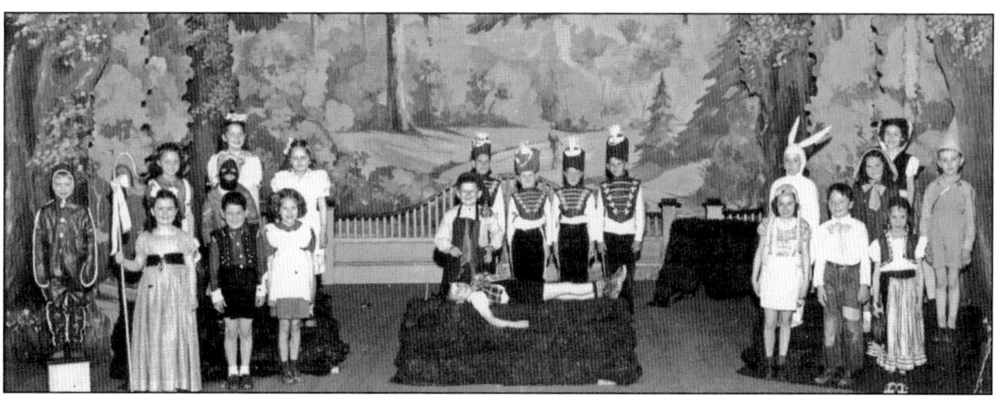

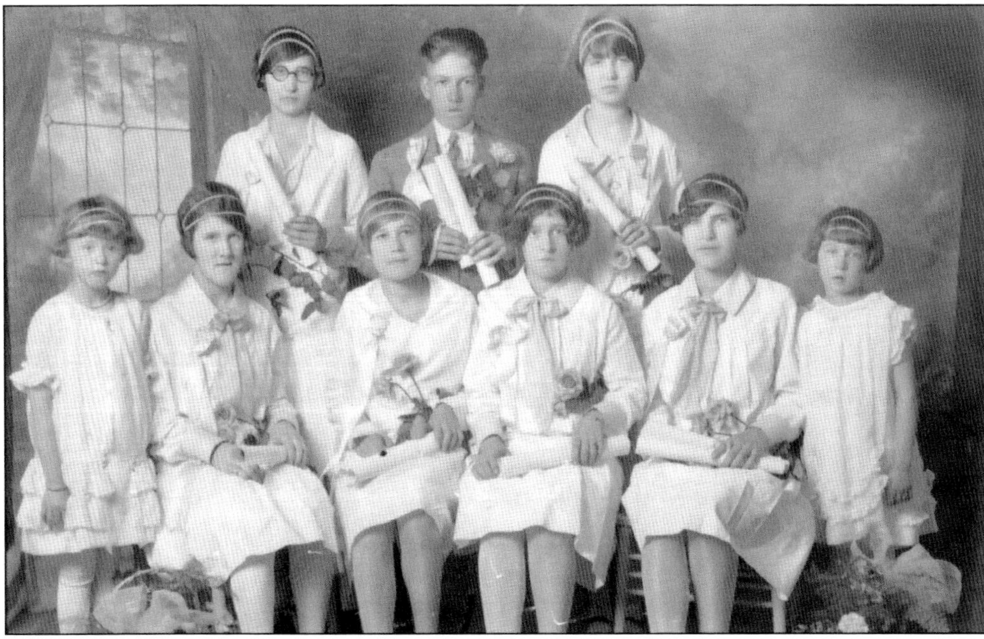

By 1924, Visitation Parish was debt-free, and a school was next on the agenda. Construction began in 1925 on the two-story building with eight classrooms, oil heat, two lavatories, and two halls. The first graduating class, shown in part in 1927, includes, in no particular order, Margaret Boehmer, Caroline Bouronille, Lucille Gerdes, Mary Jost, Frances Kopp, Theresa McMahon, Virginia Peters, Eugene Prudhomme, and Eva Thaden. (Visitation Catholic School and Parish Archives.)

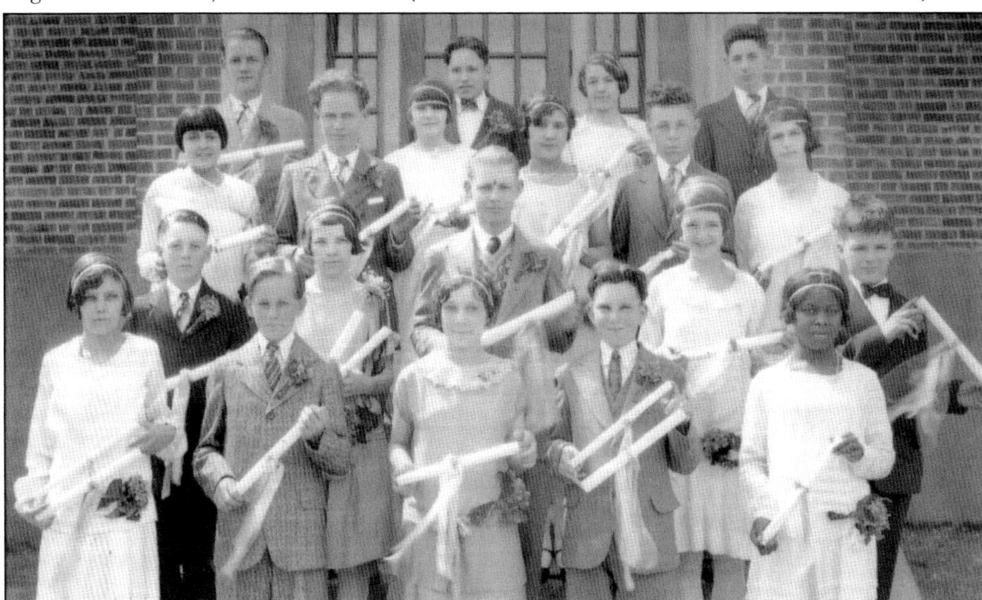

Visitation Catholic School opened in 1925, following the failure of a Ku Klux Klan–sponsored anti-Catholic voter initiative aimed at outlawing private schools. The second graduating class includes Bernice Canada (first row, right) with unidentified classmates in 1928. These 20 graduates proudly display their beribboned diplomas as they pose in front of the school. (Visitation Catholic School and Parish Archives.)

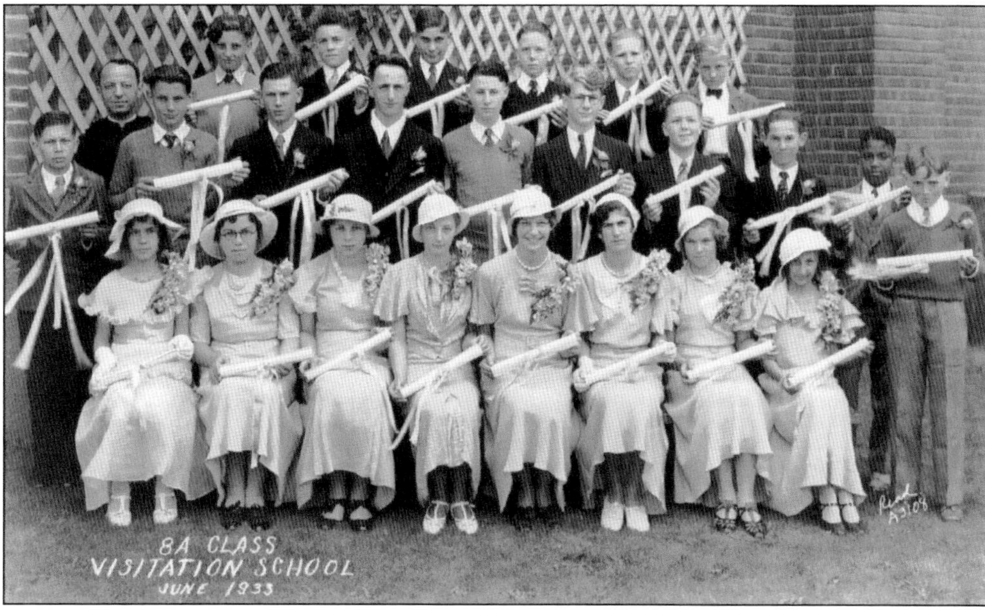

The Great Depression saw a growth in parish participation with more than 750 members and 200 students at the school in 1933. Graduation success was in store for 24 students shown with the pastor Rev. Anthony Hack, OSB. Also identified is John Hazen (second row, fourth from left). De rigueur were the ties for the boys and hats and corsages for the ladies. (Hazen family.)

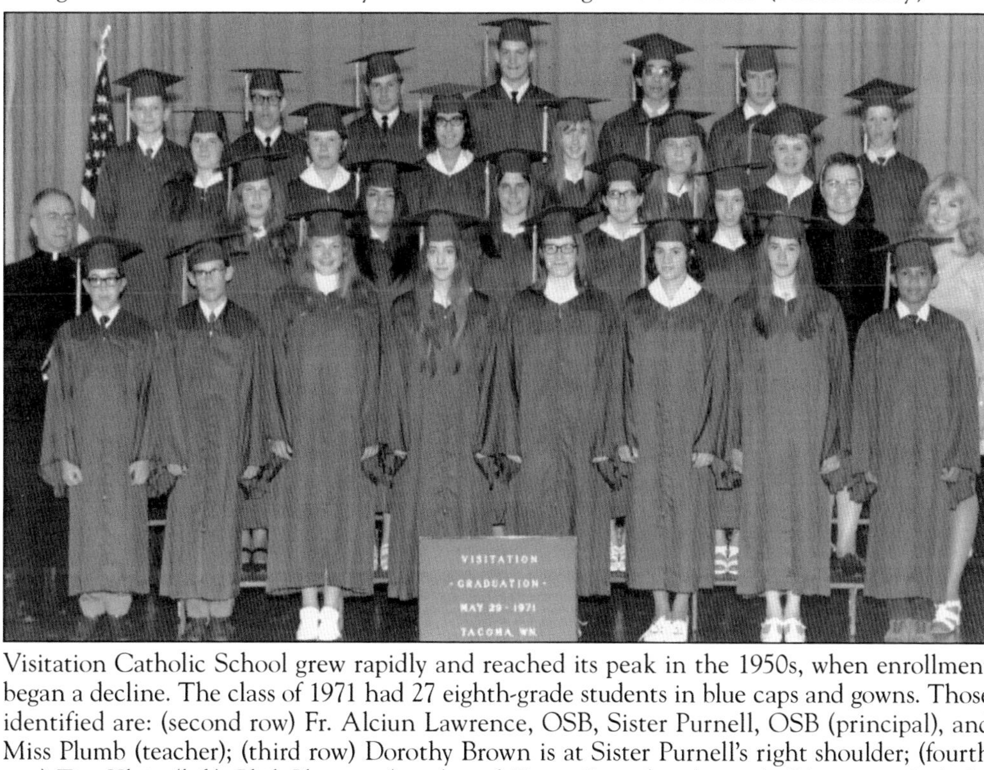

Visitation Catholic School grew rapidly and reached its peak in the 1950s, when enrollment began a decline. The class of 1971 had 27 eighth-grade students in blue caps and gowns. Those identified are: (second row) Fr. Alciun Lawrence, OSB, Sister Purnell, OSB (principal), and Miss Plumb (teacher); (third row) Dorothy Brown is at Sister Purnell's right shoulder; (fourth row) Tim Klein (left), Phil Clemens (next), and Kevin Cornelius (center). (Visitation Catholic School and Parish Archives.)

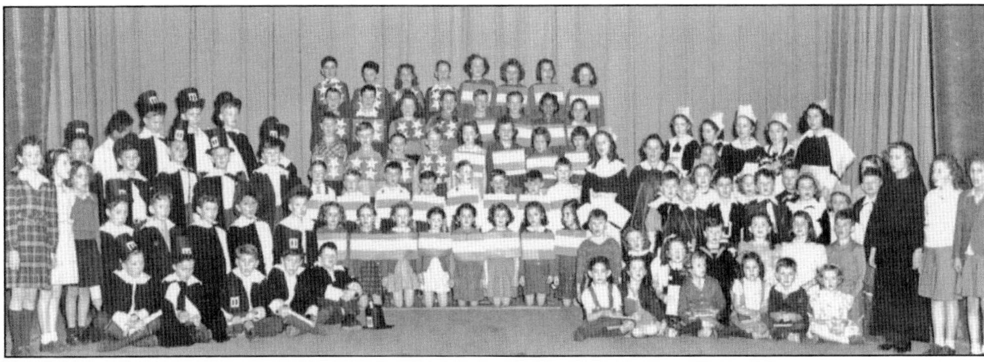

Patriotism occupied many Americans' minds, including Holy Rosary Catholic School students', in January 1947. The United States flag is creatively presented with 13 stripes taped to 28 little bodies, and 48 stars were added with three rows and four columns of squares, four stars to each square. Pilgrims flank the stars and stripes. Cathy Sleet (right pilgrim group, third row, right) joins unidentified mixed-class students. (Cathy Bunger family collection.)

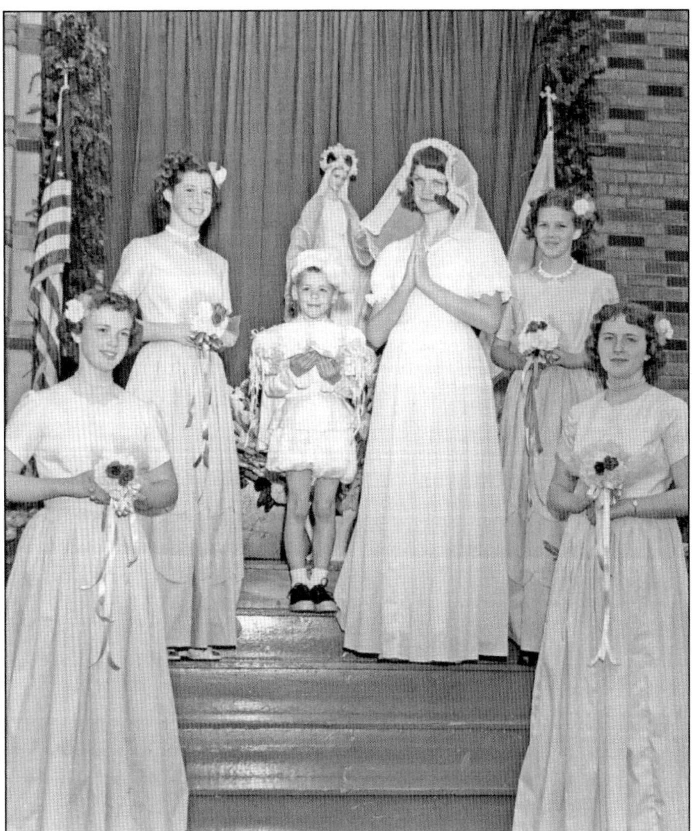

Maureen Sims (veiled), a Visitation Catholic School student, was honored as May Queen in 1953 for the crowning of a statue of the Blessed Mother at St. Edward's Seminary in Seattle, an event that included 8,000 students and faculty from around the Seattle Archdiocese. May Queen attendants included, from left to right, Karen Lavine, Marilyn Eckroth, Rickey Hutt (page), Louise Hulscher, and Patricia O'Neil. (Visitation Catholic School and Parish Archives.)

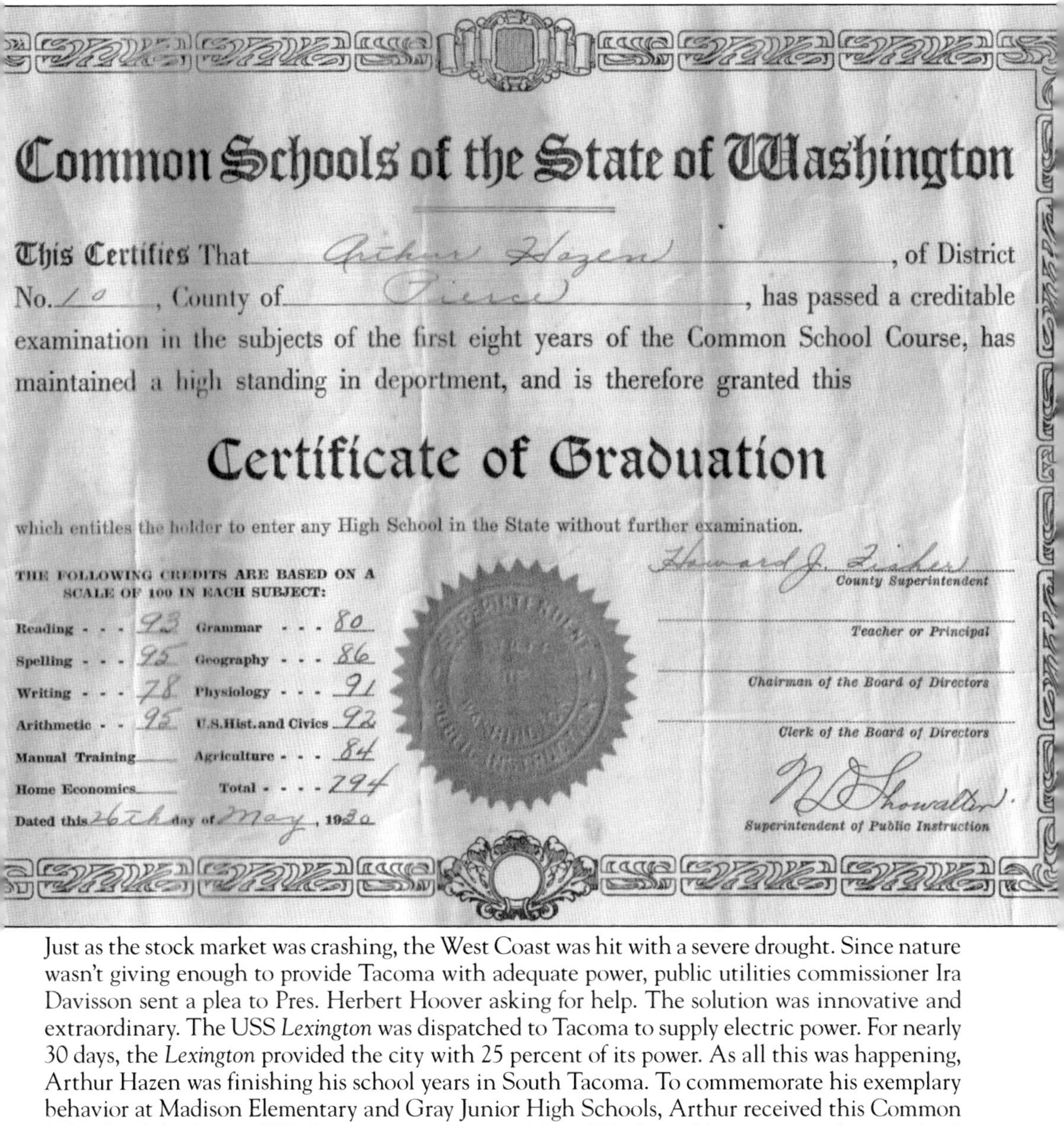

Common Schools of the State of Washington

This Certifies That Arthur Hazen, of District No. 10, County of Pierce, has passed a creditable examination in the subjects of the first eight years of the Common School Course, has maintained a high standing in deportment, and is therefore granted this

Certificate of Graduation

which entitles the holder to enter any High School in the State without further examination.

THE FOLLOWING CREDITS ARE BASED ON A SCALE OF 100 IN EACH SUBJECT:

Reading	93	Grammar	80
Spelling	95	Geography	86
Writing	78	Physiology	91
Arithmetic	95	U.S. Hist. and Civics	92
Manual Training		Agriculture	84
Home Economics		Total	794

Dated this 26th day of May, 1930

Howard J. Fisher
County Superintendent

Teacher or Principal

Chairman of the Board of Directors

Clerk of the Board of Directors

N. D. Showalter.
Superintendent of Public Instruction

Just as the stock market was crashing, the West Coast was hit with a severe drought. Since nature wasn't giving enough to provide Tacoma with adequate power, public utilities commissioner Ira Davisson sent a plea to Pres. Herbert Hoover asking for help. The solution was innovative and extraordinary. The USS *Lexington* was dispatched to Tacoma to supply electric power. For nearly 30 days, the *Lexington* provided the city with 25 percent of its power. As all this was happening, Arthur Hazen was finishing his school years in South Tacoma. To commemorate his exemplary behavior at Madison Elementary and Gray Junior High Schools, Arthur received this Common Schools of the State of Washington certificate in May 1930. Signed by county and state school superintendents, this graduation certificate entitled young Hazen to enter any Washington state high school. "Common Schools" refers to schools maintained at public expense in a school district with kindergarten through 12th grades. Today we more commonly call them public schools. (Hazen family.)

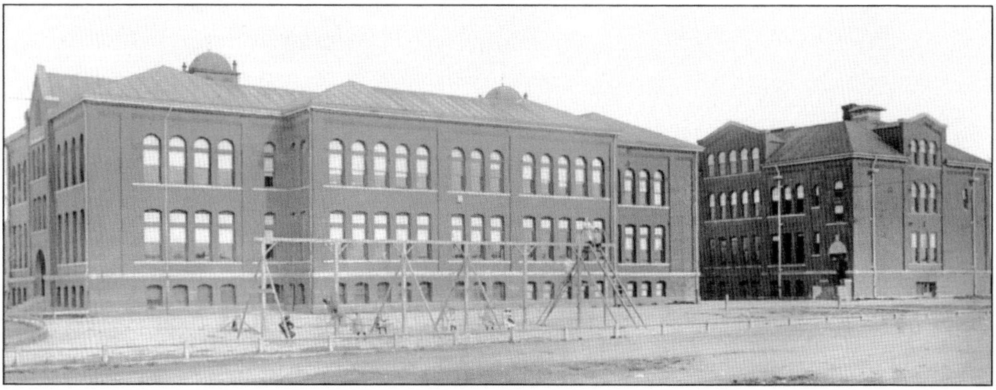

Students enjoy the playground swing set c. 1915 at Edison Elementary School (left) and the Barlow Annex. Named for the area in which it was built, Edison Elementary opened at South Fifty-eighth and Cedar Streets in 1892. Today a new building has replaced the old Edison, but the majestic Barlow Annex proudly remains where it was built in 1910. (Thomas R. Stenger collection.)

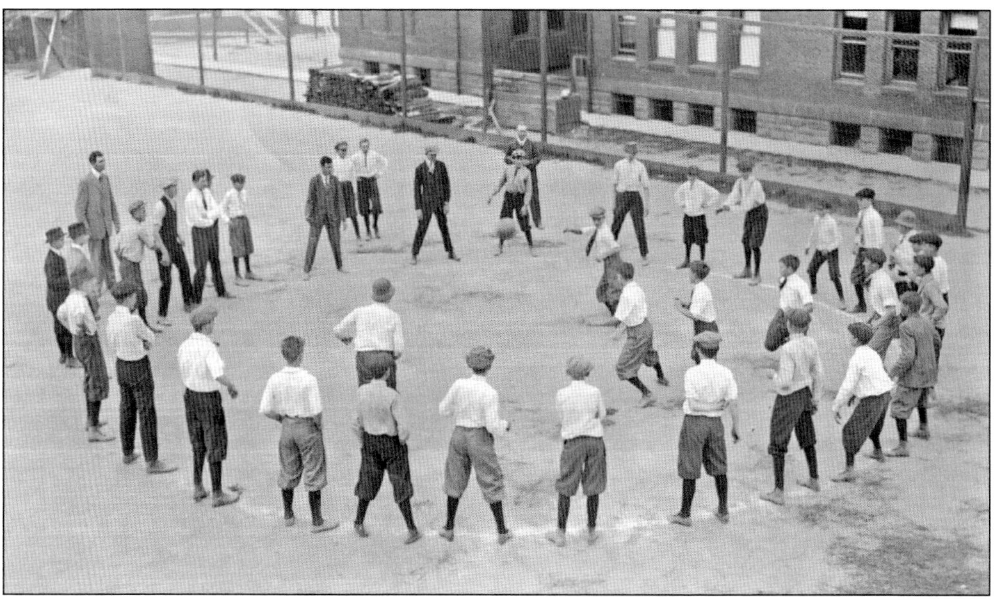

Dodge ball was a game boys played on the Arlington Elementary playfield at 3002 South Seventy-second Street around 1920. The fashion included knickers, kneesocks, midi-blouses, ankle-high shoes, and newsboy caps for the young men flanked by supervising adults dressed in suits, white dress shirts, and hats. The ball in the air, defended from approaching classmates, is the center of attention for all in the white-marked circle. (Tacoma Public Schools.)

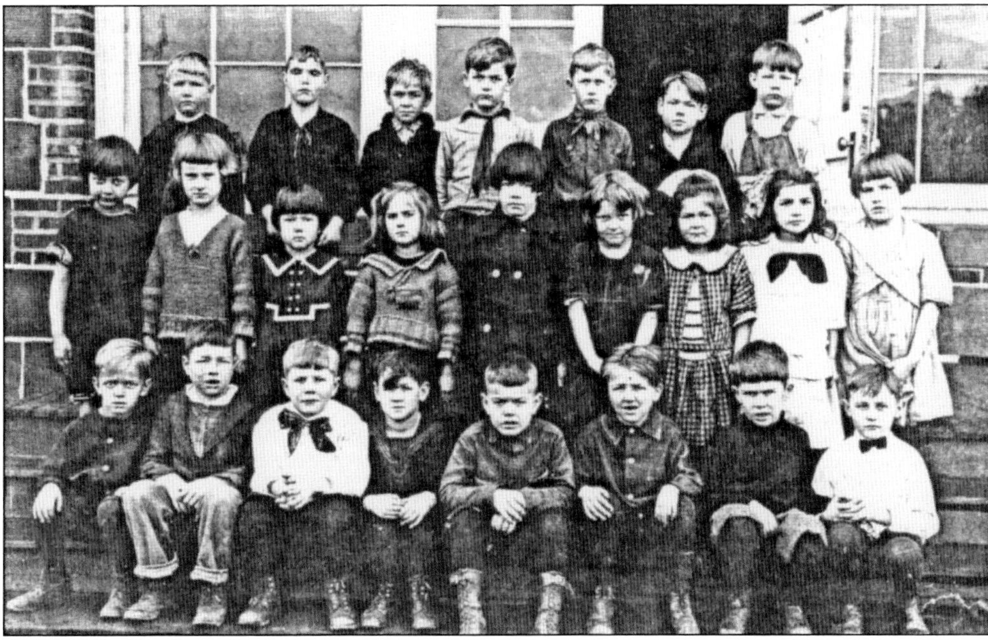

In 1912, after two years of petitioning by the Manitou Improvement Club, the school board placed a portable building on the sight of Manitou Park. A permanent building was built in 1919 on land purchased at 4806 South Sixty-sixth Street. Unidentified Manitou Park Elementary first-grade students from 1923 pose on the steps of their permanent school building just four years after it was built. (Tacoma Public Schools.)

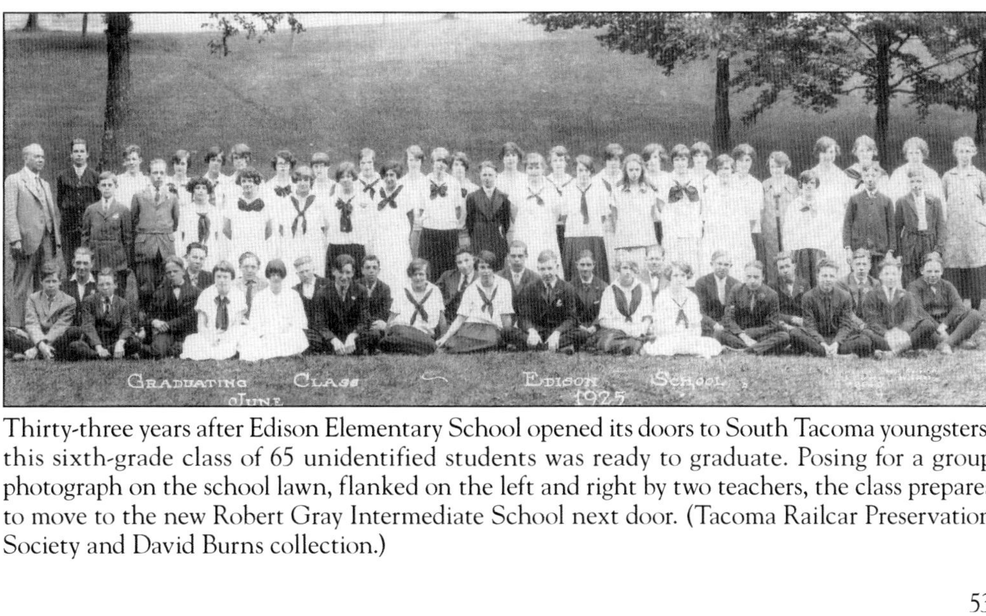

Thirty-three years after Edison Elementary School opened its doors to South Tacoma youngsters, this sixth-grade class of 65 unidentified students was ready to graduate. Posing for a group photograph on the school lawn, flanked on the left and right by two teachers, the class prepares to move to the new Robert Gray Intermediate School next door. (Tacoma Railcar Preservation Society and David Burns collection.)

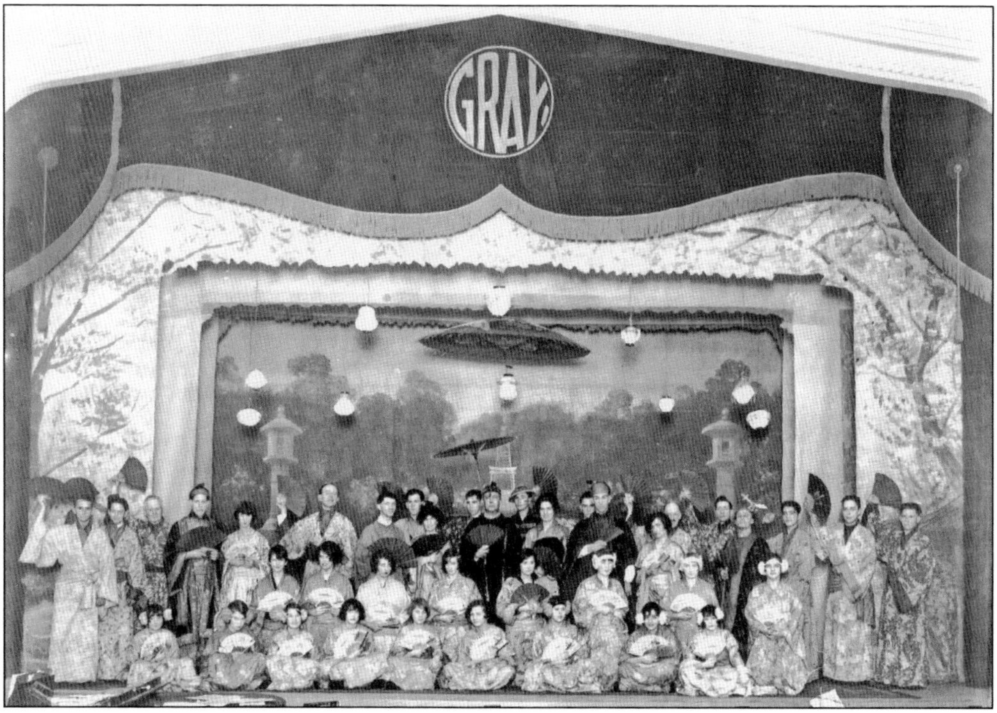

Captain Robert Gray Intermediate School, the new South Tacoma School that opened at 3109 South Sixtieth Street in 1926, was named in a contest held by *Tacoma Daily Ledger*. The name reflected the school policy to name intermediate schools after important Northwest historical figures. One year later, this unidentified cast performed the popular Gilbert and Sullivan opera *Mikado* on the new stage. (Tacoma Public Schools.)

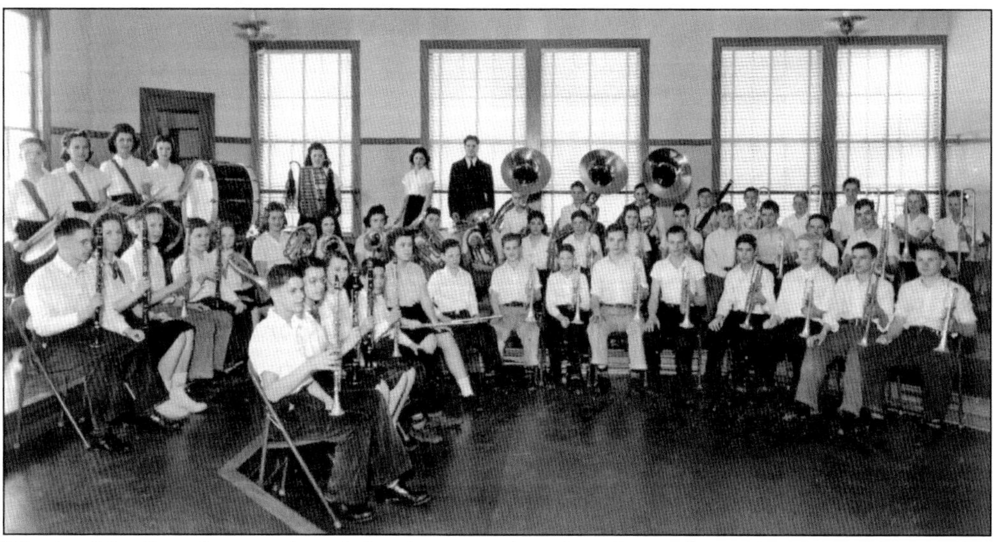

The land for Gray Intermediate School was purchased in September 1924, the same year Max Haller was born in Dickinson, North Dakota. Shortly thereafter, the family moved to the Manitou neighborhood where Max was raised. Fourteen years later, Max (first row, fifth from right, with trumpet) and other unidentified band members play in the renamed Gray Junior High ninth-grade band. (Max and Amelia Haller.)

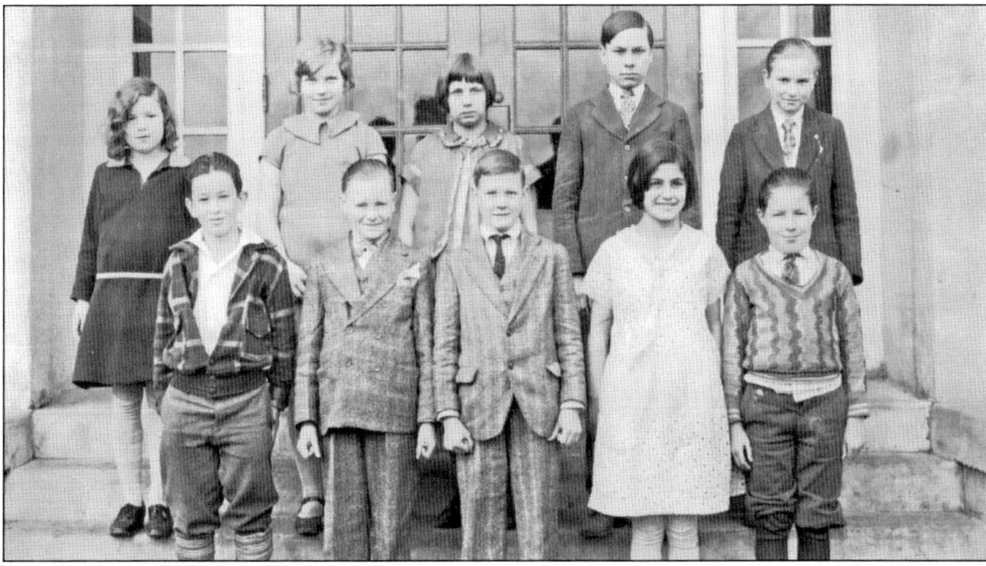

Madison Elementary opened in 1921 in a portable at 3102 South Forty-third Street. Although James Madison was the fourth president of the United States, the new school also identified the area where it was located. The permanent building was built seven years before the *c.* 1928 "6A Passing Class" (above) with Art Hazen (second row, right) and nine of his unidentified classmates reached sixth grade. The mixed 3A/4A class (below) attended the school around 1935. Students include Alice Capps (second row, second from left), Homer Capps (third row, third from left), and Joseph Hazen (fourth row, first from left). Others in unknown positions include: Donald Rockwood, James H., John Peterman, Dicky P., David ?, Russell Faller, Lorne Johnson, Barbara Page, Gladys Rorse, Herbert McCan, Fred H., Richard ?, Clara Rice, Joy ?, Barbara Heartman, Irene B., Sonny B., Billy B., Leter May, E. P., and Donald Miller. (Hazen family.)

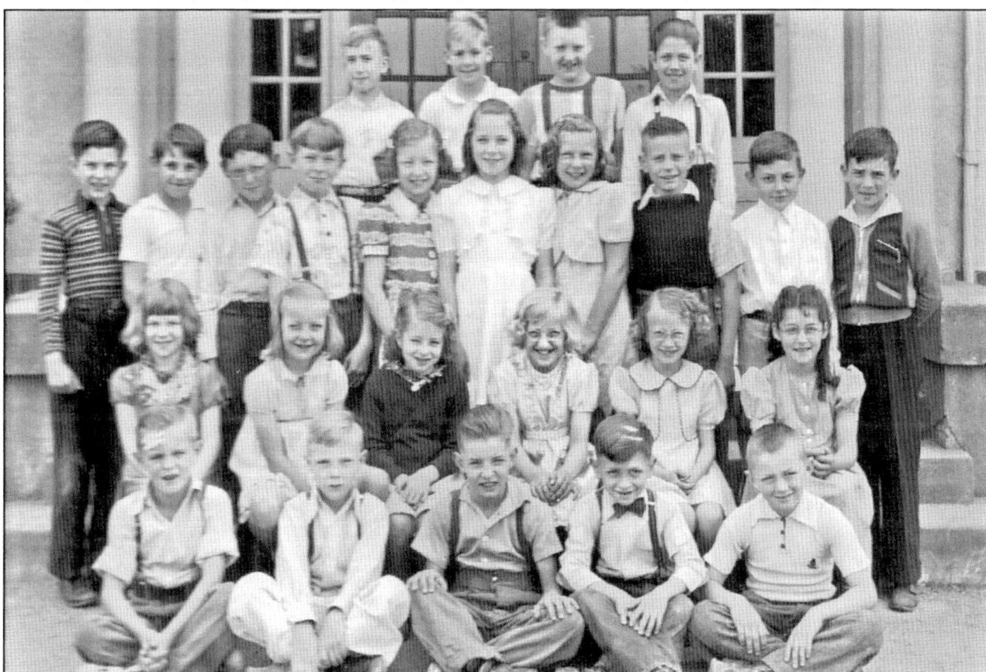

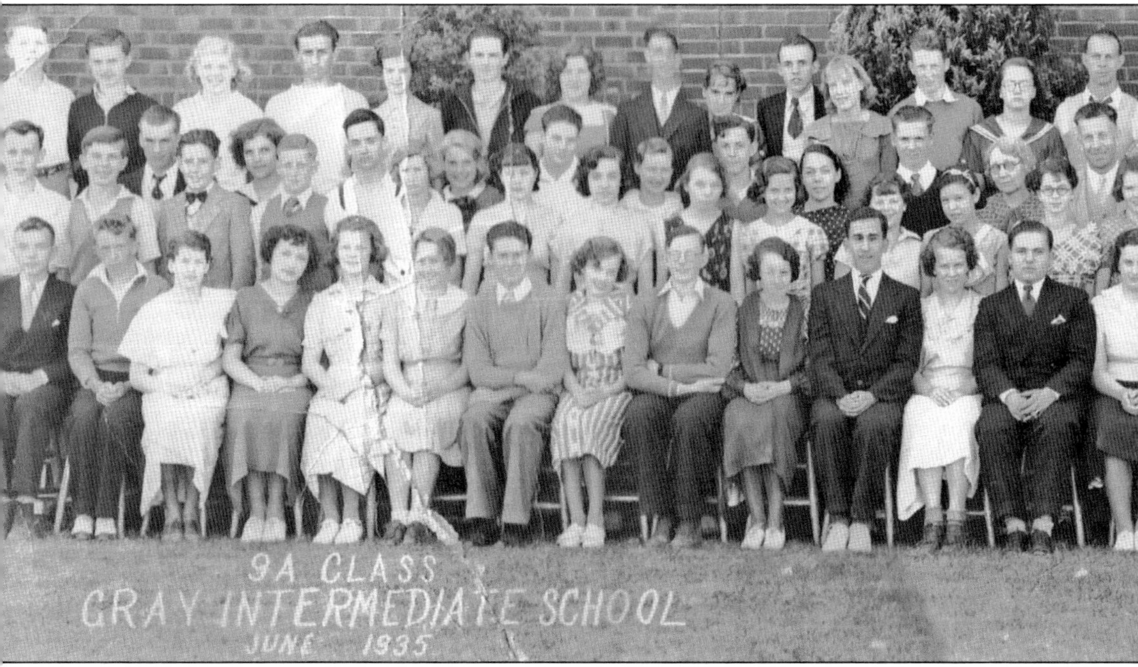

Although the South Tacoma Businessmen's Association voted in 1924 to oppose the chosen site and petitioned the school board to reconsider, the lot next to Edison Elementary School and the Barlow Annex was purchased to build Captain Robert Gray Intermediate School. Architect E. J. Bresemann and general contractors Jarl and Lasker were hired the same year, and Gray Intermediate opened two years later with more than 1,000 in attendance for the ceremony. The school was only

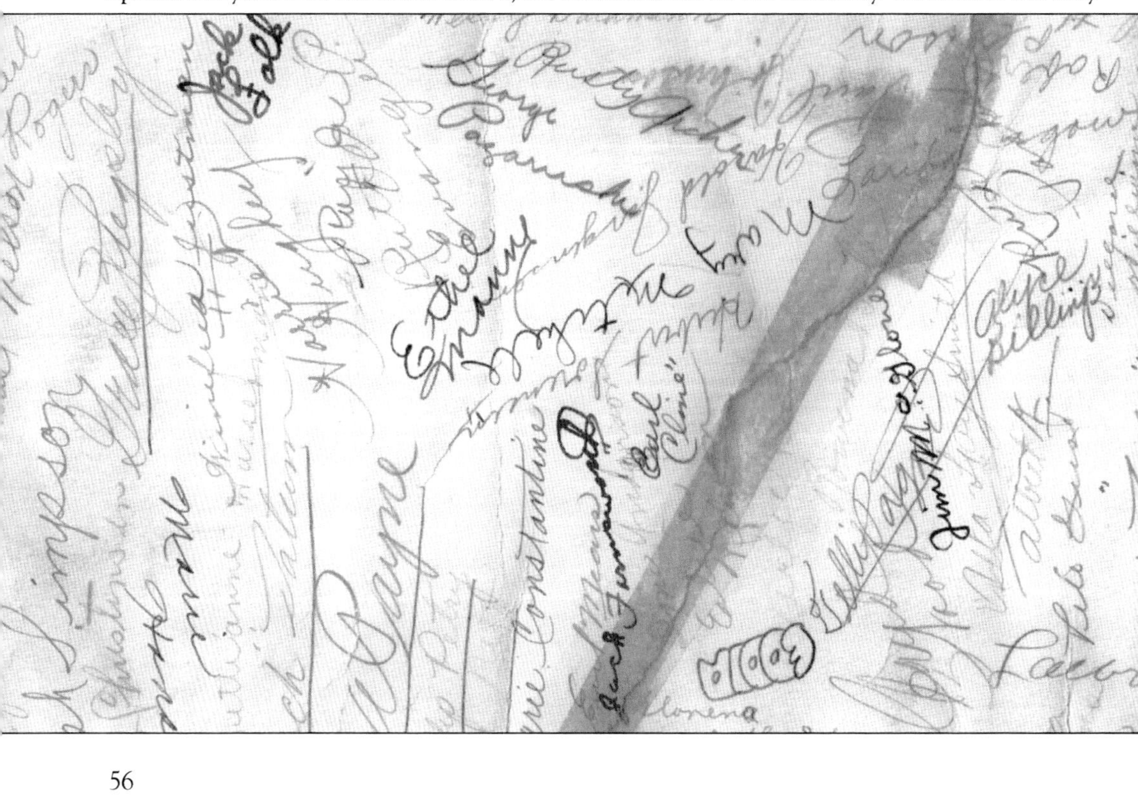

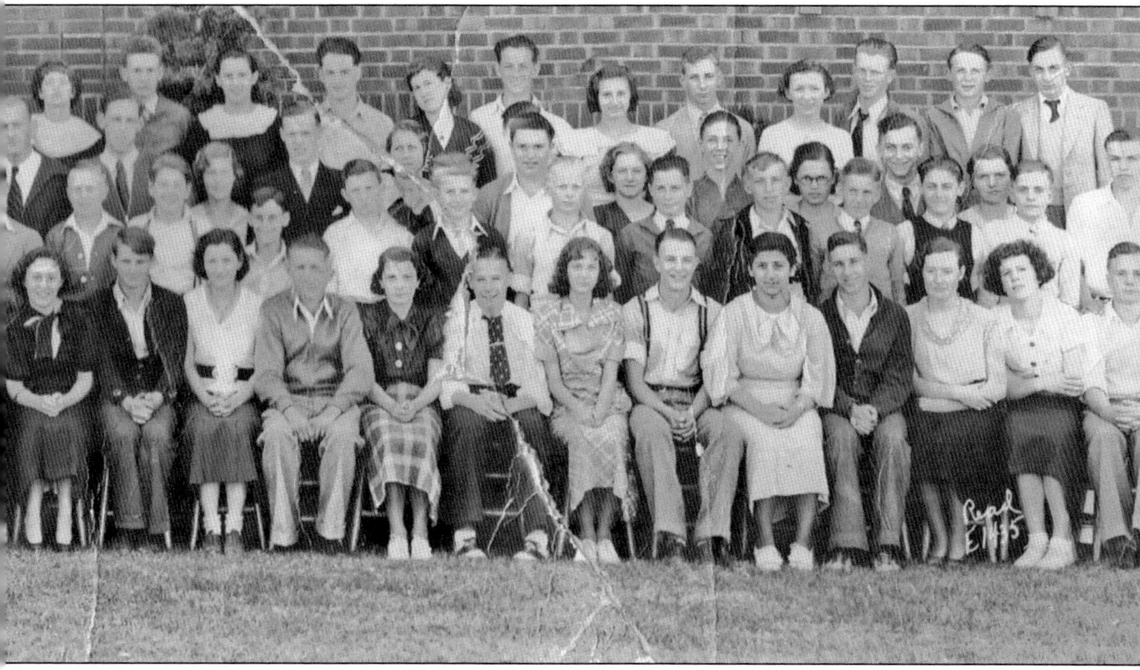

nine years old when this 9A class graduated in 1935. Lincoln High School opened in 1914 and was the next public education step for Gray Intermediate students. Not knowing what the future would bring as the students moved from Gray to Lincoln, the signatures on the reverse of the image provide a bond. Identified is Andrew Hazen (third row, sixth from left). (Hazen family.)

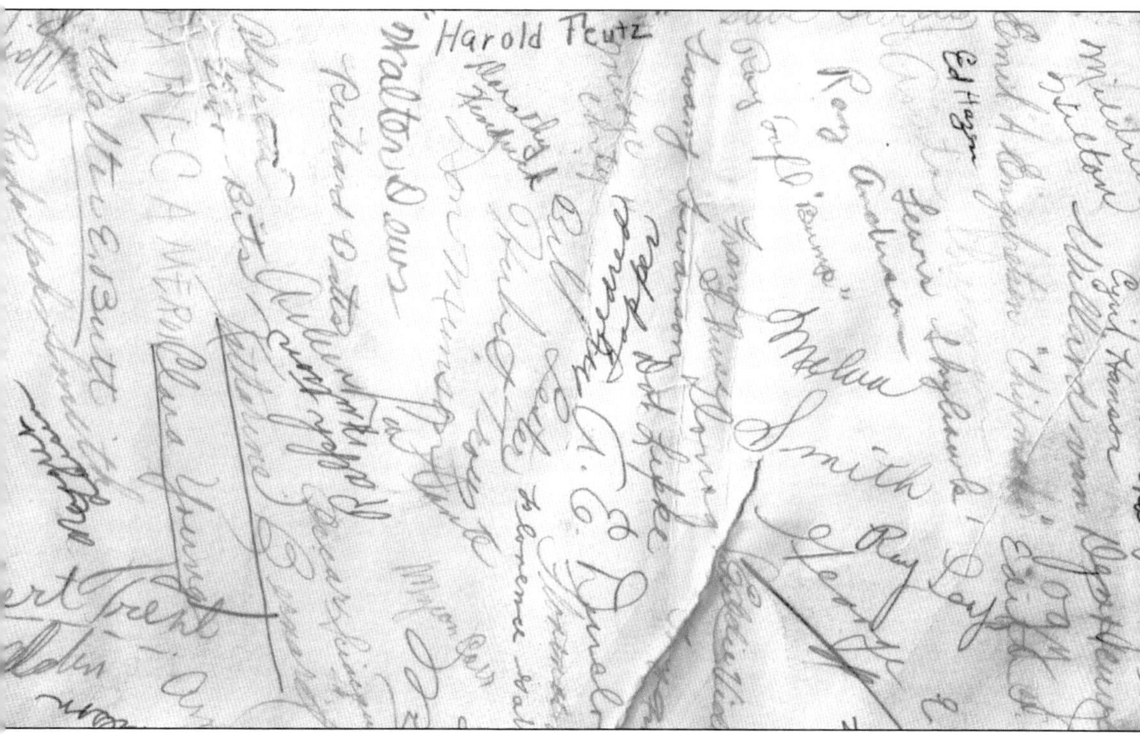

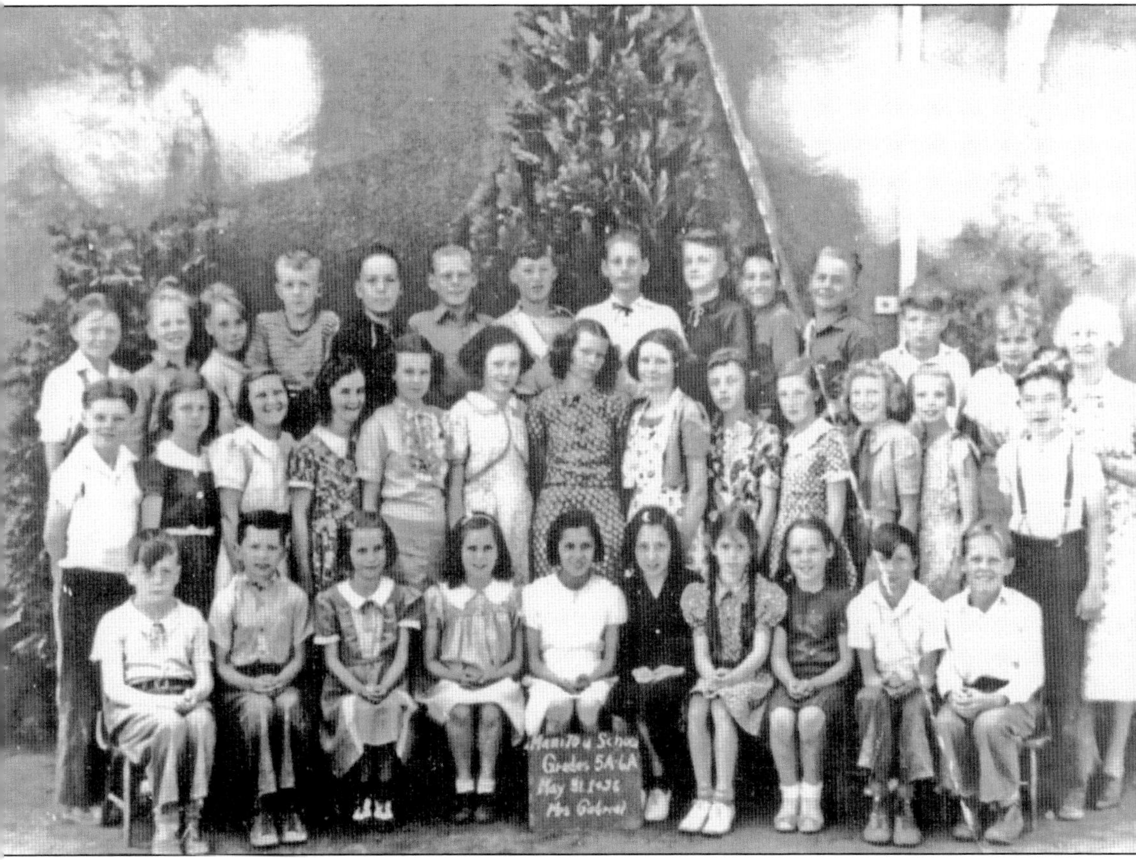

Manitou Park Elementary's 5A-6A class from May 1936 represents two grades from a school with a meager beginning. At the insistence from parents that they have a school in their neighborhood, the board relented, and by 1919, an addition was built to accommodate overcrowding and large classes such as this mixed-grade group. The students are, from left to right, (first row) Ronald Ogden, Robert Price, Helen Ritchie, Lois Gorrel, Lubicia Steponavich, Dorothy Arnora, Willmyrth Miller, Iris Morris, Robert Davis, and David McKicanie; (second row) Allen Kay, Josephine Holland, Mary Mack, Peggy Rough, May McKicanie, Billie Stairs, Mable Hicks, Viola Venebles, Alicia Mather, Sheila Campbell, Mary Gooch, Vida Everts, and Donald Walden; (third row) James Cornell, Phillip Thorson, Billie Ogden, Earl Grocote, Bob Hubert, Max Haller, Tom Ponton, Paul Dorghoy, Edwardo Rew, Earl Burkhart, Richard Feldmann, Larry Crossman, Ivan McBee, and teacher Myra Gabriel. (Max and Amelia Haller.)

Following voter approval for a new South Tacoma high school, land was purchased, the city gave adjoining park land to the school board, and Lincoln Park High School opened in 1914. "Park" was deleted from the name in 1917. Local artist Alonzo Lewis was commissioned with monetary donations to create a bronze statue of Abraham Lincoln, which was dedicated February 12, 1918. Pat Playford, wielding a broom, cleans the 9-foot statue in 1944 with other unidentified students. (Harold "Hal" Snodgrass.)

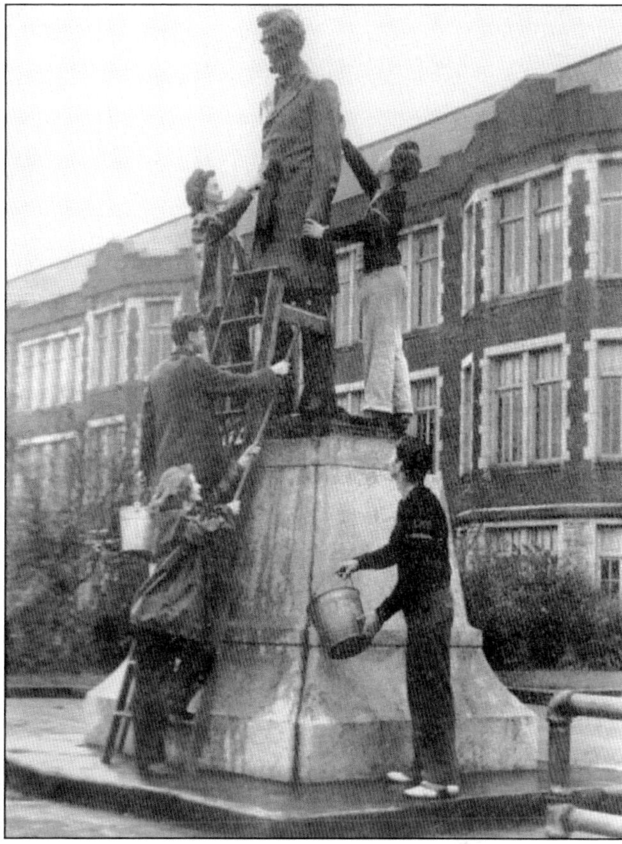

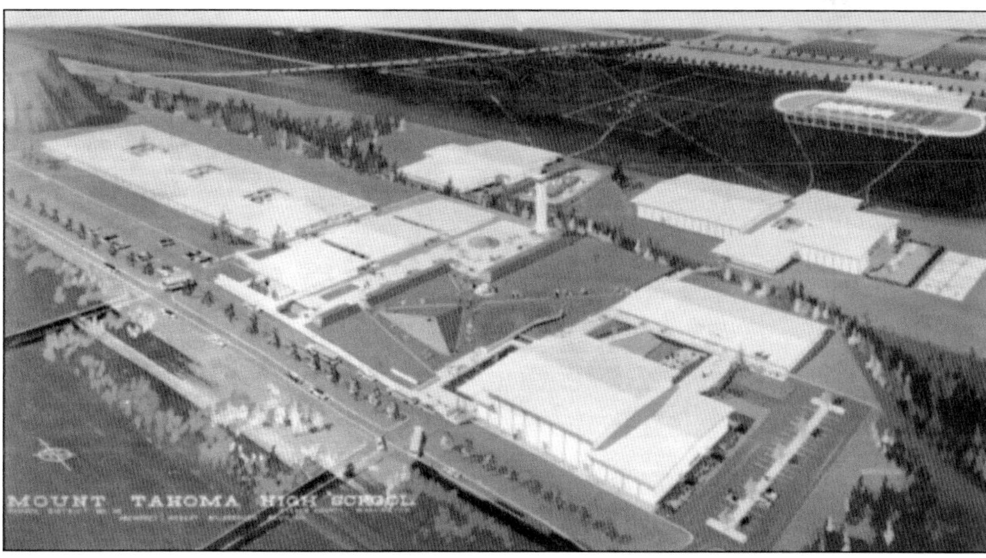

In 1952, funds were appropriated to build a new high school in South Tacoma. Mount Tahoma High School opened nine years later at 6229 South Tyler Street. This architectural drawing shows the eight-building complex of separate, self-contained units for 10th-, 11th-, and 12th-grade classes and the football field in the top right. Mount Tahoma was designed for team-teaching with a double-period schedule to facilitate lab instruction. (Eric Swanson collection.)

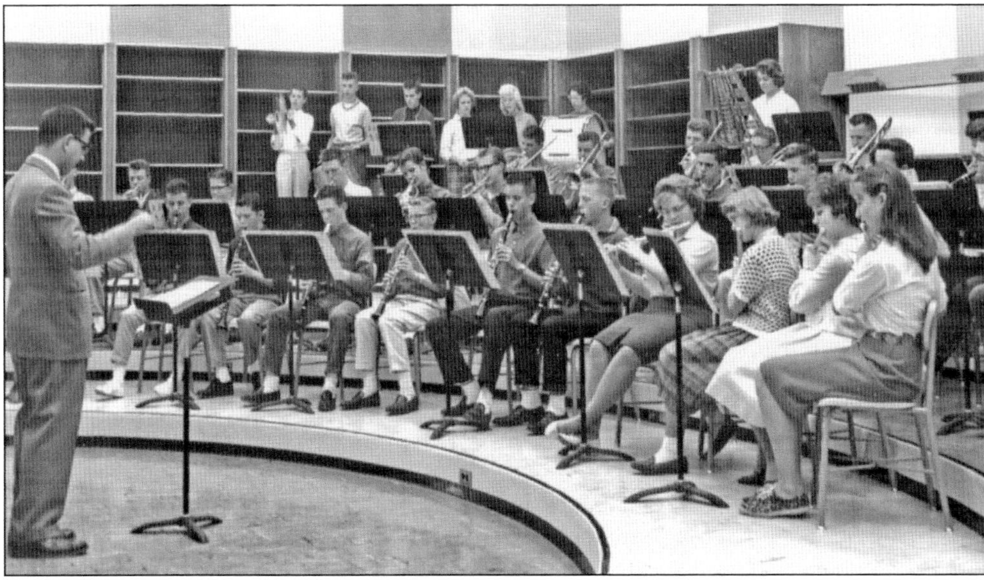

Bearing the Native American name for Piece County's mountain, Mount Tahoma High School opened in 1961 at 6229 South Tyler Street. The eight-building complex included library, arts and crafts, shop, combination auditorium/music buildings, gymnasium/pool, and 36 classrooms. This unidentified instrumental group is led by band instructor Richard Schactler in the early years. (Tacoma Public Schools.)

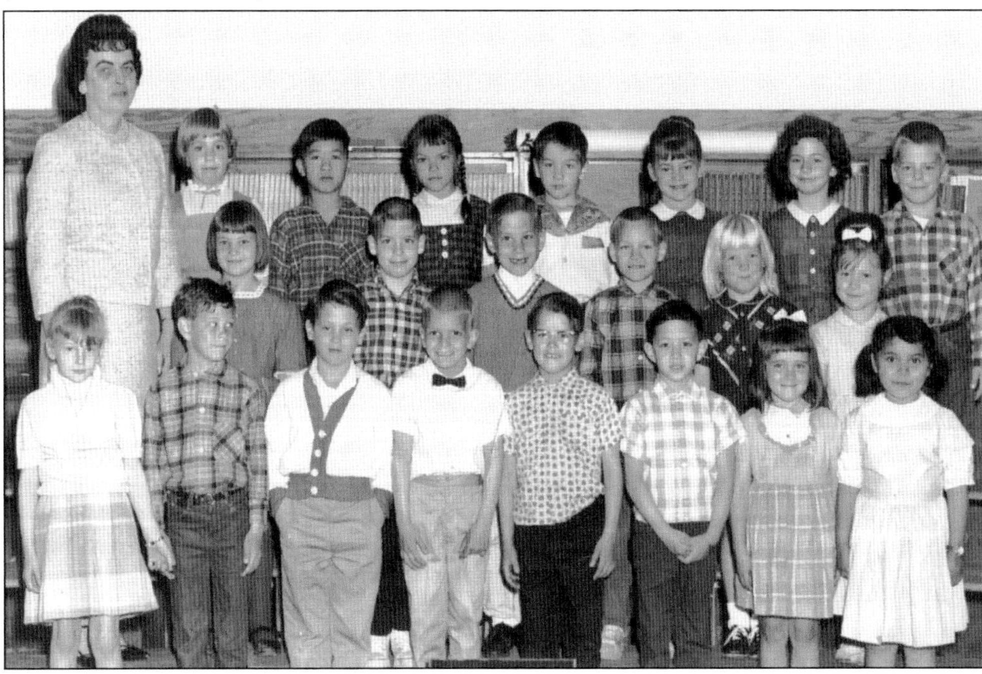

In the temporary classrooms above the feed store, the first two Edison Elementary teachers were Delia Whiting and Fannie Daly. Seventy-four years later, this first-grade class attended in the second new building constructed since Edison Elementary open at South Fifty-eighth and Cedar Streets in 1892. Identified are Mrs. Peterson (teacher) and Pat Haller (second row, third from right). (Max and Amelia Haller.)

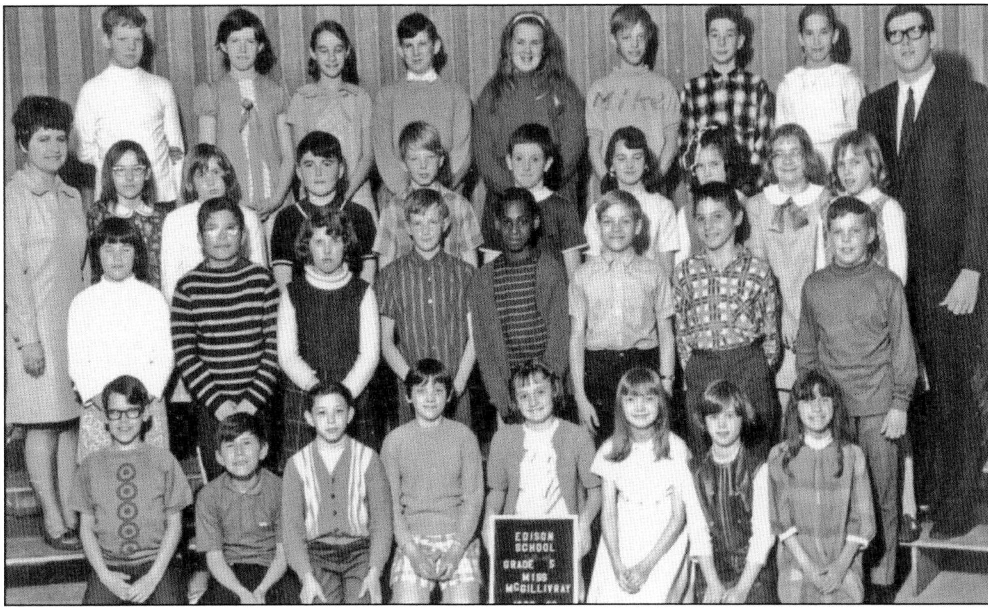

Seventy-six and 82 years, respectively, after Edison Elementary's opening day, these fifth-grade students attended classes in the new building at 3114 South Fifty-eighth Street. The 1968–1969 students from left to right are (first row) Kelly Kenyon, Mike Karch, Roy Jeske, and five unidentified; (second row) unidentified, Robert Sliger, unidentified, Robert Main, Reginald King, Pat Haller, John Miller, and Dick Dorfner; (third row) Miss McGillivray, two unidentified, Edward Greenwood, George Cougle, Chris Cox, and four unidentified; (fourth row) Mike Hollis, two unidentified, Bryan Ichiava, unidentified, Mike Larson, Ted LaFratta, unidentified, and Mr. Herbert. The 1974–1975 class includes (first row) Mike Nunes, Randy Haller, Cliff Balcom, and Harrumi Tucker; (second row) unidentified, Trista Burnston, Nancy Uren, two unidentified, Susan ?, unidentified, Steven Miller, and two unidentified, (third row) Steve Hoye, Kirby Donaldson, Frank Isaacs, Tim Church, Darlene Deleverne, two unidentified, Pam Nelson, and Mrs. Siguenza. (Max and Amelia Haller.)

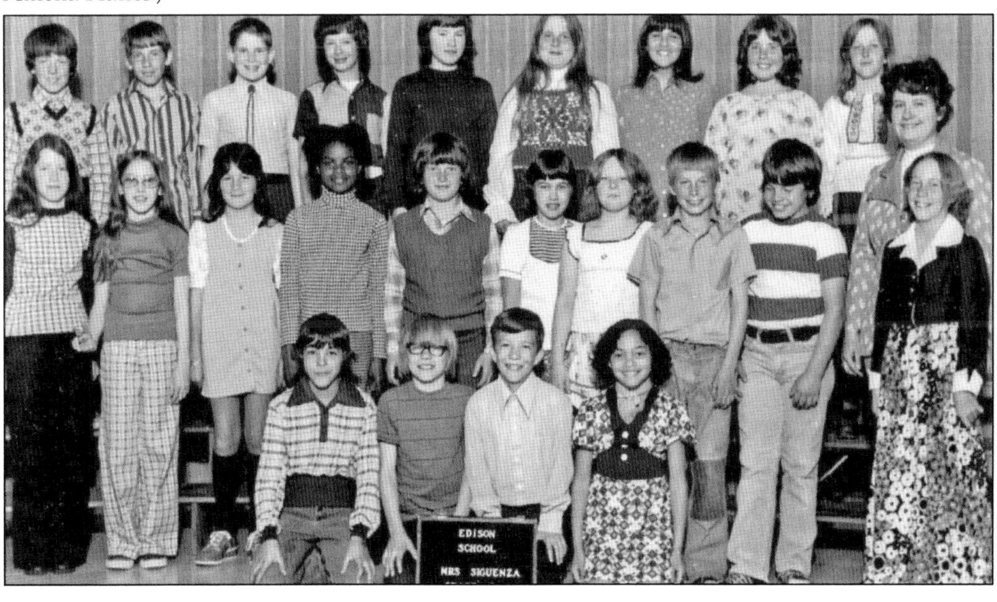

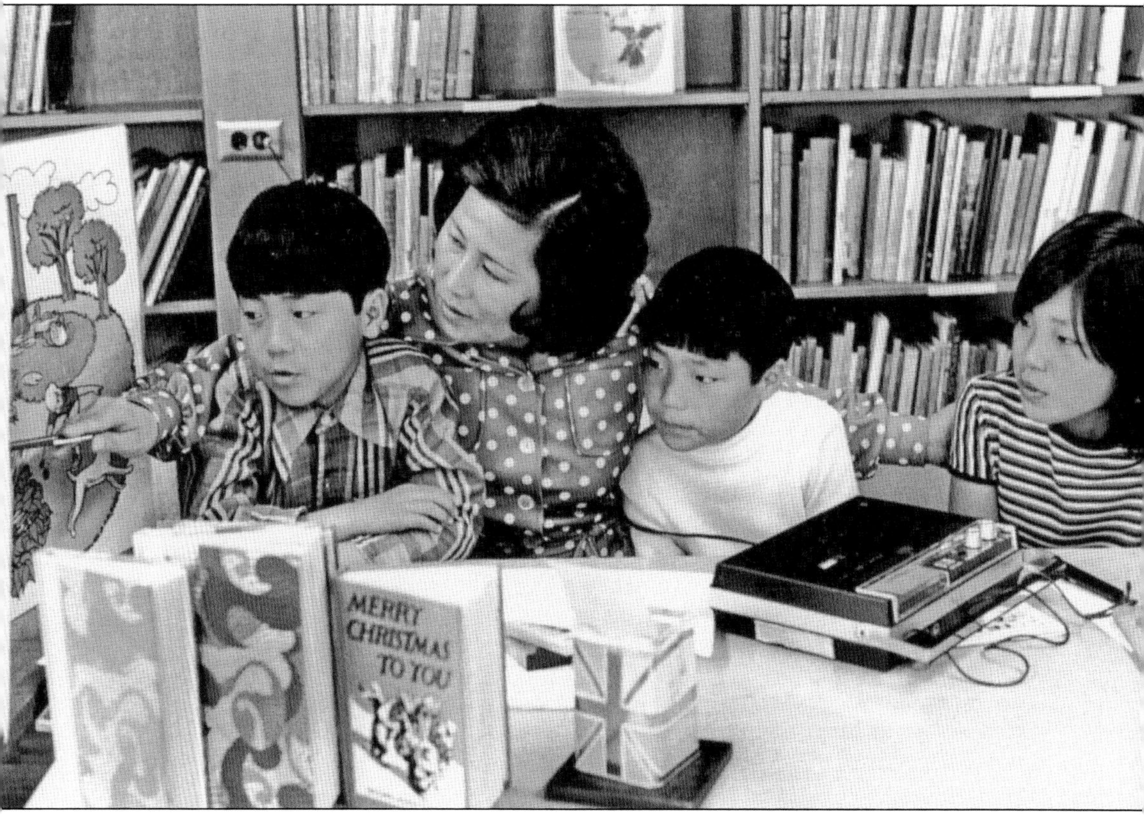

In 1919, rewarding the persistence of parents in the Arlington Park area, a one-story tiled school was built at 3002 South Seventy-second Street. The school board had denied multiple requests for a school in their area or to provide transportation for Arlington Park children to attend neighboring Edison Elementary. Alfred A. Johnson was Arlington Elementary School's first principal and also taught fourth- and fifth-grade students. The school opened with three additional teachers and a janitor. Five years later, four classrooms, an auditorium, and a gymnasium were added. In 1954, nine classrooms, a play area, and an office were added to the building. In November 1956, Mrs. Arthur's class of third-grade students wrote a get-well letter to Pres. Dwight D. Eisenhower when he suffered a heart attack, and they were thrilled to receive a reply. In-Soo Baker, a Tacoma resident and a social worker from Washington State Department of Social and Health Services, provides tutorial support in 1975 for three unidentified Korean students in Arlington's library. (Tacoma Public Schools.)

Five

The People Create a Community

South Tacoma, a community of everyday people living everyday lives, began as a melting pot of immigrants seeking a new life. As the resident population grew, the business center expanded. The people built homes, churches, and schools. Businesses provided material needs, entertainment, and neighborhood gathering places.

South Tacoma Way has changed as much as the businesses that have lined it over time. Until 1926, the section south of Forty-eighth Street was called Edison Avenue, and the segment north of Forty-eighth Street was originally known as Broadway, then Union Avenue, and finally South Tacoma Way in 1932. The small section between Pacific Avenue and South M Street was known as Wakefield Drive. The few blocks between South Sprague Avenue and South Prospect Street were once called Michigan Avenue.

Since the late 1800s, a plethora of businesses have opened, closed, and/or remain in South Tacoma. Some are large, many are small, but all play a role in creating a miniature America, epitomizing how communities formed across the land as the United States grew. Numerous hotels, inns, and boarding/rooming houses to accommodate Northern Pacific employees preceded the community of homes. Churches, clubs, organizations, sports, and entertainment, as well as neighborhood and family gatherings, all contributed to creating a community of working-class people cognizant of their social and economic needs. The census.gov Web site reports a population of nearly 22,000 people lived within South Tacoma's 98409 zip code area in the year 2000.

The demise of the railroad shops coinciding with the opening of the Tacoma Mall may have changed South Tacoma from an industrialized community to a service environment, but the spirit of the South Tacoma people lives on as they continue to follow their dreams in creating a community from the past for the future.

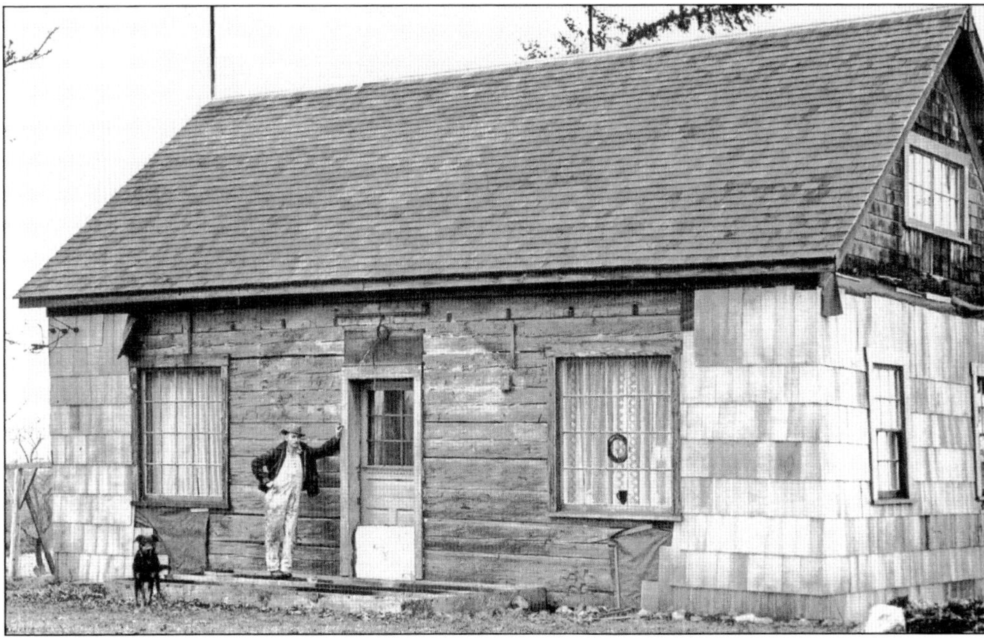

An alert dog watches the photographer as an unidentified man leans against the home pioneer John Rigney built about 1870 in what became the Manitou area. This image, taken 65 years after that construction, shows some of the original log construction of one of South Tacoma's first homes. Electricity insulators and roof antennas point out upgrades. The home at 3751 South Seventy-fourth Street was demolished in 1974. (TPL.)

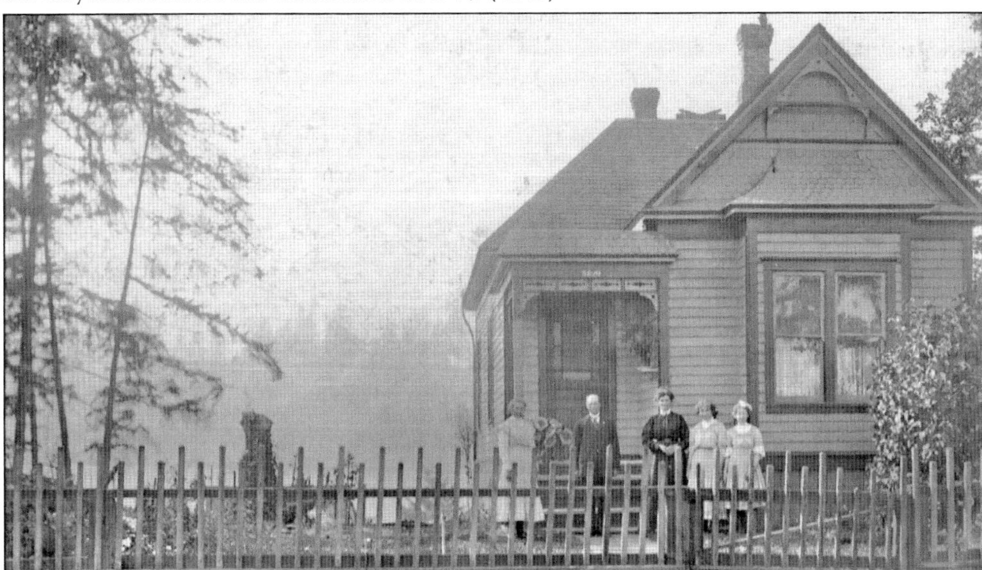

Family members stand near their gable-roofed cottage built in 1907 for Norwegian immigrant and Northern Pacific machinist Daniel Hansen. The message on the reverse states. "Dette er vart hus. Marie Hansen." Three Hansen generations occupied this typical 1900s stick-style home. The home reflects the historical significance of the early South Tacoma lifestyle and remains preserved at its original location at 5820 South Hood Street. (Tacoma Railcar Preservation Society and David Burns collection.)

This 1891 advertisement encourages one and all to bring a picnic and witness Professor Woodall's amazing feat. A 25¢ ticket included round-trip transportation to South Tacoma on the streetcar. The next day, *The Daily Ledger* reported the Mammoth Montgulfier 25-by-60-foot balloon reached a height of 3,000 feet before Professor Woodall impressed the crowd at South Park by parachuting safely to the ground. (TPL.)

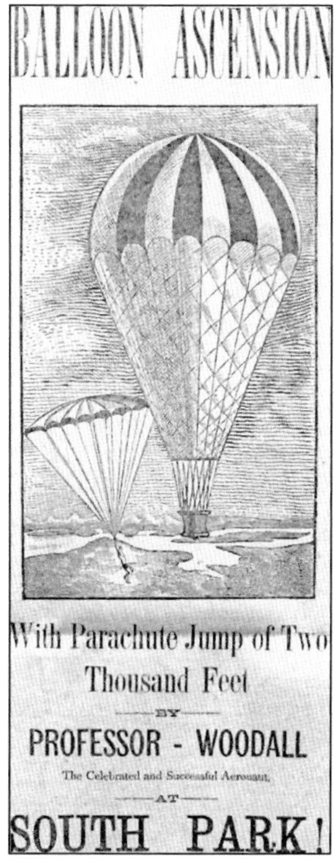

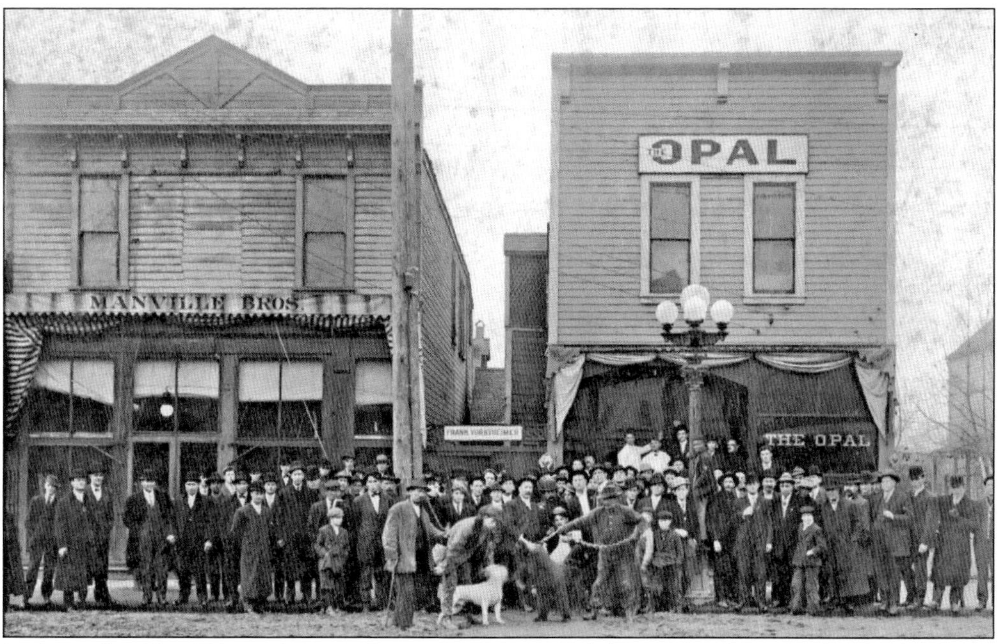

In the early 1900s, Edison Avenue's businesses were mostly between Fifty-second and Fifty-fourth Streets. Manville Brothers moved to 5228 Edison Avenue in 1903. Opal Saloon, operated by the Yorktheimer brothers, was at 5226 from 1904 to 1905. A large crowd gathers watching what may be a bear named Tiny who escaped from St. Julien Saloon on Puyallup Avenue, according to a March 1905 *Tacoma Daily Ledger* account. (Eric Swanson collection.)

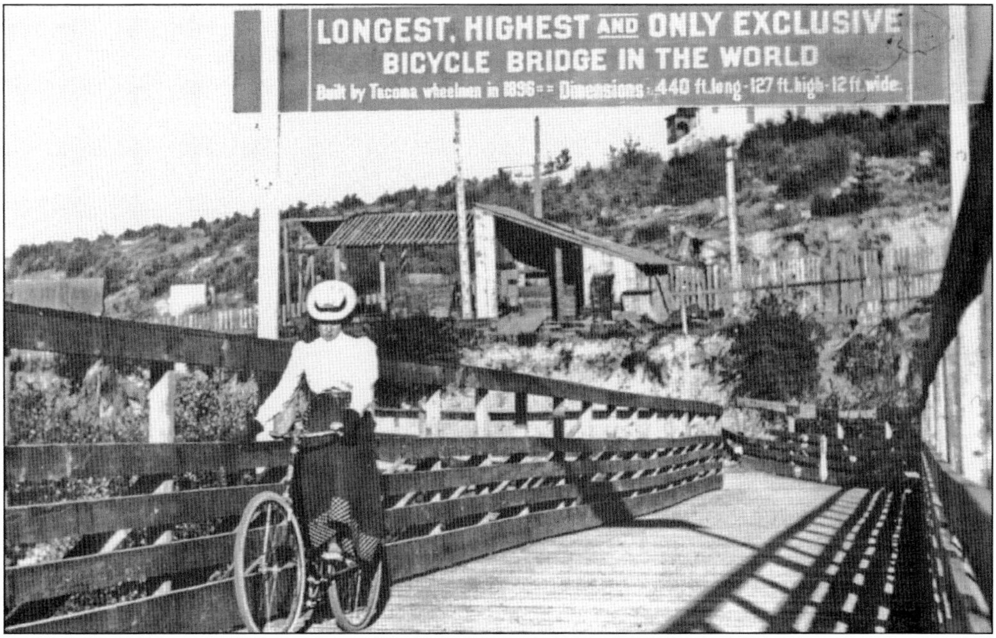

The world's longest and highest wooden bicycle bridge, built in 1896, served as a short-cut to downtown and the prairies to the south for many who lived in the Holy Rosary Church area. Although the sign states it was the "Only Exclusive Bicycle Bridge in the World," it was also used by pedestrians, motorcyclists, and occasionally a horse rider. The woman on the bicycle wears appropriate fashion of the day for a female bicycle rider. The 1906 postcard shows the bicycle bridge's steel-reinforced wooden trellis from below. A hand-written message reflects the nostalgic tone of M. M., who used this bridge as a youngster. The 440-foot-long bridge, which spanned Lincoln Park Gulch 27 feet above the bottom of the gulch between Delin Street and Yakima Avenue, slowly succumbed to decay. (Above, TPL; below, Bob Tschida collection.)

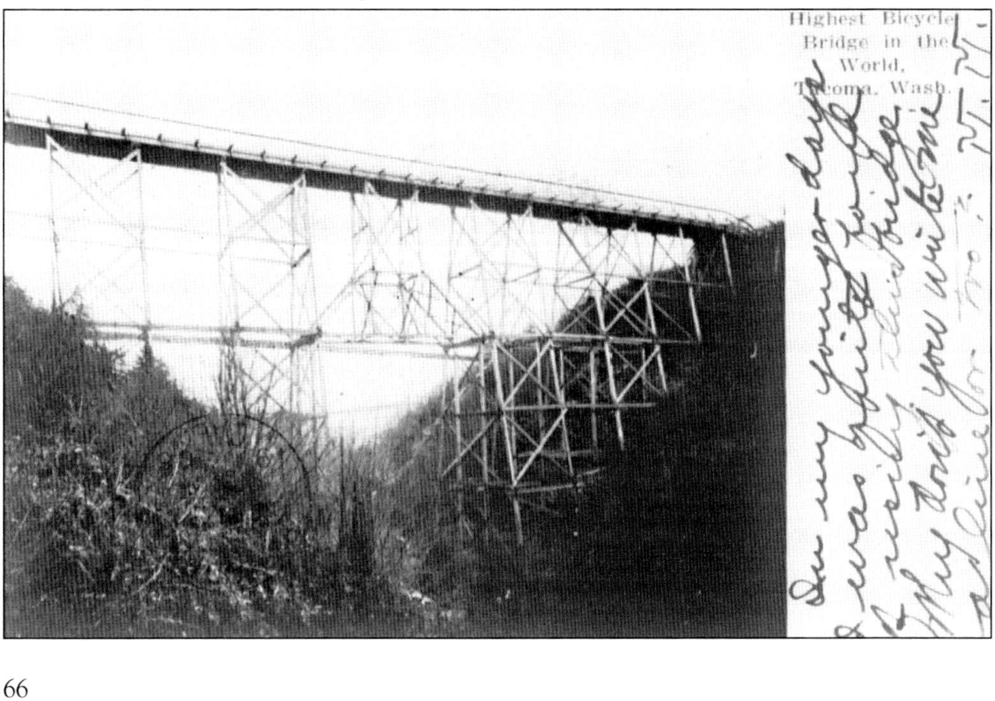

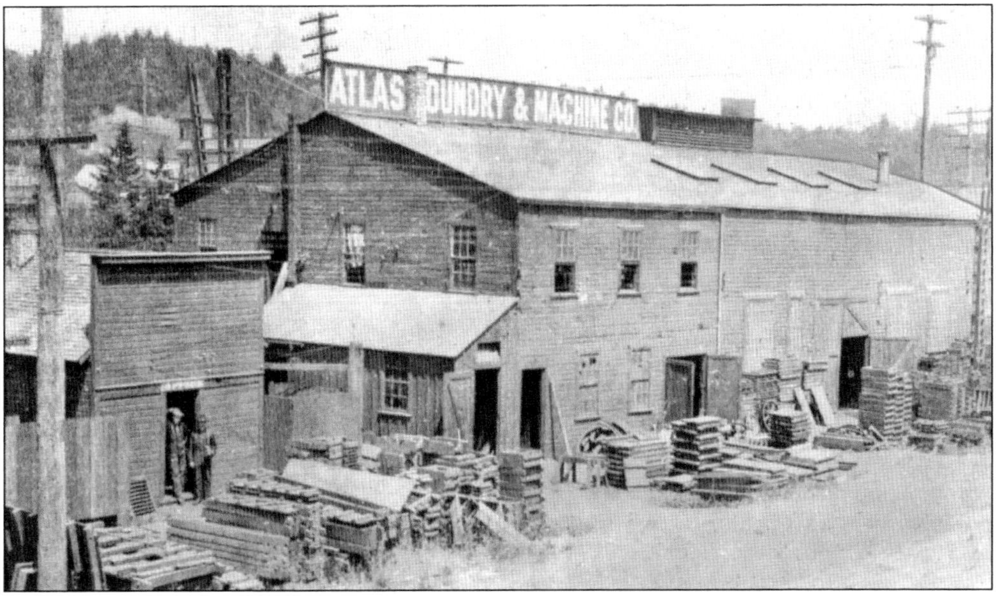

Two unidentified men lean against the door frame of the office building that was William Schiesz's butcher shop until 1899, when Atlas Foundry and Machine Company bought it and the building next door to begin the foundry business. Inside the office, two unidentified men wear ties and pose for the camera around 1900. The wallpaper adds decor to the cluttered office, where an employee sits at a rolltop desk ready to answer the phone and take a message. The office building no longer exists; however, Atlas Castings and Technology continues to use the larger building 106 years later. (Atlas Castings and Technology.)

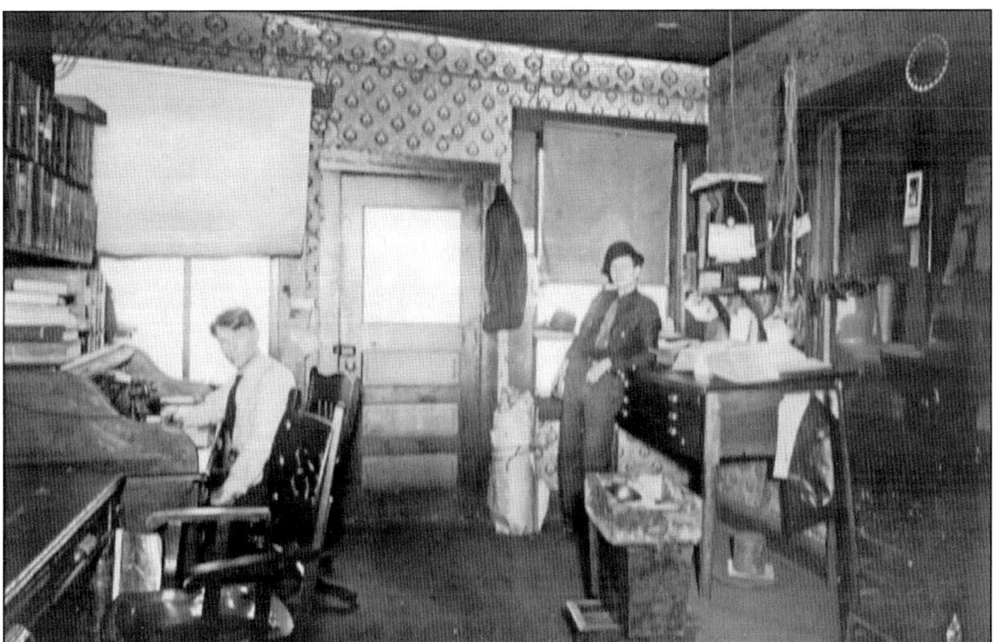

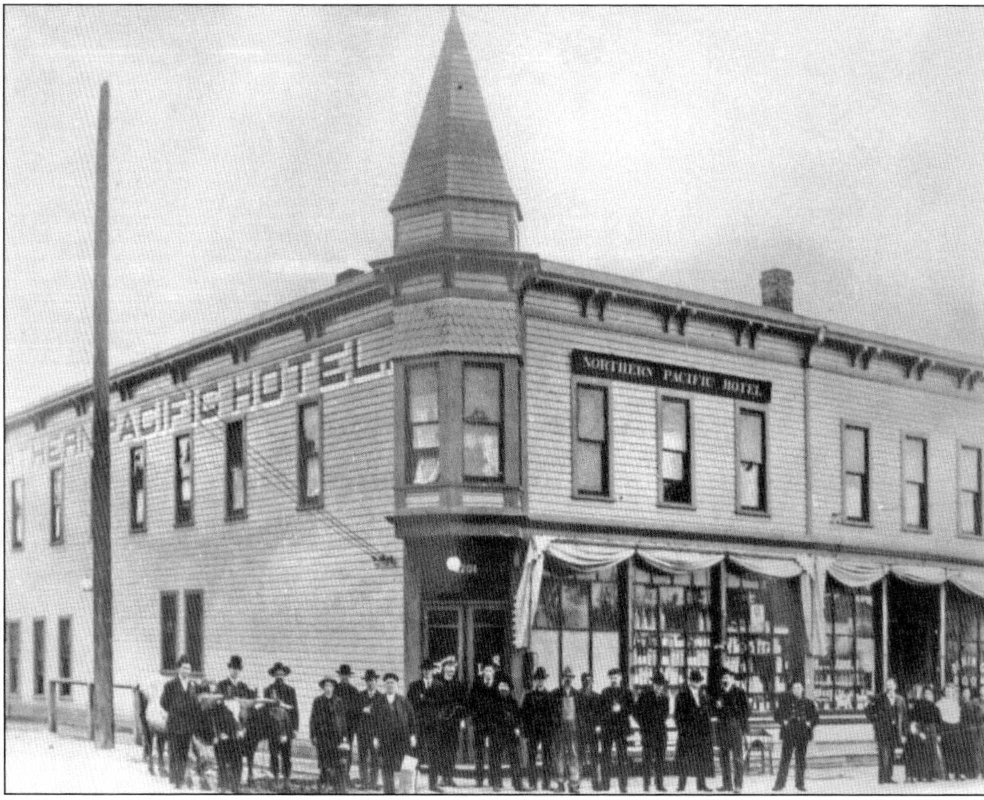

To accommodate Northern Pacific Shops workers, hotels, inns, and boarding/rooming houses were built in South Tacoma at the start of the 20th century. The Northern Pacific Hotel was built at the corner of Edison Avenue and Fifty-second Street. The hotel later burned and was razed. Two cows (left) pose *c.* 1900 with unidentified residents, a large group of men, and a family. (Tacoma Railcar Preservation Society and David Burns collection.)

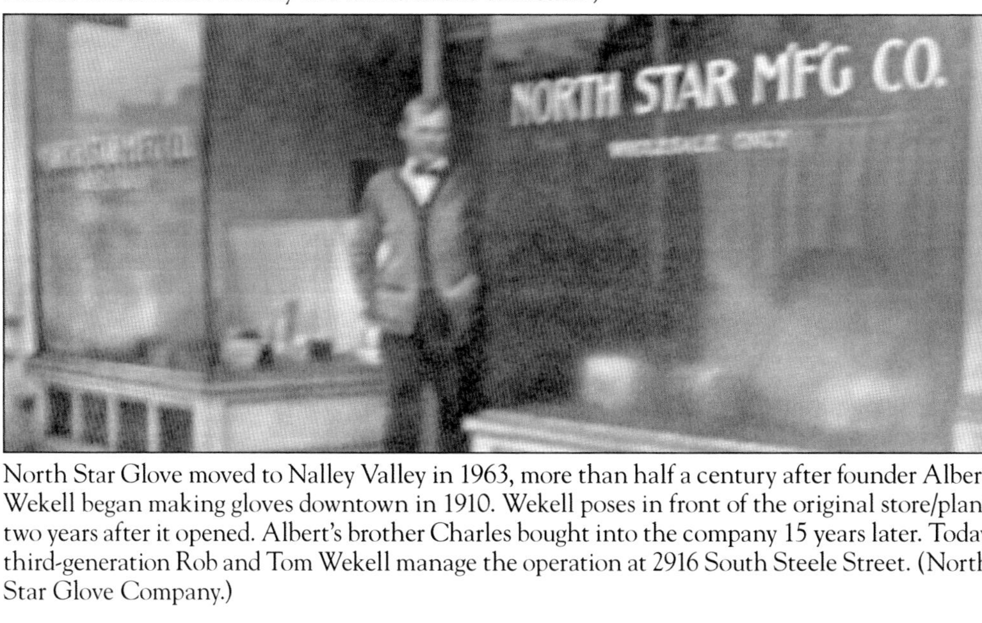

North Star Glove moved to Nalley Valley in 1963, more than half a century after founder Albert Wekell began making gloves downtown in 1910. Wekell poses in front of the original store/plant two years after it opened. Albert's brother Charles bought into the company 15 years later. Today third-generation Rob and Tom Wekell manage the operation at 2916 South Steele Street. (North Star Glove Company.)

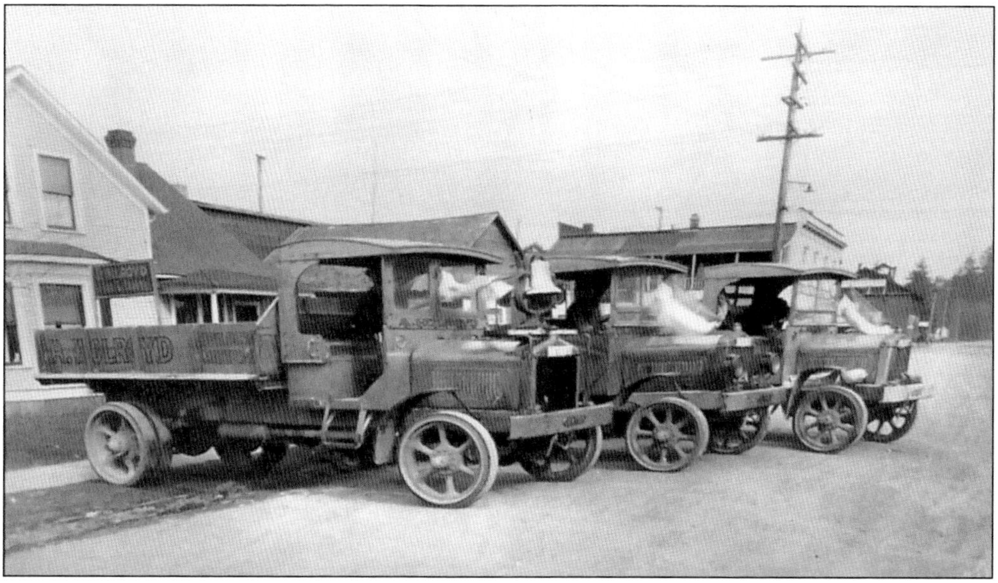

English-born Arthur Holroyd immigrated to Tacoma in 1885 via Canada. By 1906, Holroyd had established a business of buying ship-ballast cement and reselling it to contractors. Three delivery trucks are parked by the original office and Holroyd's headquarters at 5047 South Tacoma Way. Holroyd's children were actively involved in the company, as was granddaughter Margaret (in the company gravel pit *c.* 1930 below), who later became president and ran the company with husband David Nielsen and sons. Today the fifth generation is readying to carry on their great-great-grandfather's American dream of owning a business. Holroyd has been involved in many pours in the area, including the large grain elevators on Schuster Parkway. Holroyd trucks ran around-the-clock for nine days to deliver concrete for that project. (Holroyd Company, Inc., a Nielsen Company.)

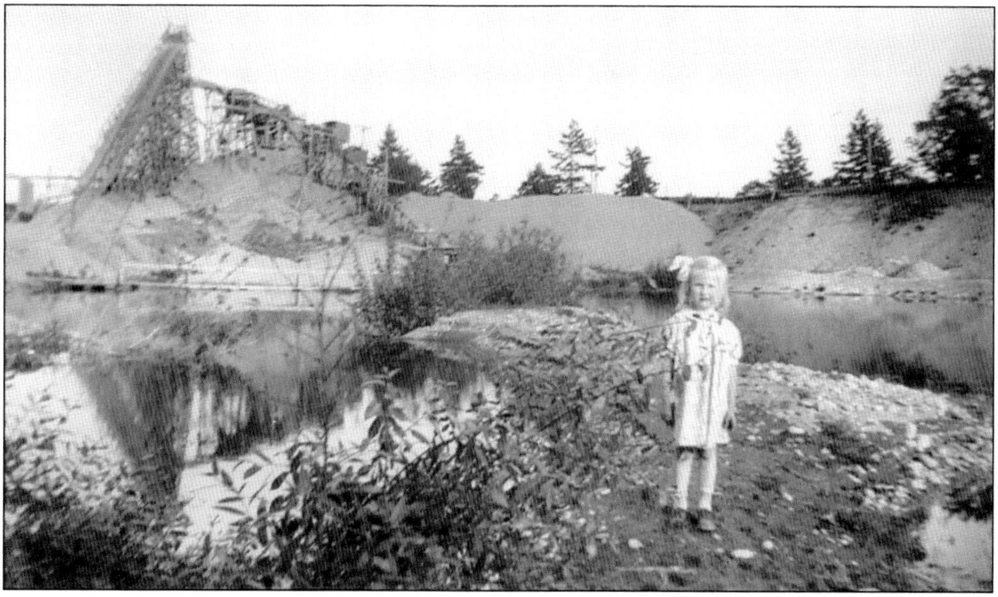

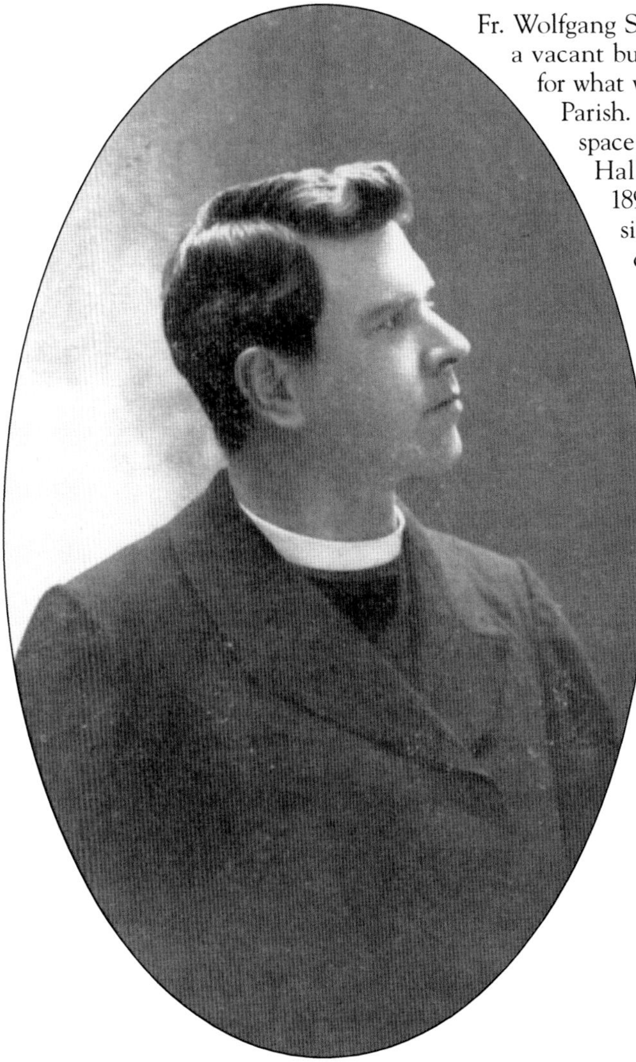

Fr. Wolfgang Steinkogler, OSB, offered mass in a vacant building in South Tacoma in 1892 for what would become Visitation Catholic Parish. The rapidly growing parish gained space by moving first to the Odd Fellows Hall and then the Edison Hotel. In 1899, two lots were purchased at Fifty-sixth and Birmingham Streets for a church dedicated to the Visitation of the Blessed Virgin Mary. (Visitation Catholic School and Parish Archives.)

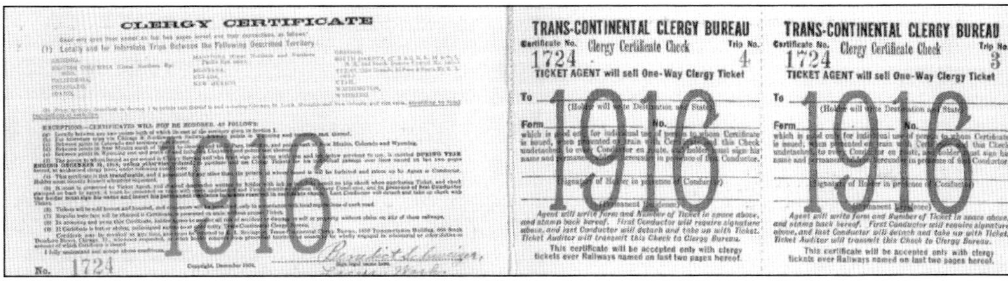

This 1916 one-way, clergy-only ticket offered by railroads allowed the religious to travel across country. Benedictine fathers from St. John's Abbey in Collegeville, Minnesota, used similar tickets in 1891. The priests came at the request of Bishop Rev. Aegidius Junger (Nisqually) to take charge of Holy Rosary Parish. The following year, they assumed pastoral care of South Tacoma's Catholics, who eventually organized Visitation Parish. (Visitation Catholic School and Parish Archives.)

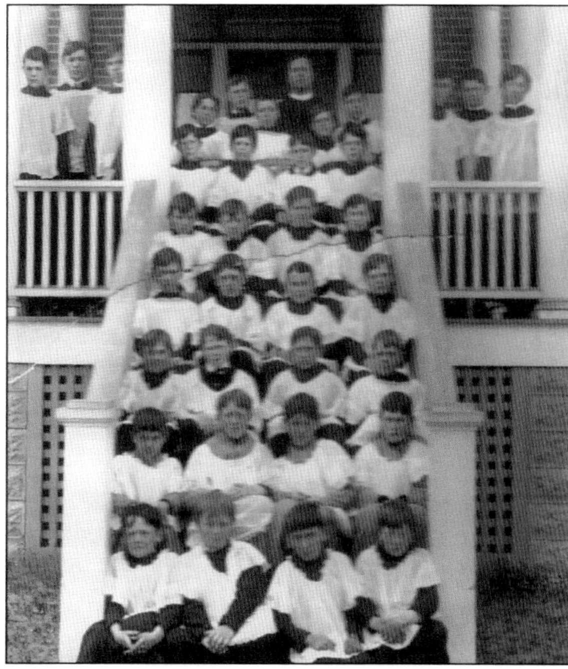

In January 1891, six lots were purchased to build a church for devout German Catholics who wanted sermons in their language. That summer, Rev. William Eversmann said the first mass at Lady of Holy Rosary, so named after seeing many roses nearby. Membership grew rapidly, as shown by this 1907 image of 35 servers, including George Bader, left balcony middle, and Frank Bader, right balcony right. (Art and Loretta Boyle.)

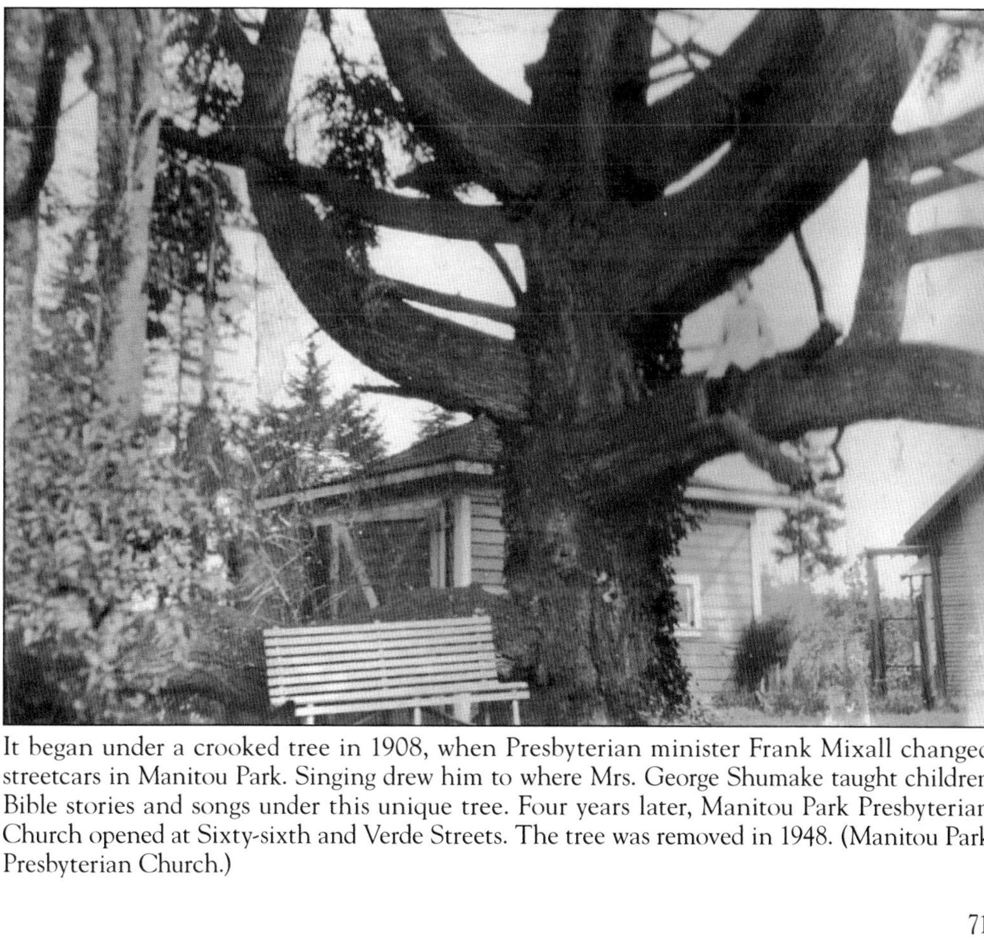

It began under a crooked tree in 1908, when Presbyterian minister Frank Mixall changed streetcars in Manitou Park. Singing drew him to where Mrs. George Shumake taught children Bible stories and songs under this unique tree. Four years later, Manitou Park Presbyterian Church opened at Sixty-sixth and Verde Streets. The tree was removed in 1948. (Manitou Park Presbyterian Church.)

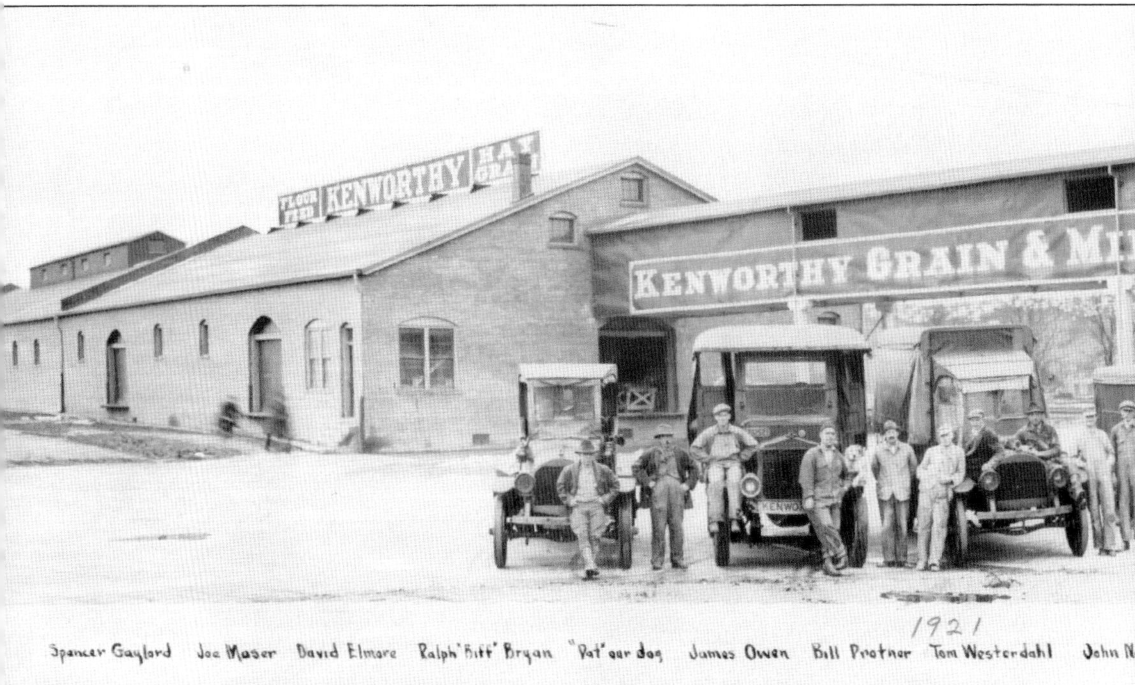

In 1907, W. H. Kenworthy took advantage of the proximity of the railroad tracks to open Kenworthy Grain and Milling Company. He later constructed an enclosed bridge over Fifty-sixth Street for handcarts to transport grain across the street to a brick storage warehouse to load on trucks/trains. The bridge has long been removed, but grain is still milled at 5436 South Washington Street. Elizabeth Sherer (left) and Rose Portmann watch from the office window as employees (from

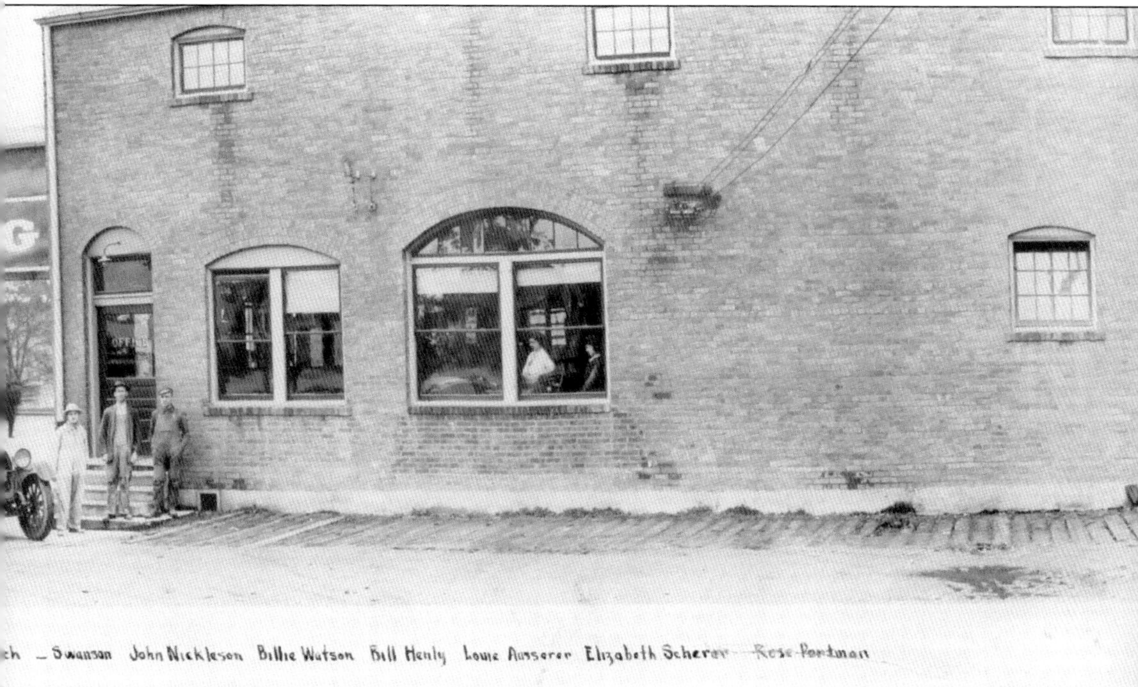

left to right) Spencer Gaylord, Joe Moser, David Elmore, Ralph "Biff" Bryon, Pat the dog, James Owen, Bill Prother, Tom Westerdahl, John Neilson, John Busch, ? Swanson, John Nickleson, Billie Watson, Bill Henley, and Louie Ausserer pose against Kenworthy trucks in 1921. Kenworthy Mill changed to General Mills in 1937 and became X-Cel Feeds, Inc., in 1962. (John Wriglesworth, X-Cel Feeds, Inc.)

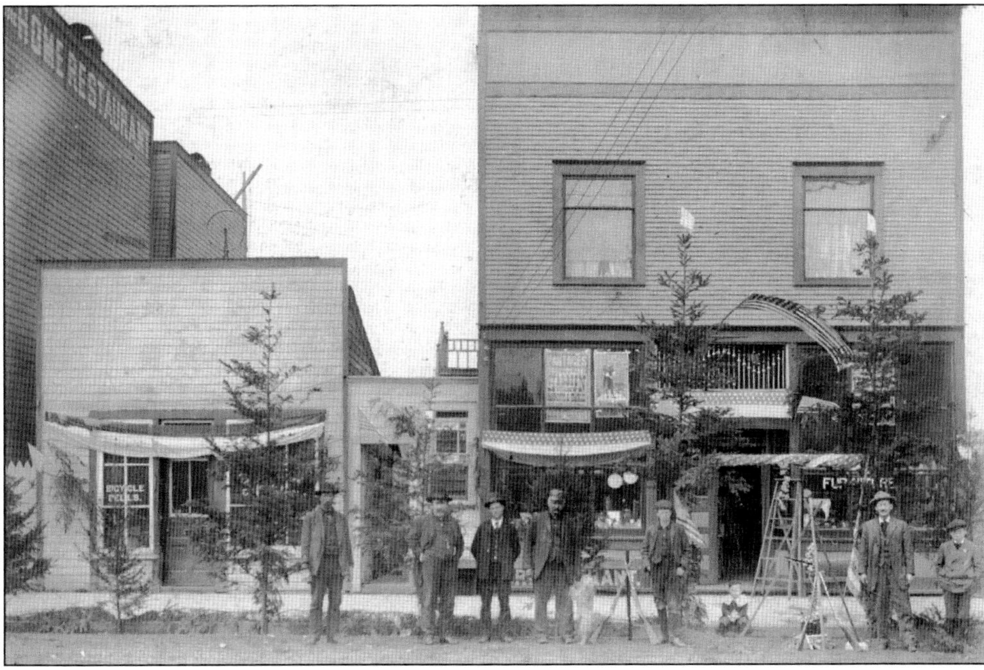

As the 20th century smiled upon South Tacoma, businesses were beginning to line the streets. According to 1906–1908 city directories, this unexplained event occurred in front of Amzie D. Browning's Bicycle and General Repairing at 5042 Union Avenue. Posters in the windows next door announce 10–25¢ Pantages tickets to see Houdini's brother, Hardeen. Barely visible on the left is a restaurant owned by G. K. Whitney. (Eric Swanson collection.)

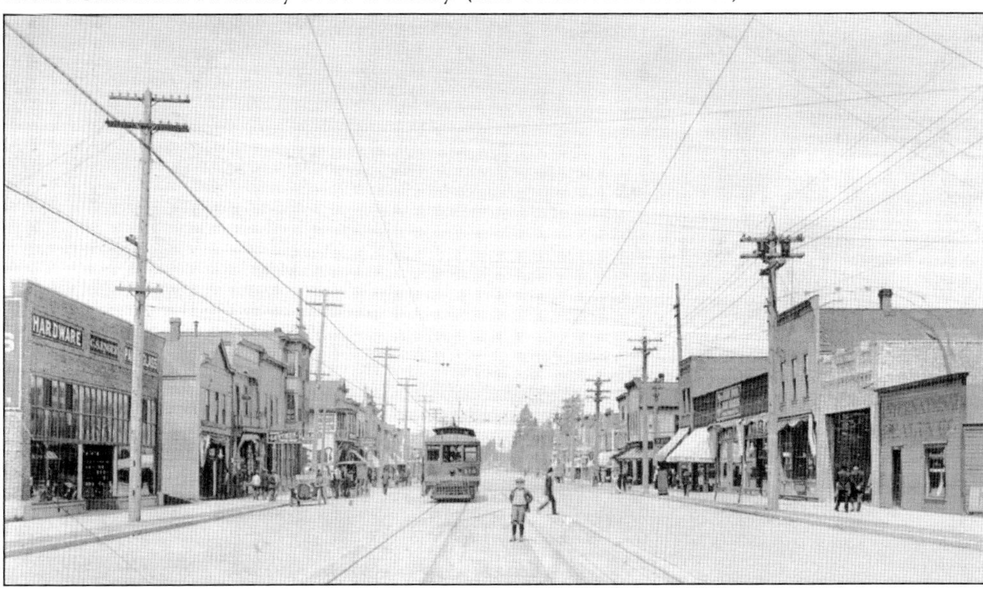

Enger Hardware (left), at 5412–5414 Edison Avenue, was at its third location around 1910. The young boy in the middle of the street posing for the photographer seems oblivious to the trolley car approaching from behind. International Realty Company is the first building on the right, and a sign identifying McLean Brothers is a few doors down next to a wallpaper store. (Eric Swanson collection.)

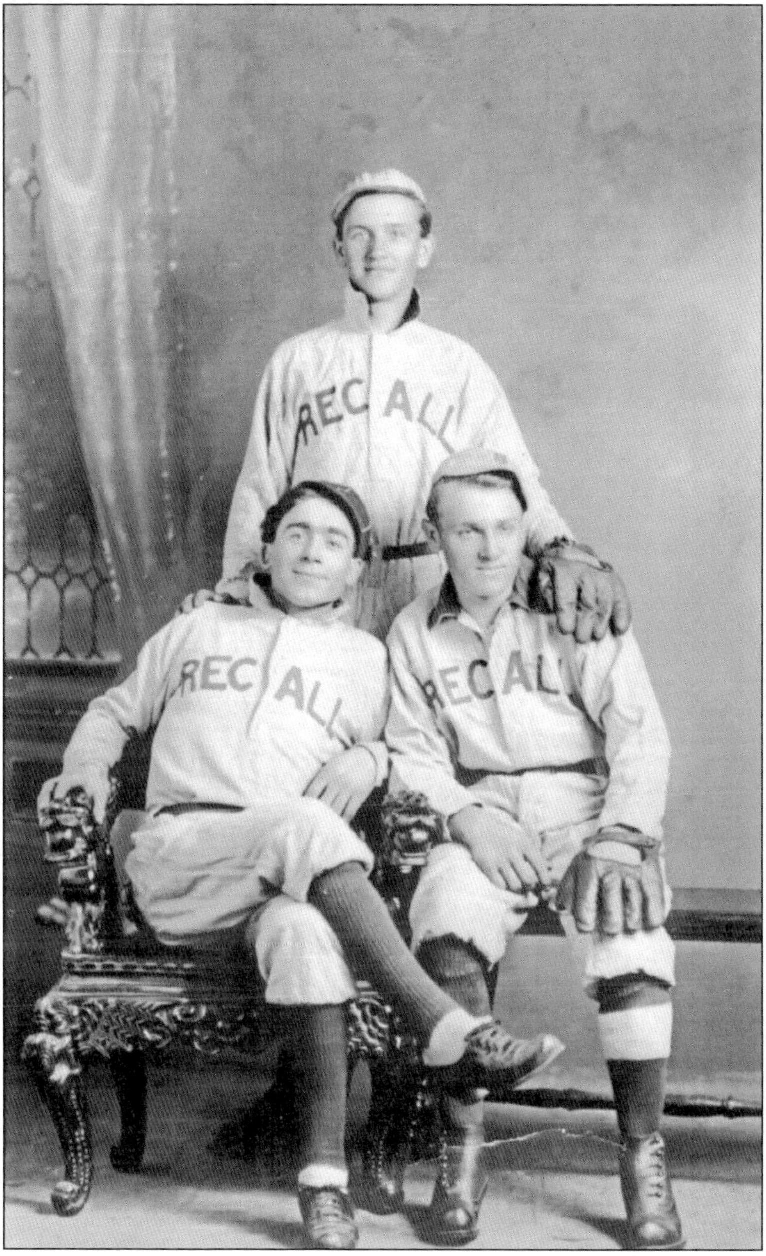

In 1910, one hundred and fifty petitions were distributed to recall Tacoma's mayor, A. V. Fawcett. According to the *Tacoma Daily News* (January 17, 1910), a list of seven charges was filed against the mayor. Concerned citizens showed support for the recall in different ways. South Tacoma resident Andrew Hazen, left front, and two unidentified friends wore baseball uniforms with "RECALL" emblazoned on the front of the shirts and posed for a photographer at Sterling Studio in downtown Tacoma. The letter A is somewhat bolder than the other letters on the shirt, which may allude to the beginning of the mayor's first name, Angelo. The ornately carved wood chair provides Hazen and his friends with a prop and the baseball mitts add a look of reality. Hazen farmed in the South Tacoma area that is now the Tacoma Mall and also had a career at Atlas Foundry. (Hazen family.)

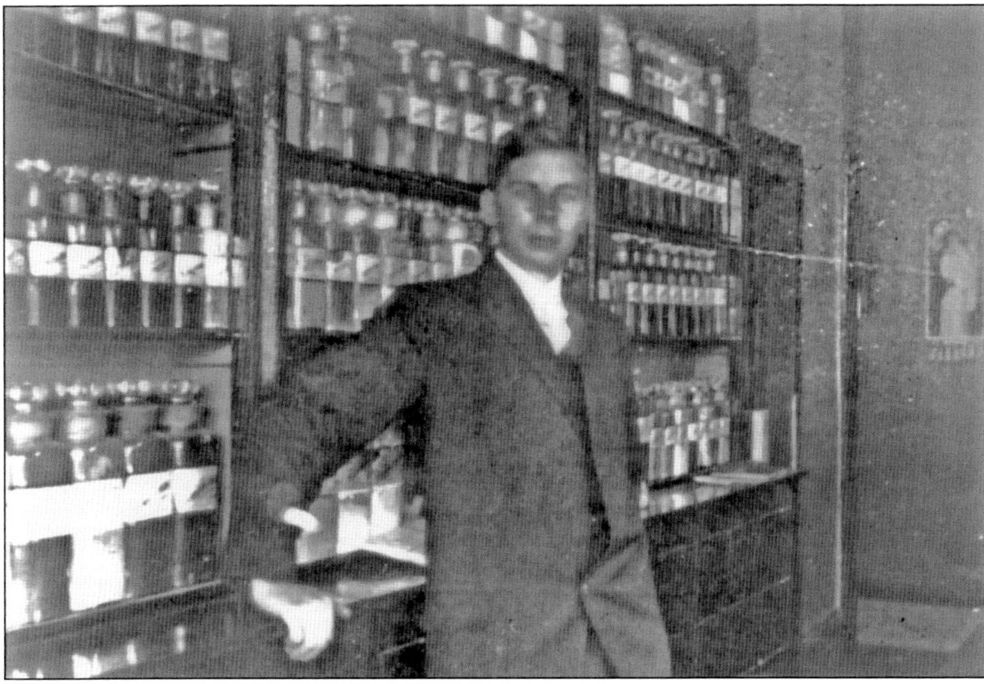

In 1910, Fredrick Ludwig poses with apothecary jars containing syrups, elixirs, and tinctures in his new pharmacy. At the age of 20, Ludwig purchased Tacoma's oldest pharmacy, Yuill and McKenzie, and moved Ludwig Drug across the street, where his son and grandson continued the business for 70 years at the corner of Fifty-fourth Street and South Tacoma Way, which was also a trolley stop. (Ludwig and North family collection.)

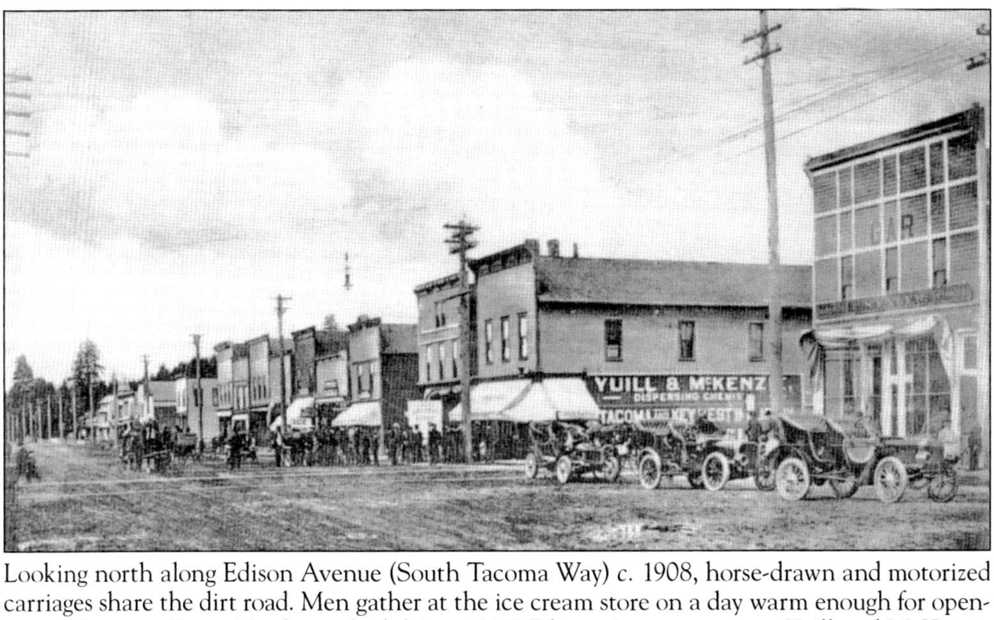

Looking north along Edison Avenue (South Tacoma Way) c. 1908, horse-drawn and motorized carriages share the dirt road. Men gather at the ice cream store on a day warm enough for open-topped buggies. Enger Hardware (right) is at 5412 Edison Avenue, next to Yuill and McKenzie Dispensing Chemistry, which was purchased by pharmacist Fred Ludwig in 1910. The following year, Ludwig Drug moved to 5401 Edison Avenue. (Eric Swanson collection.)

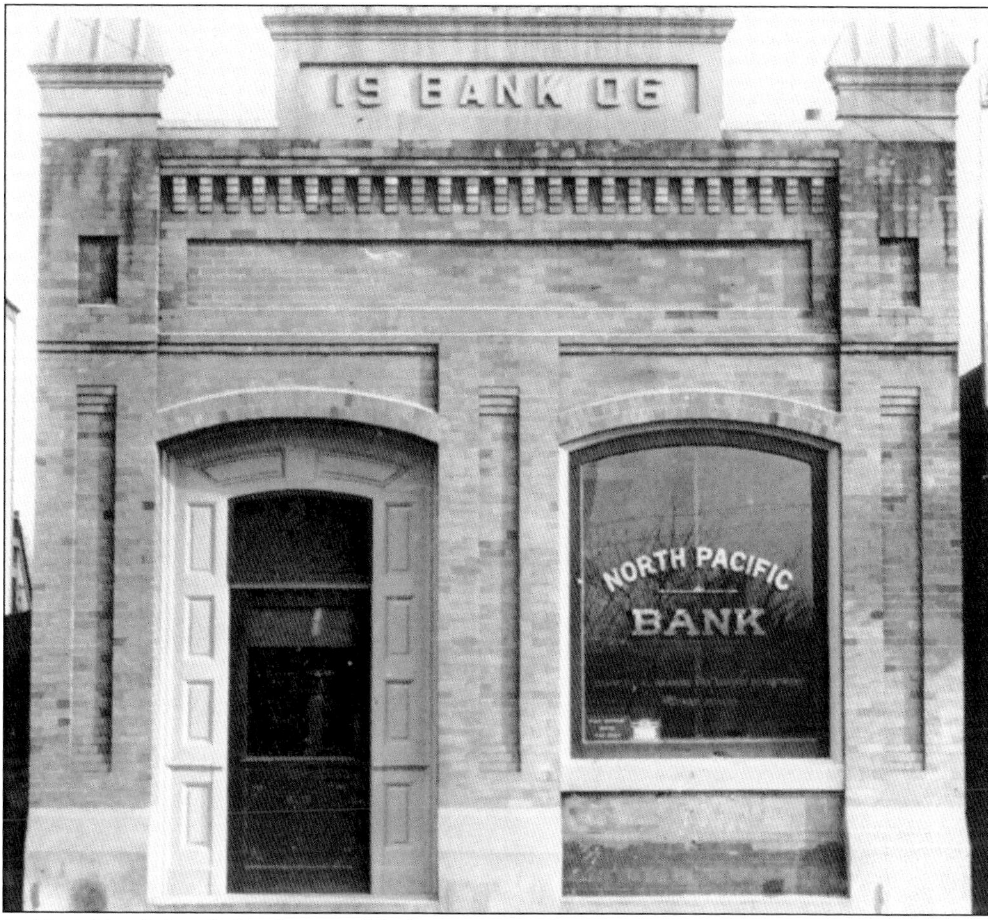

In 1906, North Pacific Bank opened for business on Edison Avenue, currently 5221 South Tacoma Way. It was named for the nearby Northern Pacific Railway Shops, whose workers it served. German immigrant and railroad telegrapher Peter Wallerich purchased the bank in 1912 when he heard of the bank's uncertain financial situation from a message he was relaying. In the early days of little security, money was kept in a shoe box and Wallerich took it home every night on the streetcar. In 1914, the bank constructed a new building at Fifty-sixth Street and South Tacoma Way, pictured below around 1950. Wallerich's son, Clarence, joined the bank in 1928 and remained until 1960, when grandson Peter K. Wallerich took over. North Pacific Bank became Heritage Bank in 1998. (Peter K. Wallerich.)

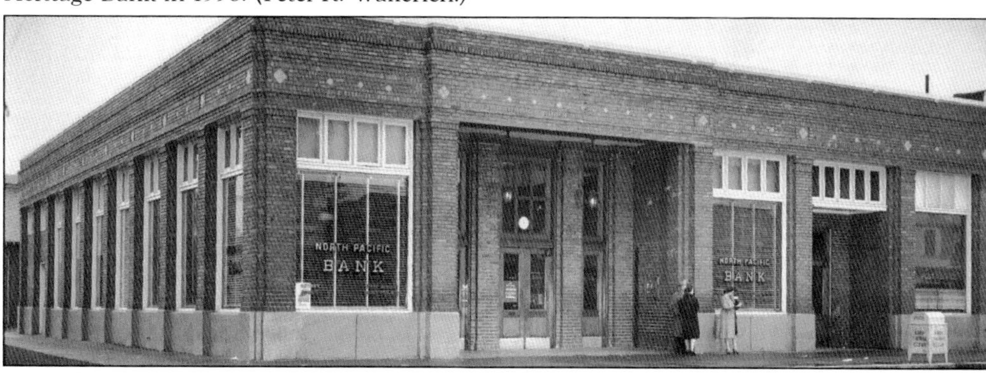

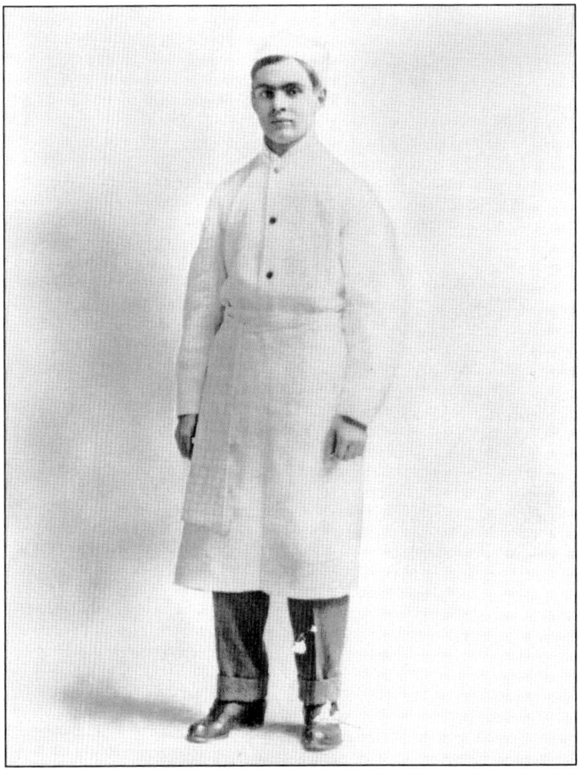

When Yugoslav immigrant Marcus Nalley arrived in the United States in 1903 at age 13, he knew no English and 13¢ were the young man's assets. By age 21, Nalley was chef at a fine Chicago restaurant and had mastered English. At age 25, Nalley married Elizabeth Cook, and they moved to Tacoma. While master chef (left) at Tacoma's Bonneville Hotel, Nalley learned how much guests liked Saratoga Chips. By 1918, Nalley was making chips in his home and selling them door-to-door to local merchants. Nalley sliced, fried, salted, and marketed the first 50-pound batch, guaranteeing merchants he would buy back any that did not sell. Success moved the business out of the home and into a one-room plant (below) where mayonnaise and maple syrup were added to the production. (Birds Eye Foods, Inc.)

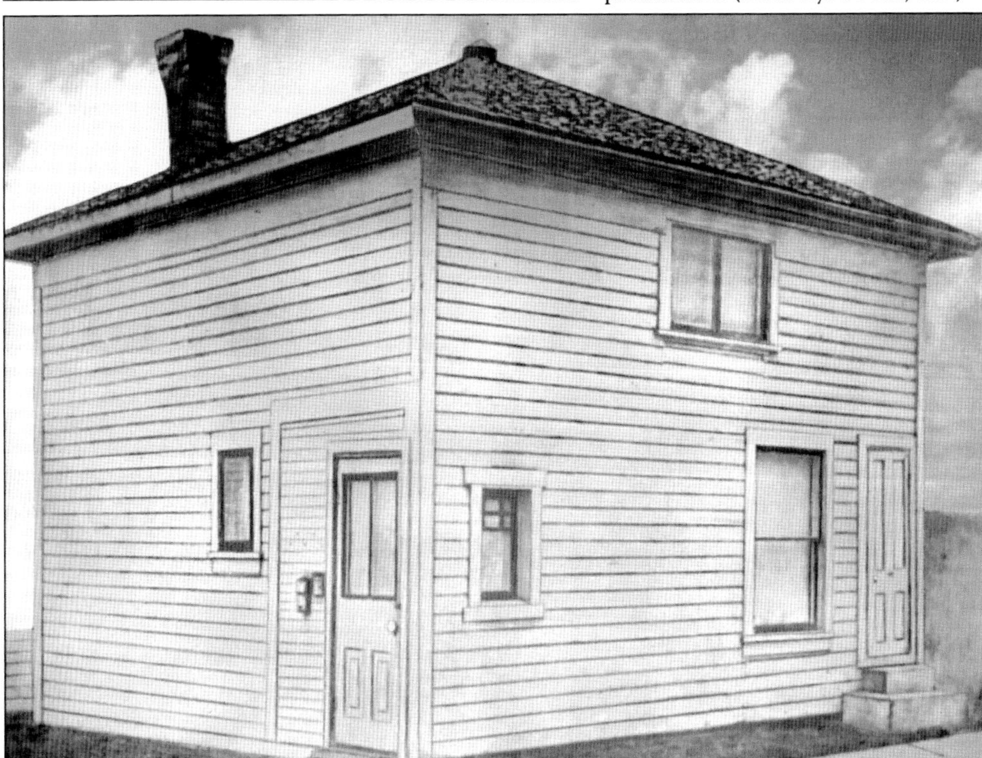

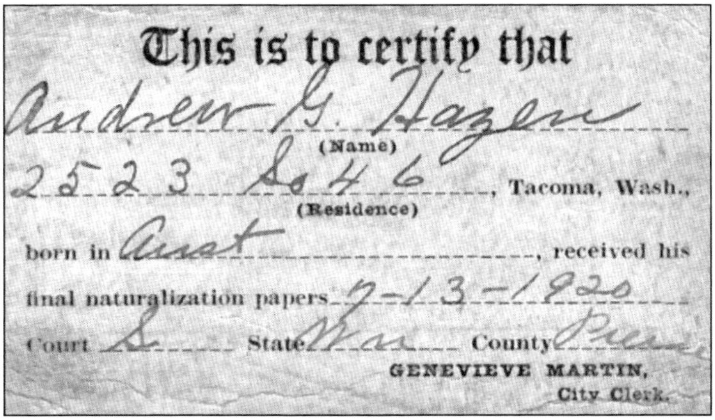

This is to certify that
Andrew G. Hazen
(Name)
2523 So 46, Tacoma, Wash.,
(Residence)
born in Aust, received his
final naturalization papers 7-13-1920
Court S State Wa County Pierce
GENEVIEVE MARTIN,
City Clerk.

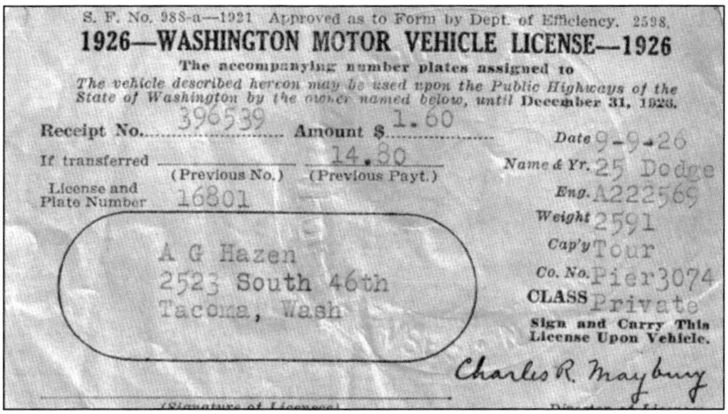

S. F. No. 988-a—1921 Approved as to Form by Dept. of Efficiency. 2598.
1926—WASHINGTON MOTOR VEHICLE LICENSE—1926
The accompanying number plates assigned to
The vehicle described hereon may be used upon the Public Highways of the State of Washington by the owner named below, until December 31, 1926.
Receipt No. 396539 Amount $ 1.60
Date 9-9-26
If transferred 14.80
(Previous No.) (Previous Payt.)
Name & Yr. 25 Dodge
License and Plate Number 16801
Eng. A222569
Weight 2591
Cap'y Tour
Co. No. Pier3074
CLASS Private
A G Hazen
2523 South 46th
Tacoma, Wash
Sign and Carry This License Upon Vehicle.
Charles R. Maybury

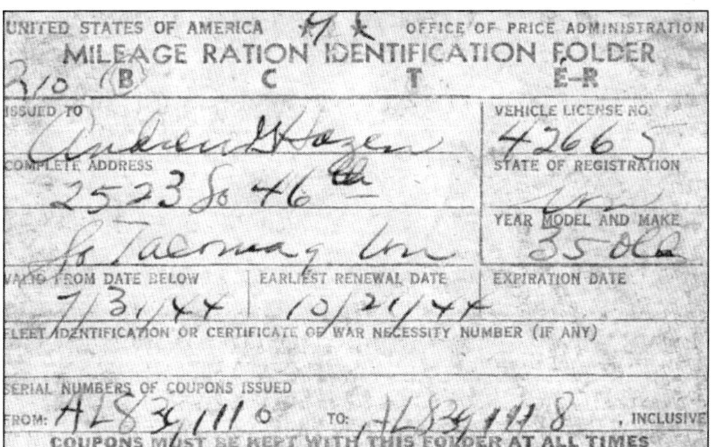

UNITED STATES OF AMERICA OFFICE OF PRICE ADMINISTRATION
MILEAGE RATION IDENTIFICATION FOLDER
B C T E-R
ISSUED TO Andrew G Hazen
VEHICLE LICENSE NO. 42665
COMPLETE ADDRESS 2523 So 46th
STATE OF REGISTRATION Wn
So Tacoma Wn
YEAR MODEL AND MAKE 35 Old
VALID FROM DATE BELOW 7/31/44
EARLIEST RENEWAL DATE 10/21/44
EXPIRATION DATE
FLEET IDENTIFICATION OR CERTIFICATE OF WAR NECESSITY NUMBER (IF ANY)
SERIAL NUMBERS OF COUPONS ISSUED
FROM: AL834111 0 TO: AL834111 8, INCLUSIVE
COUPONS MUST BE KEPT WITH THIS FOLDER AT ALL TIMES

These documents depict the life of a typical United States immigrant who lived and worked in South Tacoma. Austrian-born Andrew Hazen, who lived at 2523 South Forty-sixth Street, was certified as a naturalized citizen by Tacoma's city clerk on July 13, 1920. On August 9, 1926, Hazen paid $1.60 to put a license plate on his 1925 Dodge, which allowed him to drive that vehicle on the public highways of the State of Washington until the end of that year. During World War II, from the U.S. Office of Price Administration Hazen received eight mileage ration coupons good for nearly three months so he could drive his personal vehicle to Atlas Foundry on South Tacoma Way, where, in addition to farming, he had a career. (Hazen family.)

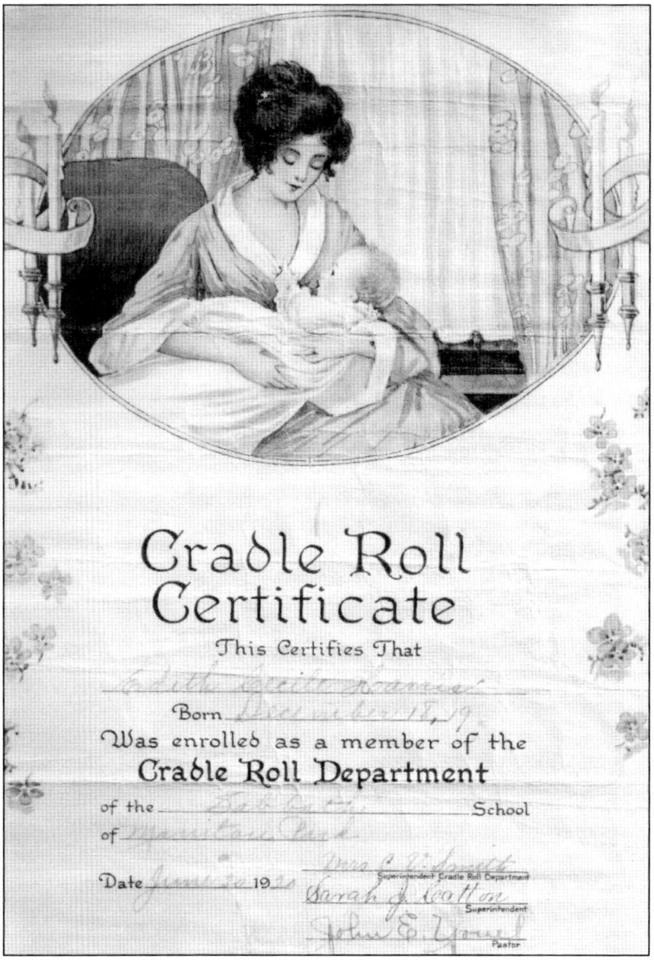

Cradle Roll Certificate

This Certifies That

[illegible]

Born [illegible]

Was enrolled as a member of the

Cradle Roll Department

of the [illegible] School

of [illegible]

Date [illegible] 19[illegible]

[illegible]

Superintendent Cradle Roll Department

[illegible]

Superintendent

John E. Youel

Pastor

Manitou Park Presbyterian Church began in a tent in the woods in 1908 in what eventually became Manitou Park. When Pacific Traction Company asked them to remove the tent from their property, the church's Ladies Aid Society purchased a small triangular lot across the street. The Little Brown Church, named because it was stained brown, was built in time for the first service in 1911. A Cradle Roll Certificate, the church's way of ensuring that babies and young children knew they belonged to God, announces the enrollment of Edith Cecile Harris in 1920. It is signed by Cradle Roll superintendents and Pastor John E. Youel. A large group poses by the little church they soon outgrew. The congregation built a larger church in 1928. In 2007, Rev. Kenneth Sikes leads the parish as they approach their centennial. (Manitou Park Presbyterian Church.)

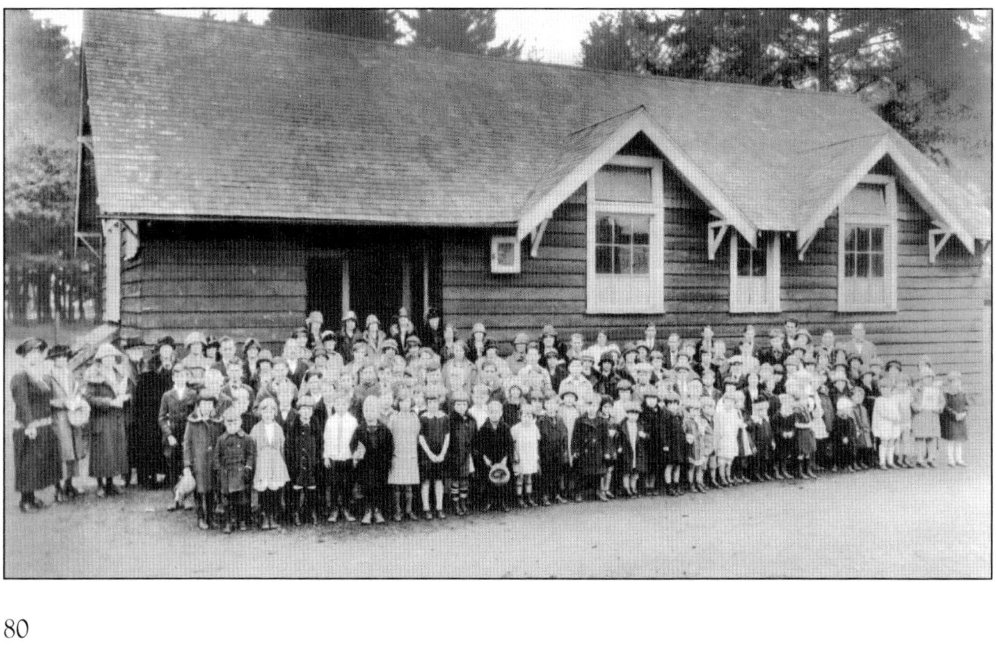

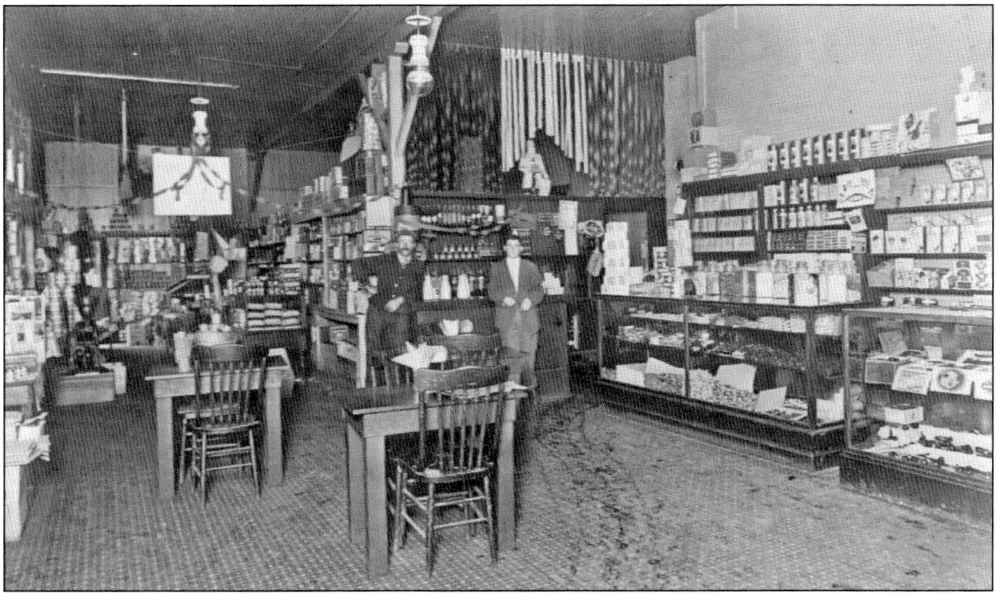

The 1910 Tacoma City Directory lists Joshua Jemison Confectionery as the occupant at 5244 South Puget Sound Avenue. The obvious traffic pattern in the floor leading from the entrance to the back room of the South Tacoma candy store *c.* 1920 indicates deliveries occurred often. Two unidentified workers await customers to sit at the dinette tables or select from the well-stocked display cases. (Hazen family.)

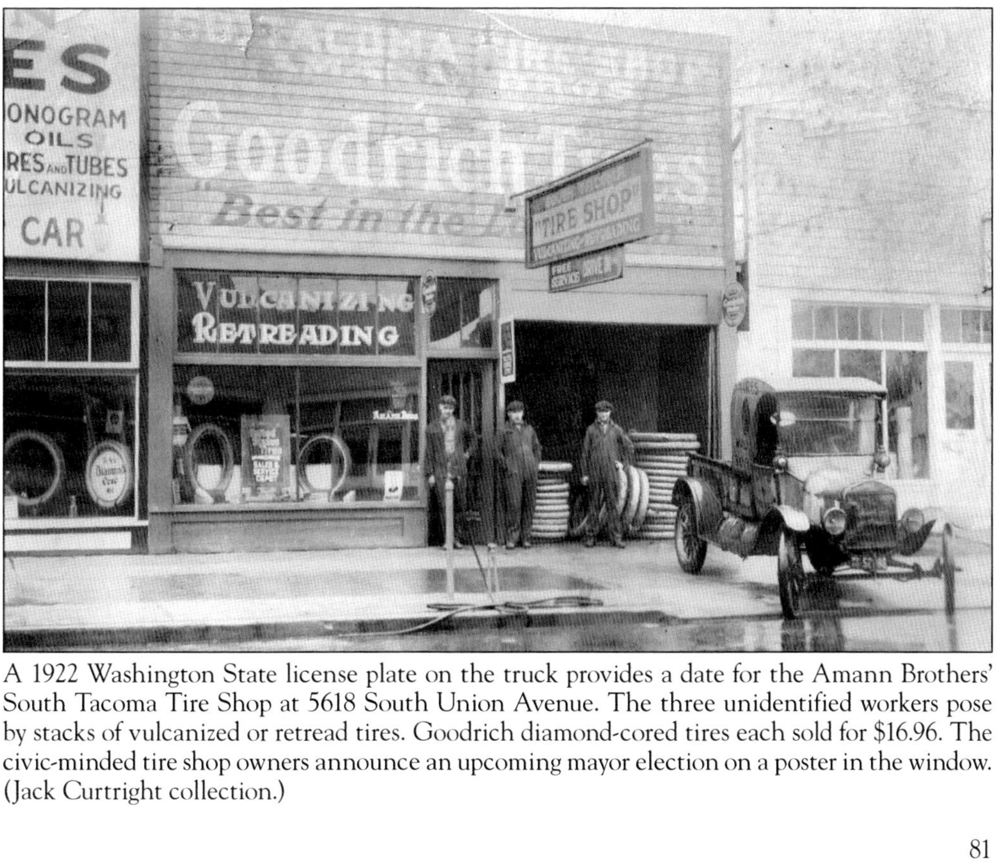

A 1922 Washington State license plate on the truck provides a date for the Amann Brothers' South Tacoma Tire Shop at 5618 South Union Avenue. The three unidentified workers pose by stacks of vulcanized or retread tires. Goodrich diamond-cored tires each sold for $16.96. The civic-minded tire shop owners announce an upcoming mayor election on a poster in the window. (Jack Curtright collection.)

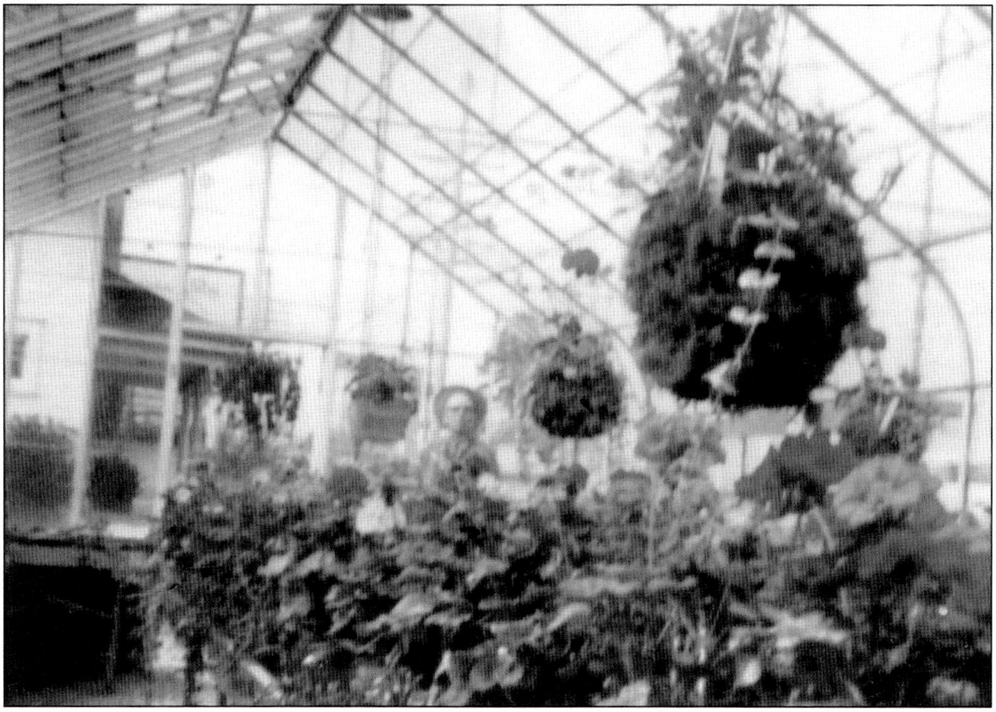

English immigrant Charles Cliff traveled west to work in Northern Pacific's Reclaiming Plant in South Tacoma. Cliff and his wife, Mabel, bought property for growing flowers and plants, built greenhouses, and founded Cliff Florists at 7630 Edison Avenue in 1923. By 1941, Edison Avenue had changed to South Tacoma Way, and son Harry had married Dolores. The second Cliff generation managed the business during World War II and until 1979, when the third generation, Bob and wife Dory, took over. They changed the name to Cliff's Flowers and continued the family legacy until 2003, when South Tacoma Honda purchased the land. Founder Charlie is shown in his beloved greenhouse surrounded by flowers. Harry, a member of the second generation, poses beside a new Deluxe four-door sedan in front of a 1936 panel truck and a 1935 two-door, all Fords purchased from South Tacoma's Mallon Motors. (Cliff's Flowers.)

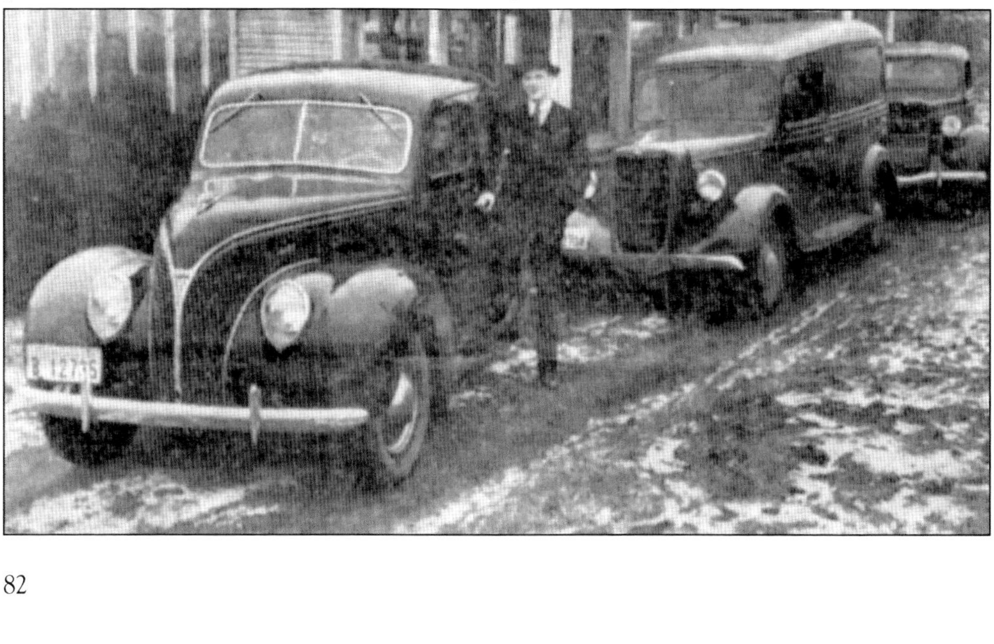

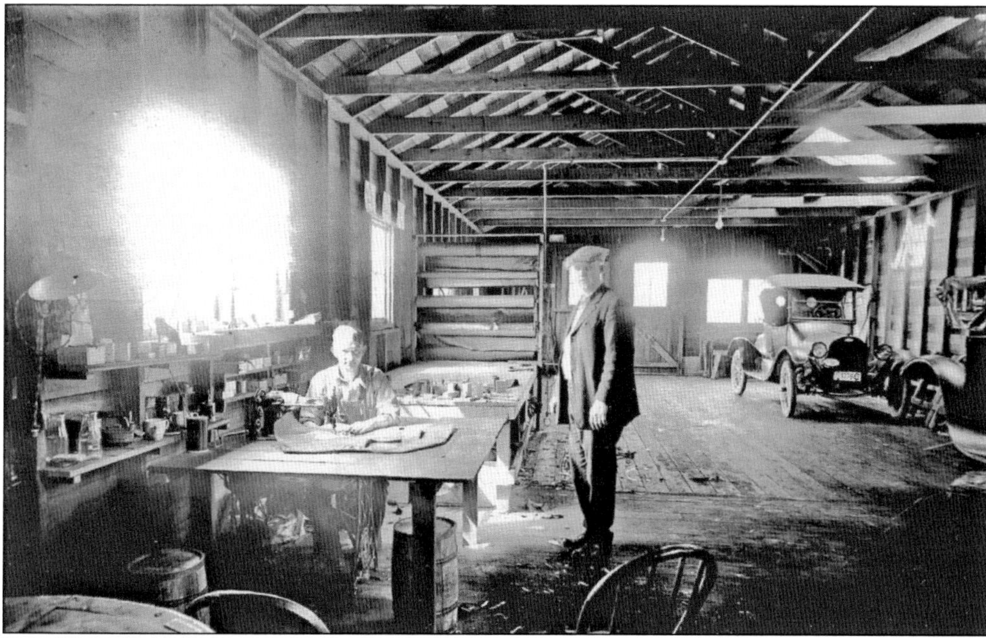

Fritz Dietz watches Auto Tops founder John Dolge Sr. sewing celluloid for the 1917 Chevy parked in the corner. The 1923 license plate indicates it has been one year since Dolge opened his one-of-a-kind business on South Tacoma Way. Celluloid isinglass and other canvas products were custom made to replace worn or damaged side curtains for vehicles. (Dolge family.)

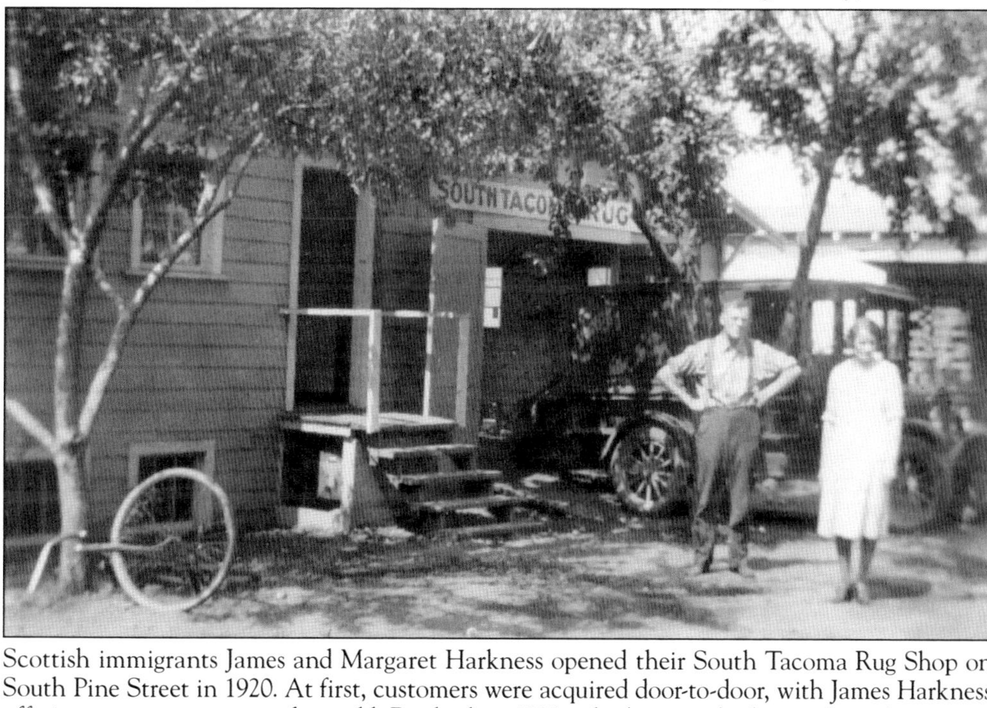

Scottish immigrants James and Margaret Harkness opened their South Tacoma Rug Shop on South Pine Street in 1920. At first, customers were acquired door-to-door, with James Harkness offering to weave new rugs from old. By the late 1920s, the business had moved to what is now South Tacoma Way. The Harknesses pose with their company vehicle at their new plant in 1927. (Dorothy Harkness personal collection.)

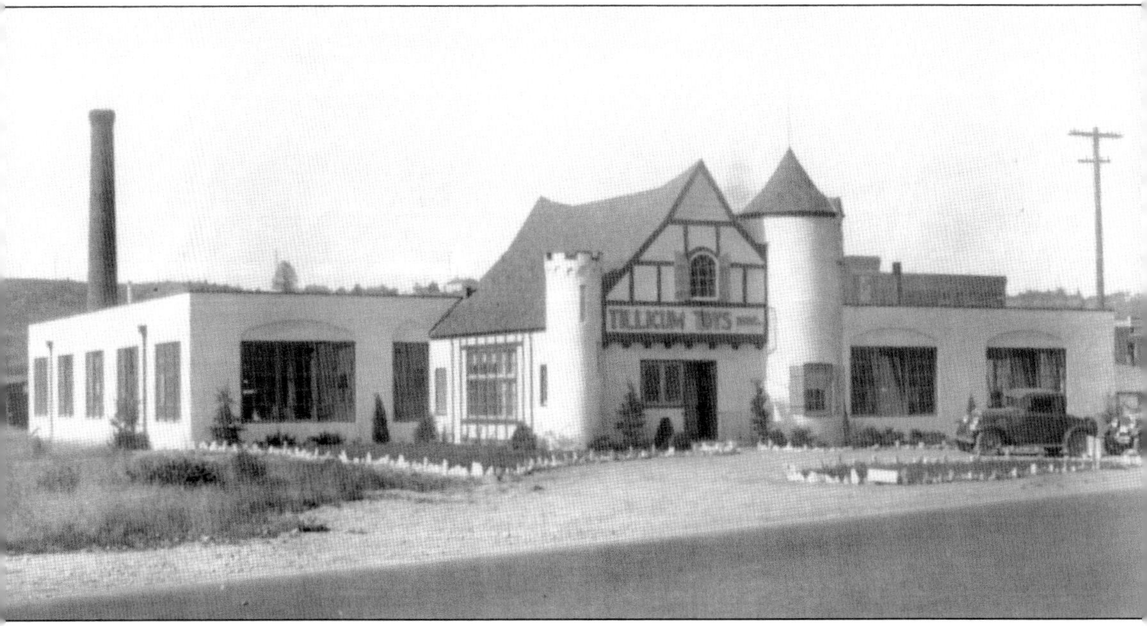

J. K. Weddell made his first toys by hand on a carpenter's workbench using waste from the lumber industry, 100-percent Northwest wood, and no breakable mechanisms. In 1929, Weddell built a castle at 2515 South Tacoma Way for his three-year-old company. Within two years, Tillicum Toys, Inc., was selling wooden toys all over the world from the South Tacoma factory. Weddell explained the name Tillicum was chosen because of its simplicity and expressiveness and not until after it was adopted did the company discover it is a Native American name meaning "good friend." Five years after the castle was built, a new plant was added, and Weddell announced they would be "in direct competition with Santa Claus Manufacturing of the North Pole. Fifteen workers will produce 1,200 wooden boats, automobiles, and battleships every day in the fairyland castle." In the past 80 years, other businesses have occupied the building, including a cheese factory and Darigold Farms Dairy. Currently, MCD Technologies, a food processing company, occupies the building. (TPL.)

Weddings, elaborately decorated with flowers, were an occasion to celebrate. Hilda Leisinger's and George Bader's families were lifetime friends and of the Swiss community. All belonged to Holy Rosary Church, where Hilda and George (right) married in 1921 when he returned from the war. They raised a family at 224 South Thirtieth Street, two blocks from the church. The house was moved when the freeway was built. In 1928, as stated in a newspaper clipping, "The wedding of one of South Tacoma's favorite girls, Margaret Harkness, to Archie Thompson was solemnized. The bride is the daughter of Mr. and Mrs. James Harkness of 6612 South Union Avenue, owners of South Tacoma business, Harkness Rug Company." From left to right are Mrs. Walter Frazier, Mrs. Archie Doty (bridesmaids), Marion Harkness (maid of honor), and Virginia Parker (flower girl). (Above, Art and Loretta Boyle; below, Dorothy Harkness personal collection.)

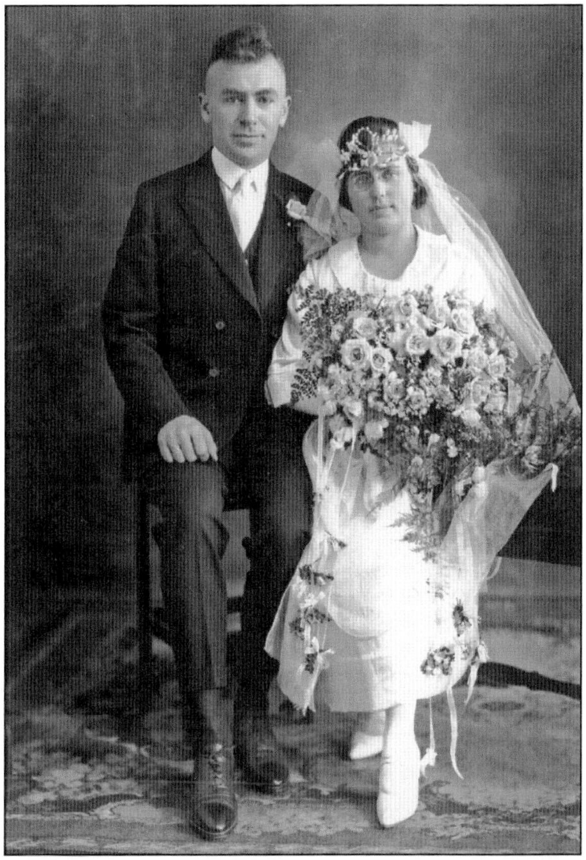

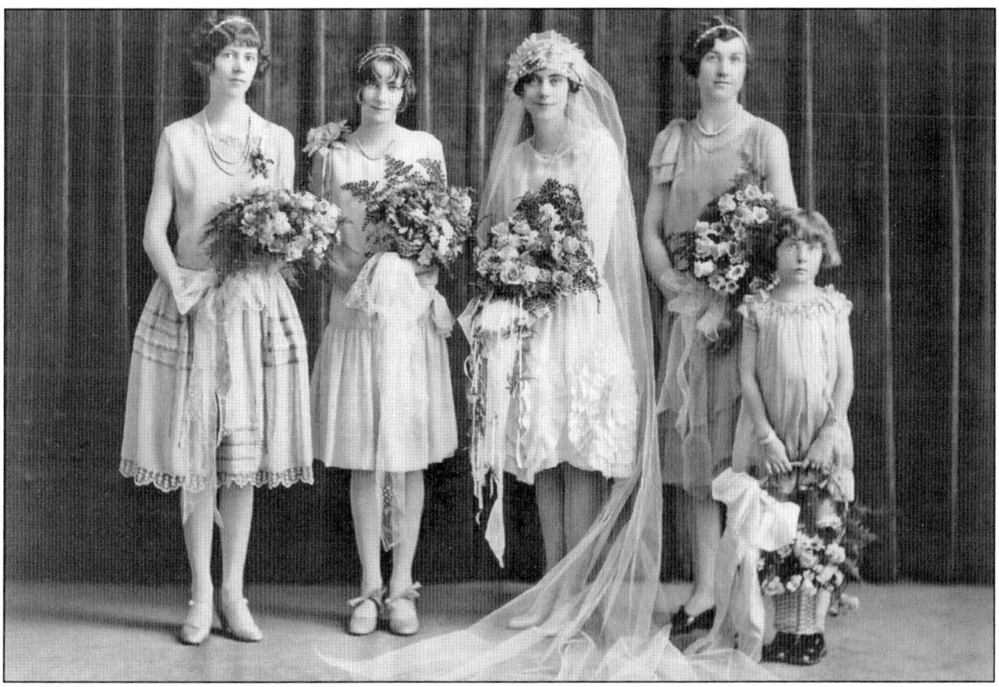

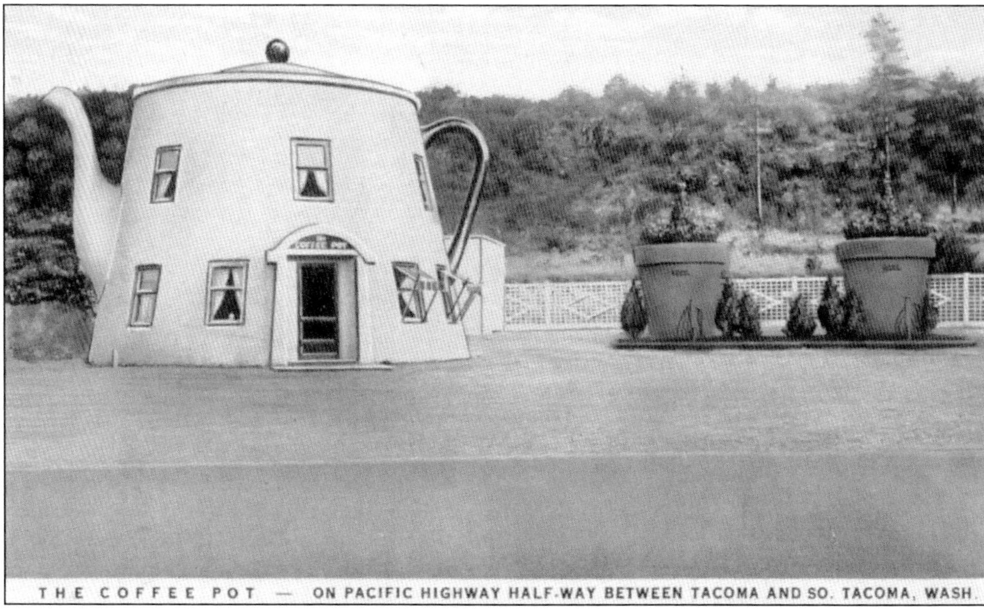

In 1929, Tacoma veterinarian Otis Button commissioned local artist Bert Smyser to design a coffeepot 25 feet high and 30 feet in diameter. The Coffee Pot restaurant, with supplementary, camouflaged, outdoor toilets labeled "Mom" and "Pop," was built in South Tacoma beside Highway 99. The coffeepot-shaped building, an American icon, was listed on Tacoma's Register of Historic Places in 2003 as Bob's Java Jive. (Thomas R. Stenger collection.)

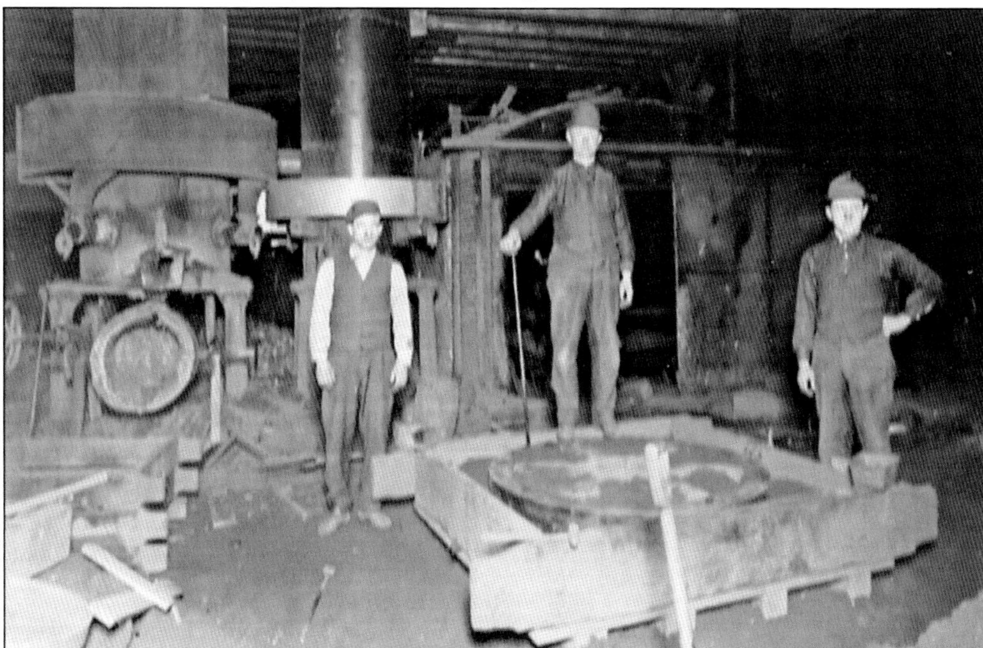

In 1932, Bill Aloof (left), unidentified, and Heinie Bering (right) prepare to pour a mold with molten metal at Atlas Foundry. A small keel block mold, used to provide test specimens for destructive testing, sits on the forward right corner of the large mold. In the 1930s, one half of Atlas's production was steel castings. (Atlas Castings and Technology.)

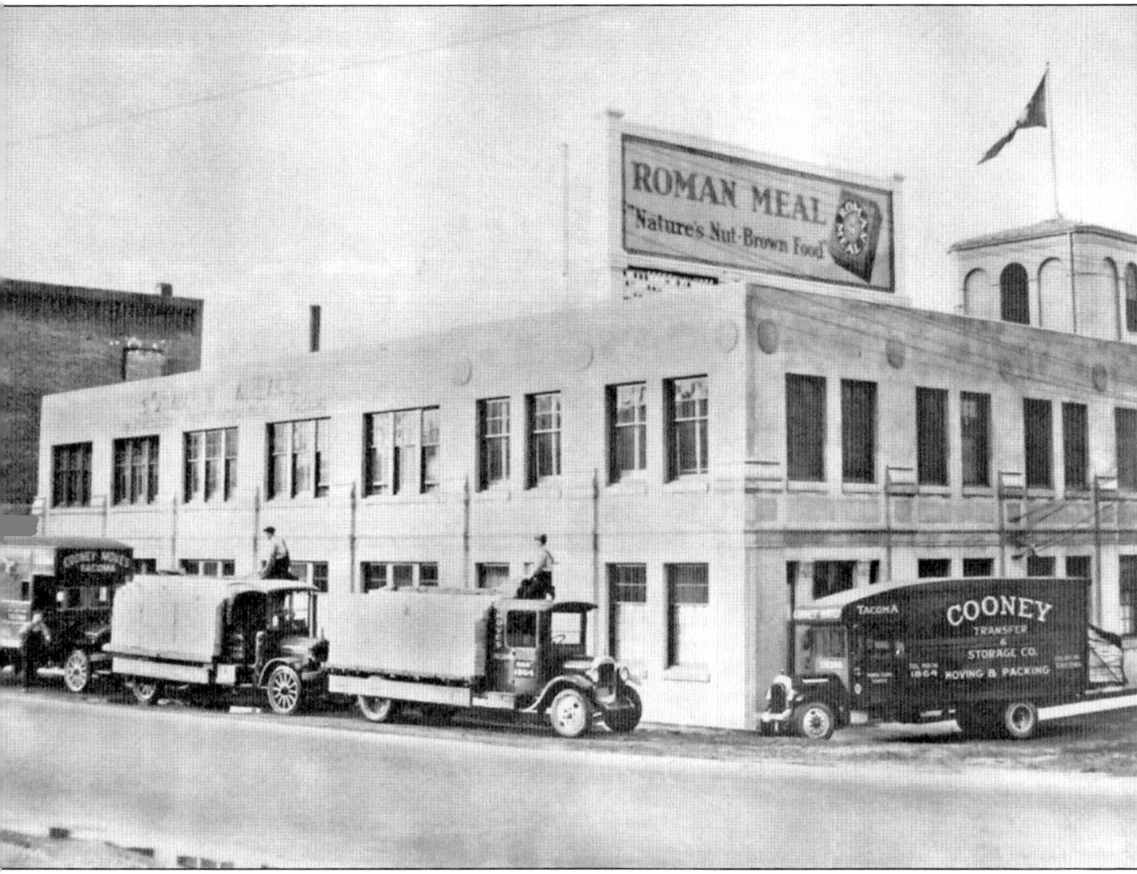

In 1910, ailing physician Robert Jackson devised a hot breakfast porridge that corrected his vitamin and mineral deficiency. Based on Roman foot soldiers' daily ration of wheat or rye, he developed Dr. Jackson's Roman Health Meal. William Matthaei, son of Henry Matthaei, a Kansas City, Missouri, master baker, who had moved to the United States from Germany, purchased Roman Meal Company from Dr. Jackson's successors in 1927. The South Tacoma business, known for its healthy bread, quickly became a familiar name to people around the world and is still owned and operated by the Matthaei family—nearly 100 years after Dr. Jackson created the solution to his health concern. This c. 1930 image shows the Roman Meal building at 2101 South Tacoma Way and Ferry Street with delivery trucks waiting to be loaded. Two unidentified men pose atop freight trucks flanked by the Cooney trucks that belonged to a drayage company used for handling shipments and deliveries to and from Roman Meal Company. A U.S. flag with 48 stars flies above the building. (Roman Meal Company.)

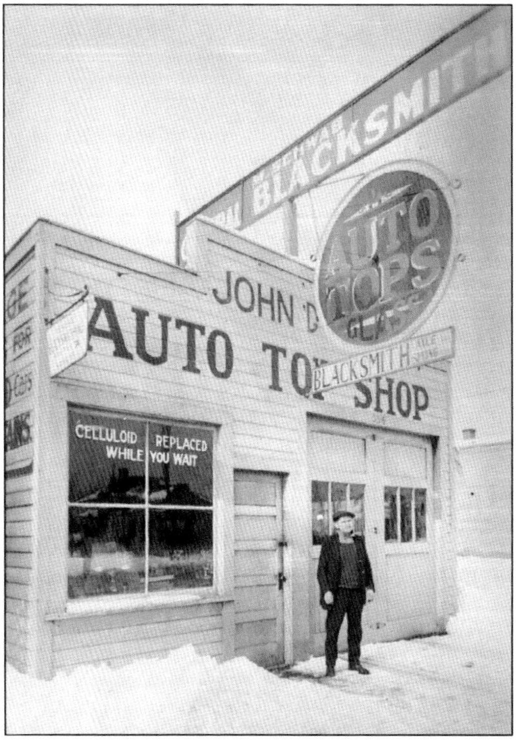

German-born John Dolge Sr. landed in the West in 1906 after sailing around Cape Horn as a seaman. For the next 16 years, Dolge worked in various jobs until opening his Auto Tops shop in South Tacoma. In 1932, Dolge stands in the snow in front of the building he shares with Michael Schwab, a blacksmith who shod horses until the automobile became popular. (Dolge family.)

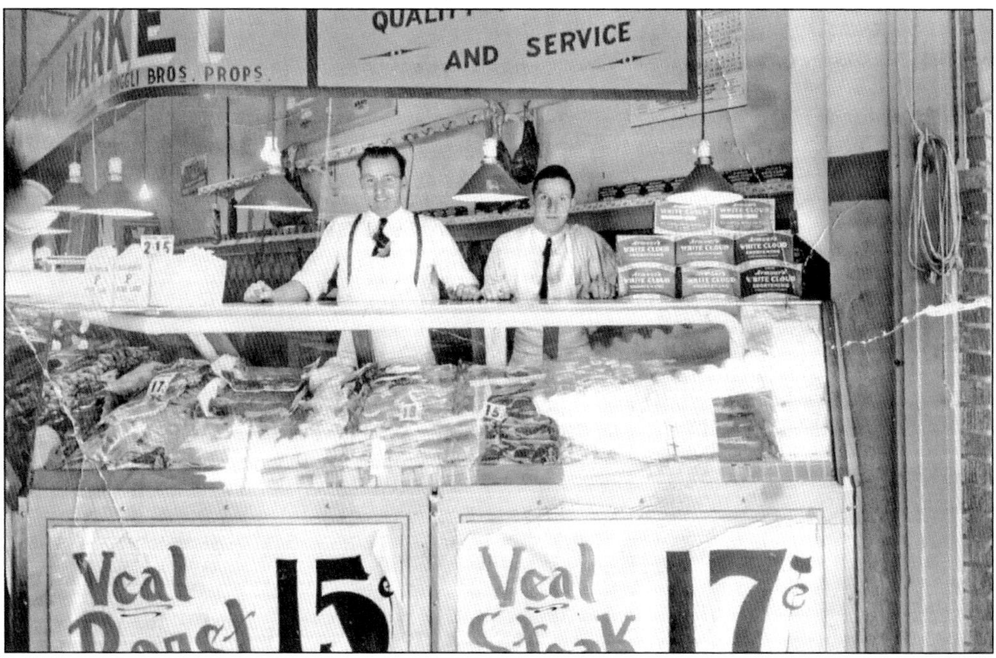

In the middle of South Tacoma's business district, brothers Martin (left) and Tony Renggli opened Renggli Meat Market at Fifty-fourth and South Tacoma Way on the east side of the street. The brothers' well-stocked meat case advertising "Veal Roast, 15¢ cents lb." and "Veal Steak 17¢ lb." would be a considered a bargain today. Diamond Pure Lard and Amour's White Cloud Shortening were sold to cook the meat at home. (Roy Renggli.)

Baker Boys Northwest has been baking bread and pastries for South Tacoma neighbors and local restaurants since 1919, when Greek immigrants Louis Evans (née Lazarous Evangelou) and his brother Peter founded Evans Bakery Company, Inc. In 1935, Ernie, the youngest of Louis Evan's children, stands in front of his uncle's home holding a large loaf of bread. The home, built around 1920 for Peter and Lois Evans, remains today at 3811 South Wright Avenue across the street from the bakery. Ernie's image, seen on the original sign (below), was used in the bakery's earliest logo and is still seen today on all Baker Boys bread wrappers. Current owners Gavin and Cindy Jury know the value of recognition when marketing a good product. (Baker Boys Northwest.)

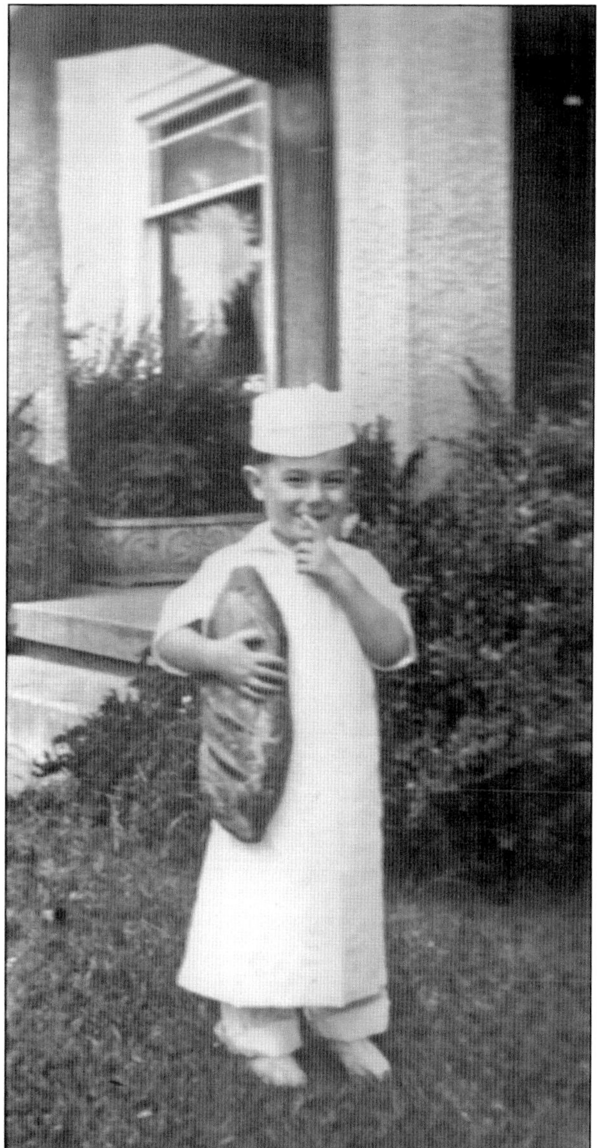

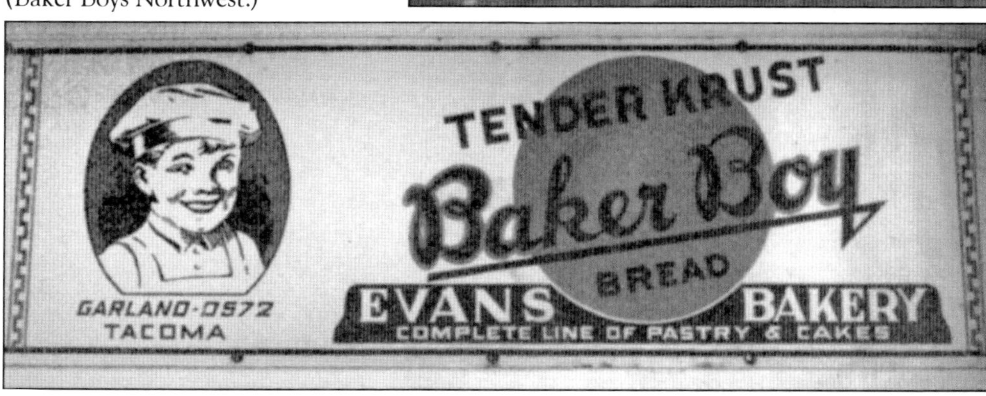

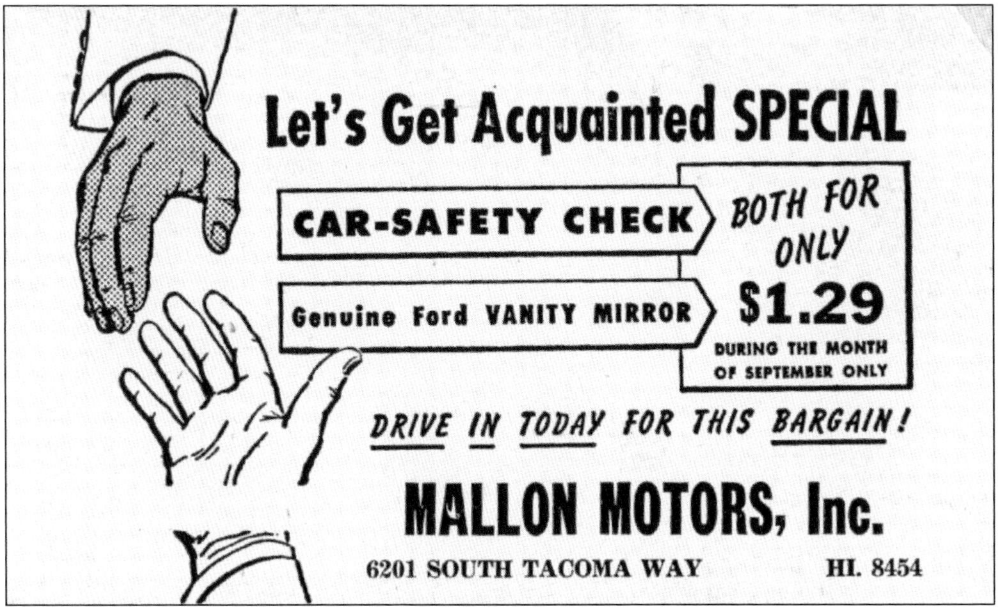

The words "cars" and "South Tacoma" in the same sentence often include "Mallon." Tommy Mallon's life with cars began in 1916 at South Tacoma's Leonard Motor Company. Mallon Ford and son Bob were both born in 1935. A used-car lot and a truck center soon joined the venture—all on South Tacoma Way. In 1952, Mallon Motors offers a get-acquainted special for $1.29. (Thomas R. Stenger collection.)

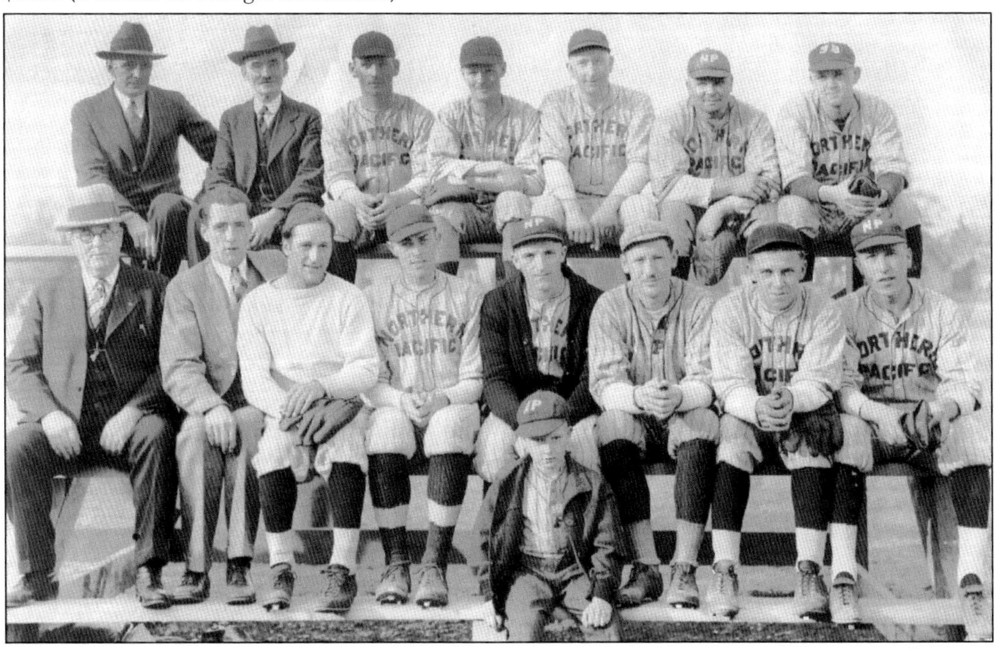

Northern Pacific workers played in A and B baseball divisions around the Puget Sound region. Identified in this c. 1930 image are (first row) Julius Crosetto (third from left), Primo Artoe (fifth from the left), and Kody Larson (second from the right); (second row) Happy Earth (middle) and shops superintendent H. A. Lyddon (second from the left representing the management). (Jim Fredrickson collection.)

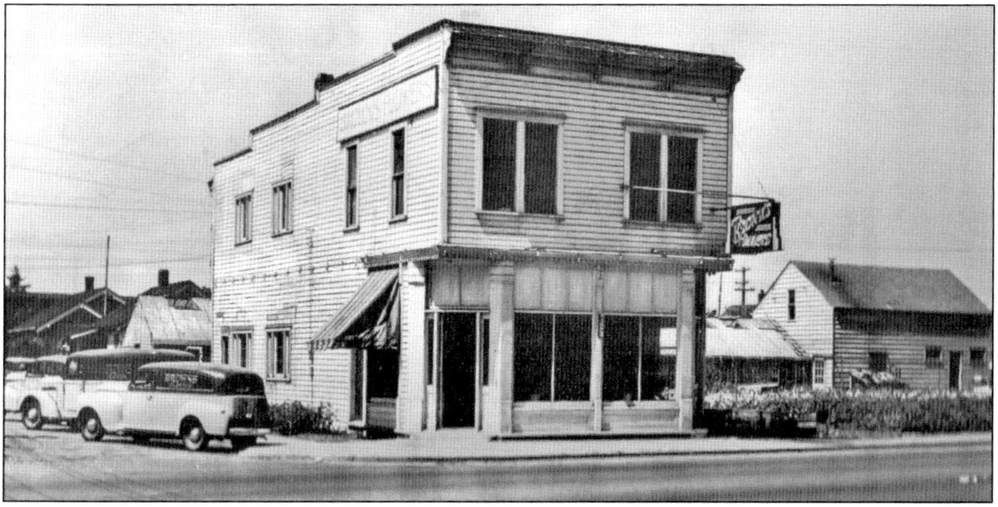

Herbert Brown, gardener for a Gravelly Lake family, received greenhouses from his employer to open a flower shop on property Brown had purchased on Steilacoom Boulevard. Because of the Depression, the Brown family lost the property, but not the business. In 1934, civic leader Norton Clapp loaned Brown's 18-year-old son Bill $4,000 to purchase an old grocery store (above) at 4734 South Tacoma Way, which the family converted to Brown's Flowers. Between 1946 and 1948, after Bill returned from World War II service, he and wife Avonelle expanded, remodeled, and built a large greenhouse, a two-story conservatory, and a corsage room while growing the flower business. Bruce Petersen, a 20-year employee, purchased the business in 1990 and a few years later bought the property. Bill Brown holds a bouquet of flowers in front of the greenhouse in 1937. (Brown's Flowers, Inc.)

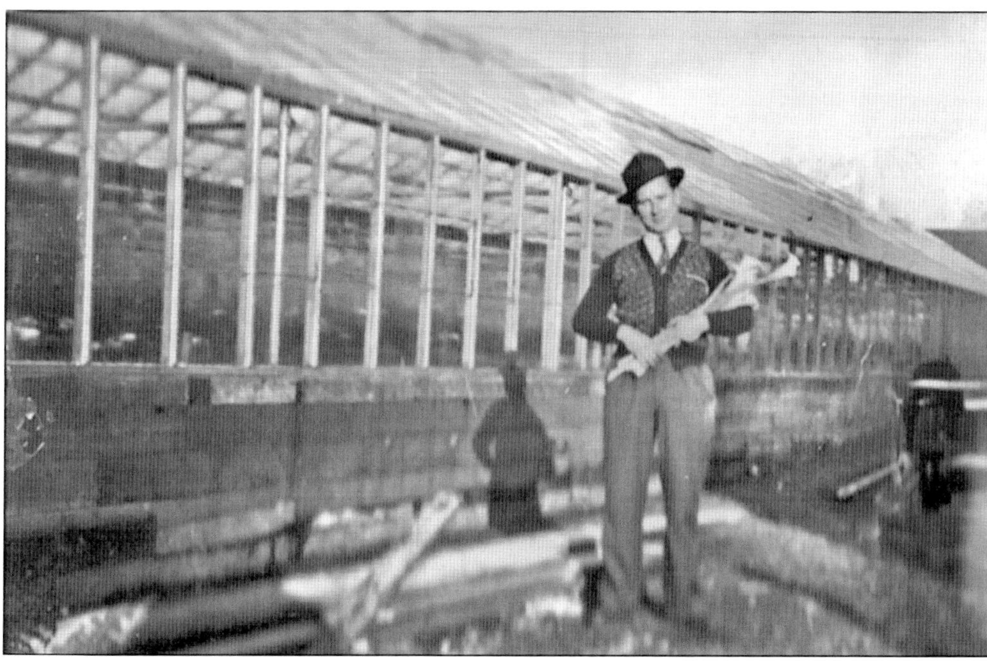

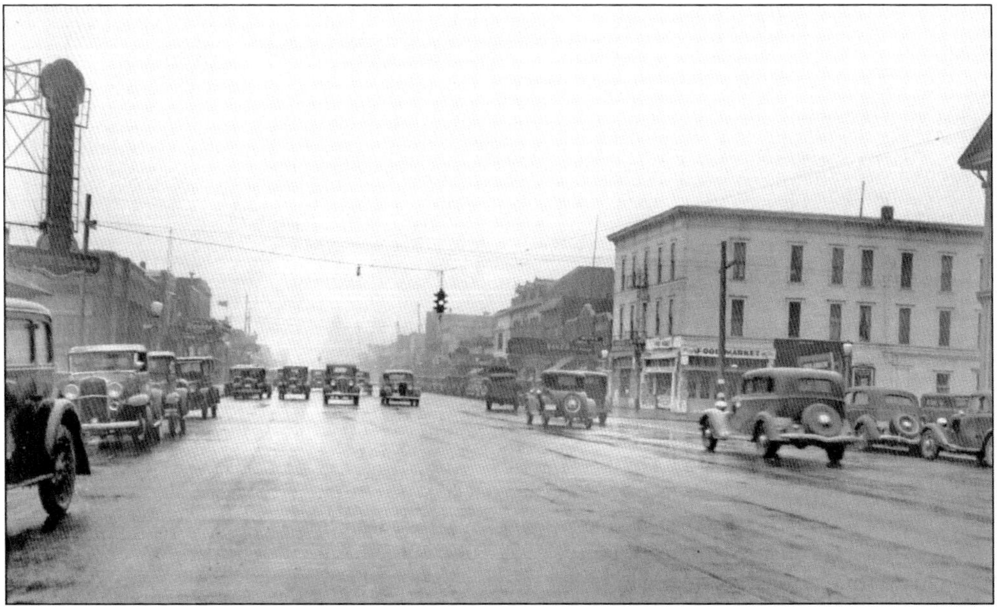

Looking north along South Tacoma Way in 1936, automobiles move slowly in the rain as drivers prepare to stop for the traffic light at Fifty-sixth Street. South Tacoma Chevrolet (left) is on the southwest corner, North Pacific Bank is across Fifty-sixth Street, and Martin's offers lunch next door. Across South Tacoma Way from left to right are a drugstore, a bakery, a men's store, and McCoy's Food Market. (Tacoma Public Utilities.)

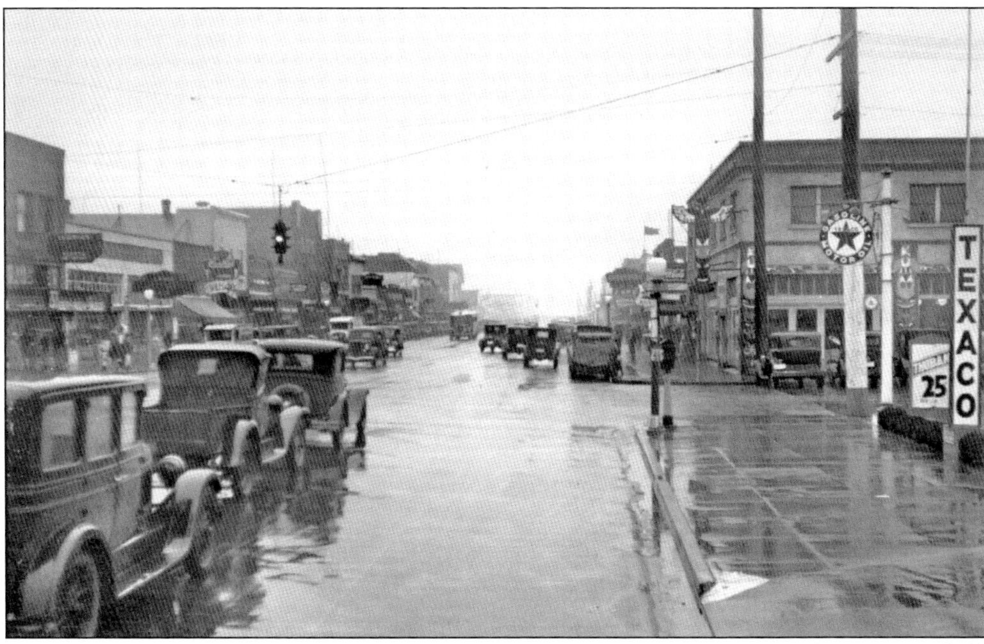

Looking south along South Tacoma Way in 1936, automobiles cruise past Ludwig's Drug (left), Lang Hardware, Central Store, a meat market, and a candy store. Across the street, beside the Highway 99 sign at the Fifty-fourth Street intersection, a police call-box is seen in front of a Texaco station. This photograph may have been taken to check South Tacoma Way traffic flow, street lighting, or traffic lights. (Tacoma Public Utilities.)

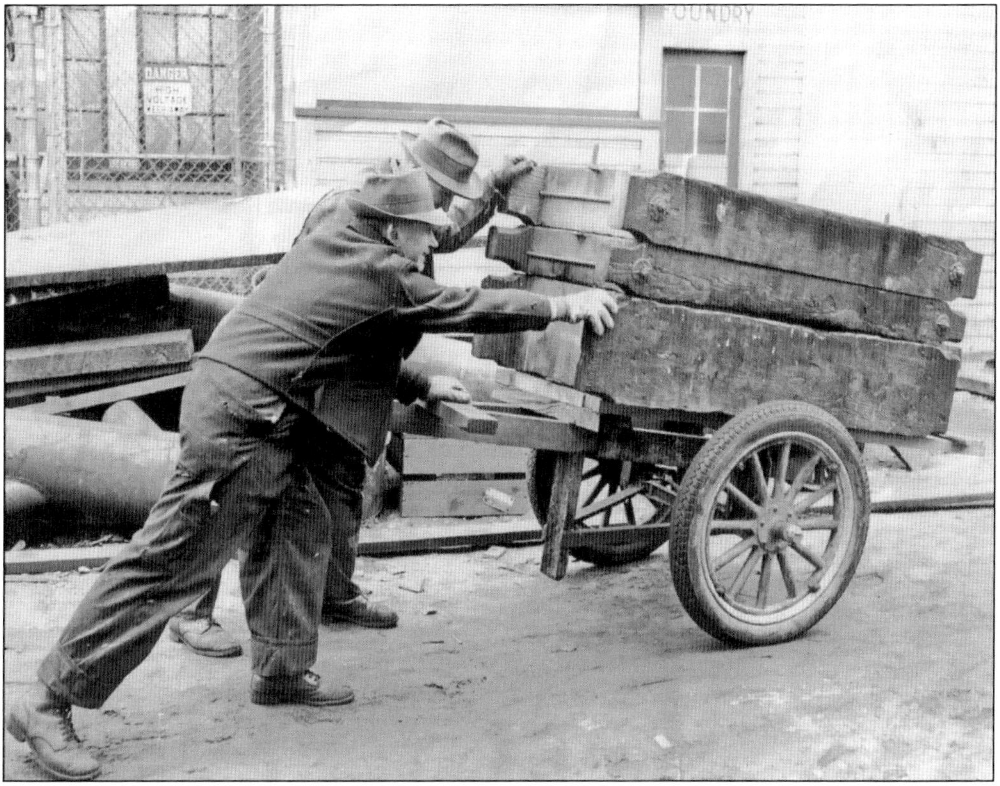

In September 1919, Andrew G. Hazen began his 44-year career at Atlas Foundry building wooden "flasks" for sand molds. Around 1937, Hazen and a helper push a cart of the wooden flasks through the Atlas facility. Today the flasks are made out of steel at the same Nalley Valley location. (Hazen family.)

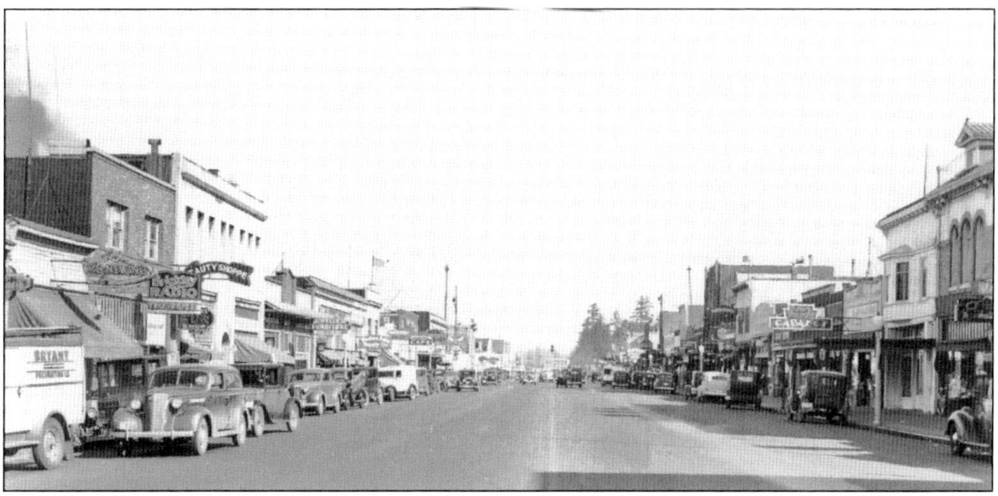

In 1938, South Tacoma Way was bustling at the 5400 block with cars double-parked and pedestrians and automobiles waiting for the traffic light. From the left to the right, some shops include J. Weisner Shoes, Brickley Radio (changed to Andersen's Penny-Wise in 1939), a fur shop, a beauty shop, Kelly Furniture, Western Auto Supply, and a café. Across the street, Ludwig Drug, Harrison's, and Holmes Cabaret are identified. (Thomas R. Stenger collection.)

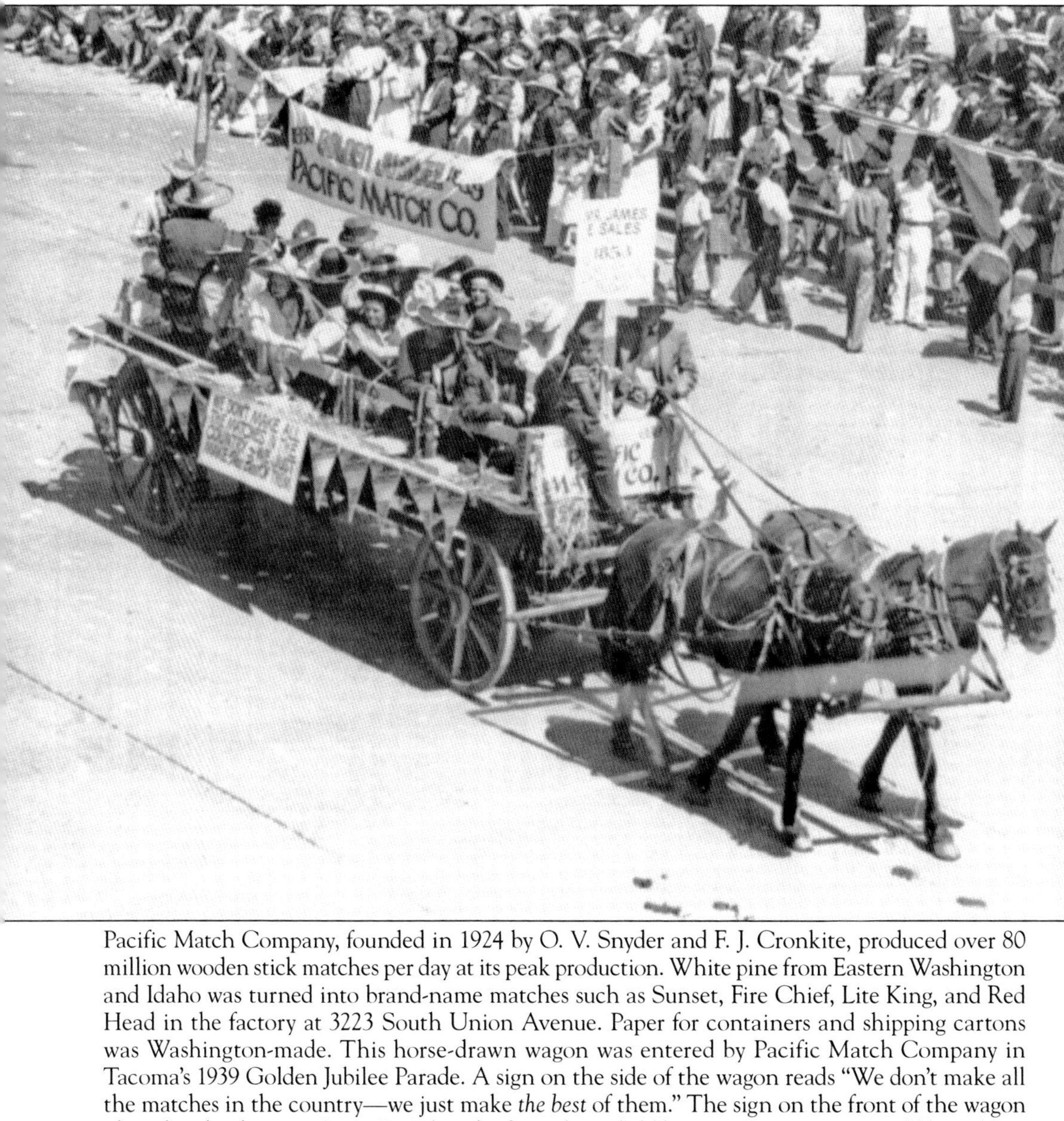

Pacific Match Company, founded in 1924 by O. V. Snyder and F. J. Cronkite, produced over 80 million wooden stick matches per day at its peak production. White pine from Eastern Washington and Idaho was turned into brand-name matches such as Sunset, Fire Chief, Lite King, and Red Head in the factory at 3223 South Union Avenue. Paper for containers and shipping cartons was Washington-made. This horse-drawn wagon was entered by Pacific Match Company in Tacoma's 1939 Golden Jubilee Parade. A sign on the side of the wagon reads "We don't make all the matches in the country—we just make *the best* of them." The sign on the front of the wagon identifies the driver as James E. Sales, the first white child born in Tacoma. He would have been 86 years of age at the time of the parade. Pacific Match Company manufactured matches until competition forced them to close in 1964. The property was later acquired by Tacoma School District. (TPL.)

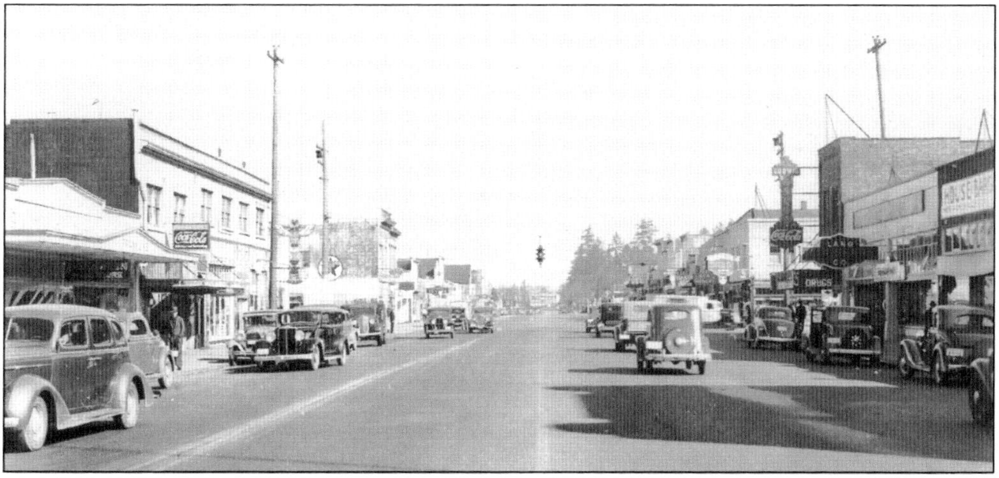

Shoppers stroll past South Tacoma Way storefronts c. 1939. Businesses on the west side of the street include, from left to right, Franklins (became Peoples in 1947), Totem Food at 5402 South Tacoma Way (became Thriftway in 1945), and Texaco. Across the street, Electric Company, Oasis Tavern, a shoe store, a drugstore, Ludwig Drug, and the Lang Company are pictured. Looking north, a traffic light hangs in the middle of the intersection. (Eric Swanson collection.)

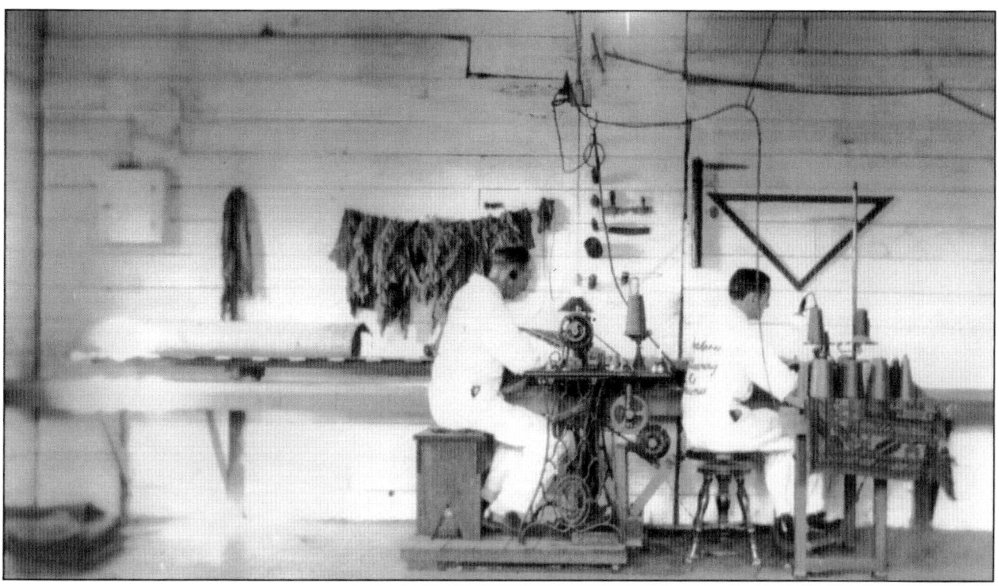

According to Margaret Harkness's diary, she and husband James lived and worked in their first home/business at 6637 South Pine Street until 1927, when they moved "down to the Ave" (Union Avenue) and built a rug weaving/repairing plant. In c. 1935, Jack Ehler (left) and the family's older son, George Harkness, repair rugs in the shop. (Dorothy Harkness personal collection.)

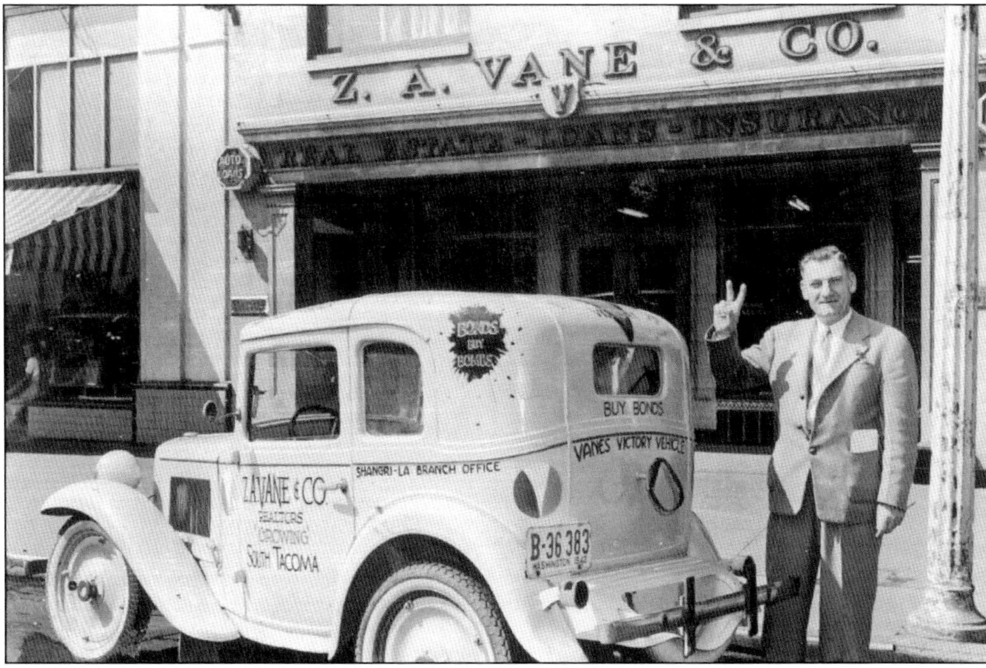

The 1942 license plate on Z. A. Vane's Austin and the *V* for victory brandished by Vane all add up to World War II, which brought material shortages to Americans. Vane suffered, but drove a smaller vehicle to economize. Vane, standing in front of his 5420 South Tacoma Way real estate office, was running for a fifth term as state representative for the 29th District. (Thomas R. Stenger collection.)

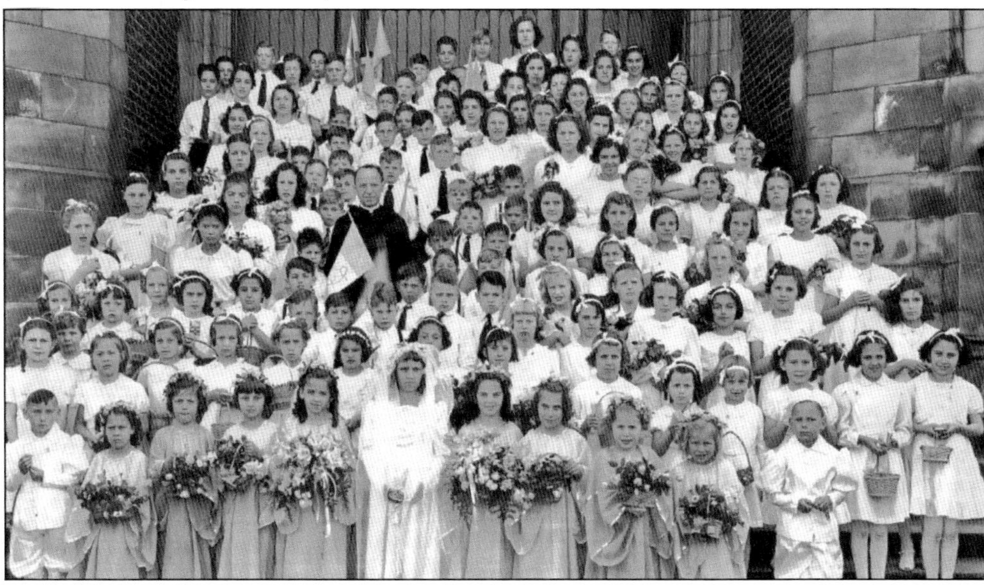

Fr. Anthony Hack, OSB, celebrates his silver jubilee at Holy Rosary Church with no shortage of children to show how much they appreciate him. Those identified are, from left to right, (first row) Brian Hendrickson, unidentified, Phyllis Bucsko, unidentified, Mollie McCormick, three unidentified, Loretta Bader, unidentified, and Hugh Weber; (second row) unidentified, Rosemary Bader, eight unidentified, and Lois Zajec. (Art and Loretta Boyle.)

Many people knew Peter Wallerich as the North Pacific Bank founder and South Tacoma Motor Company owner, but few knew him as an author and a poet. In 1938, Wallerich wrote a book of poems titled *Motor Spark: Boys, Business, Bankers, Motors, Politics, and Humorous Compositions*, printed by South Tacoma Publishing Company. In addition to banking, the poet wrote 181 pages about relationships, family, and love. (Peter K. Wallerich.)

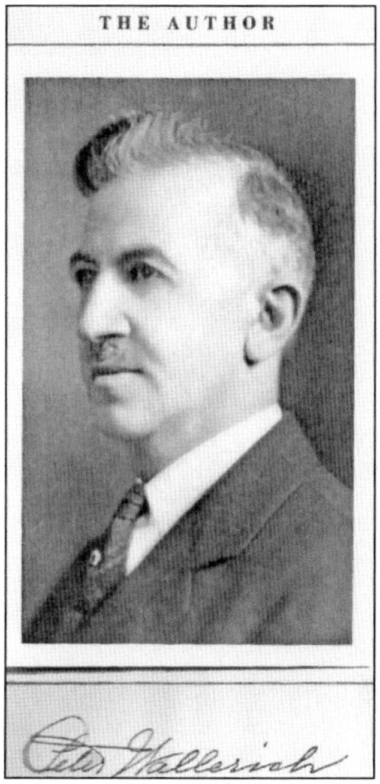

Your Banker

If a banker is polite,
As every banker ought to be,
He'll always treat you right,
At least as far as he can see.

He may not always cash your check
Because your bank is out of town,
But consideration he will give
Before he turns it down.

He may not agree with you
To loan you money for a year,
Perhaps the most that he can do
Is to politely lend his ear.

What security you offer for a loan
May be rating pretty punk,
And all the stories you bemoan
May distinctly be the bunk.

Please don't get angry in disgust
Because unable to borrow for the year,
He's still the man that you should trust
So long as he will lend his ear.

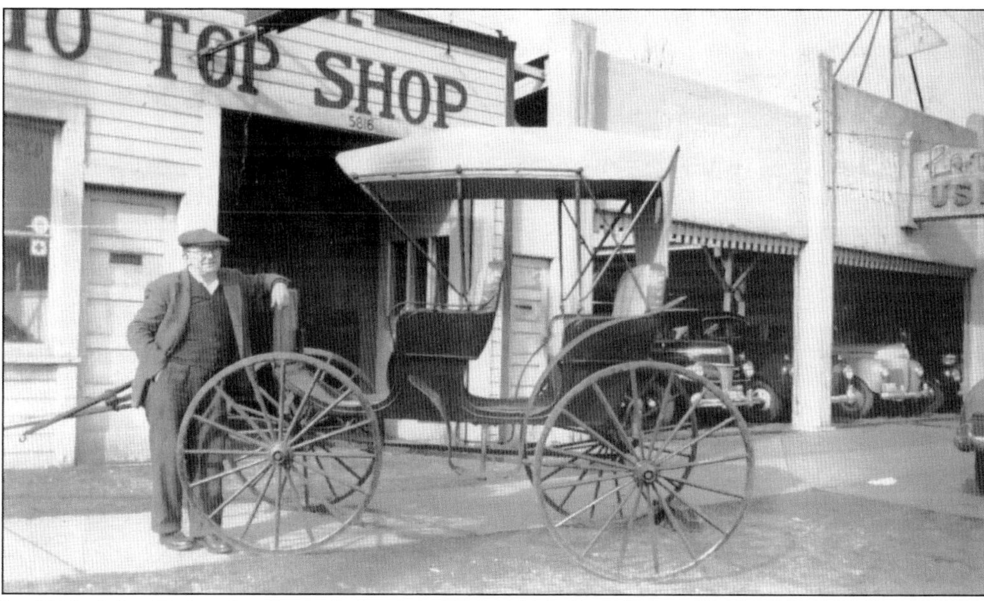

In 1922, John Dolge Sr. opened the Auto Top Shop, building and repairing convertible tops for touring cars and horse buggies. Dolge poses here with a buggy in 1944. When World War II ended, veteran John Dolge Jr. joined his father in the business. Third-generation grandsons John, Jim, and Mark Dolge continue to operate Auto Specialties, Inc., in the original location at 5816 South Tacoma Way. (Dolge family.)

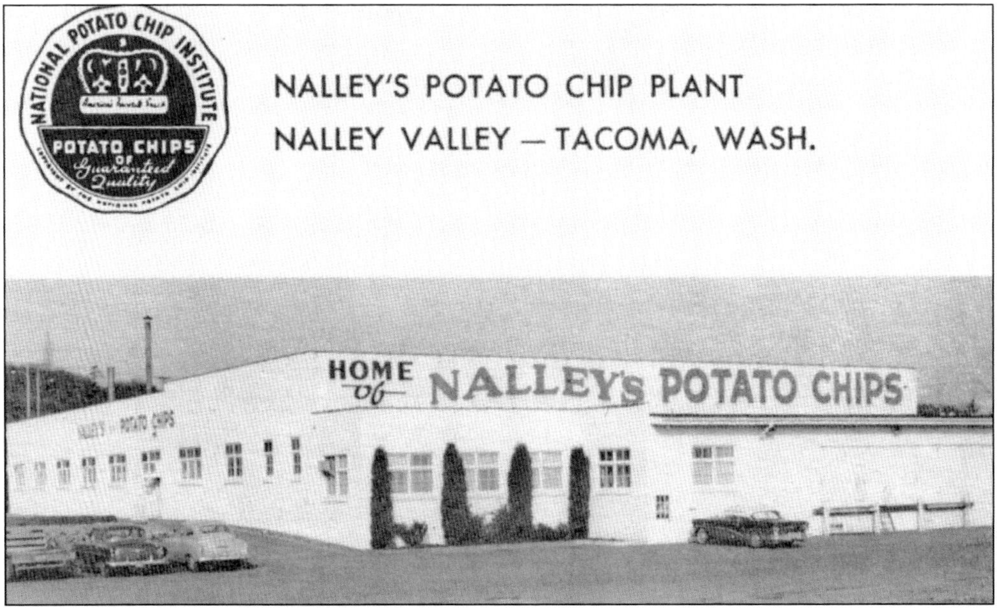

In 1940, Marcus Nalley purchased 20 acres along the railroad tracks and the area was dubbed "Nalley Valley." This first building produced pickles, potato chips, canned foods, and salad dressings. As the company grew, Nalley's foods became known around the world. With the 1997 Birds Eye acquisition, "Nalley" became a brand name, rather than a company. Today a cannery and a salad-dressing plant operate in Nalley Valley. (Birds Eye Foods, Inc.)

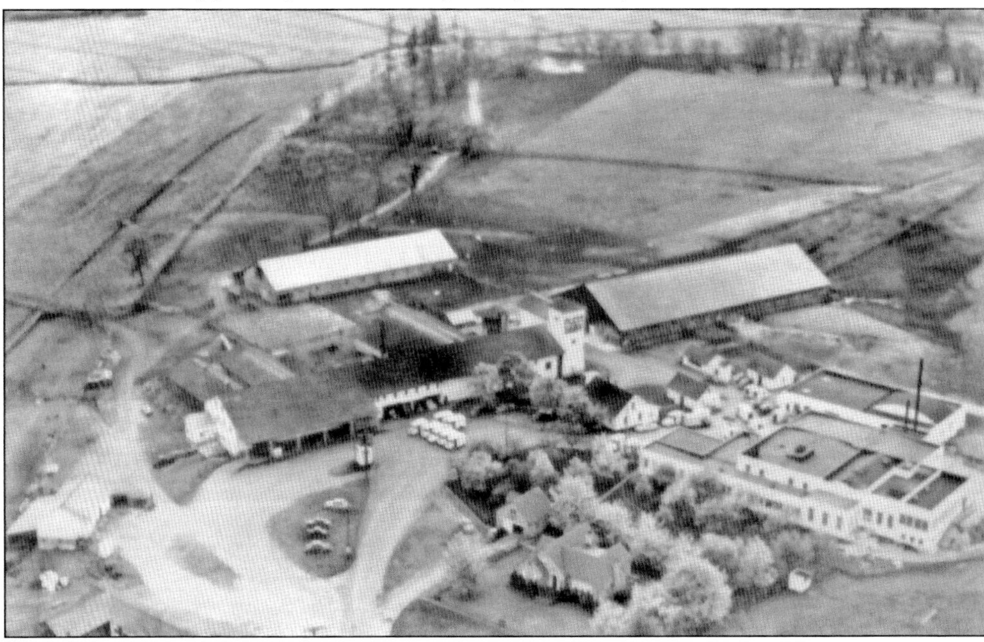

Founded in 1903 by George Chapman, Flett Dairy was named for Chapman's wife, Annie Flett. The Flett name stayed, even though Gottfried and Mary Fuchs began operating the dairy in 1913. Located at 7920 South Verde Street, Flett dairy was one of the largest dairies in Washington State. When closed in 1994, 106 acres were dedicated to Natural Resources. This aerial view shows the layout c. 1940. (Tom Jacobson.)

In 1911, Griffin Wheel Company produced 350 railway wheels a day, according to Dr. A. G. Nace in a 1936 column he wrote for the *Star*. Ray Haller, shown working at Griffin around 1940, ran an overhead crane that picked up a hot wheel and placed it in a cooler to cool slowly to prevent breaking. (Max and Amelia Haller.)

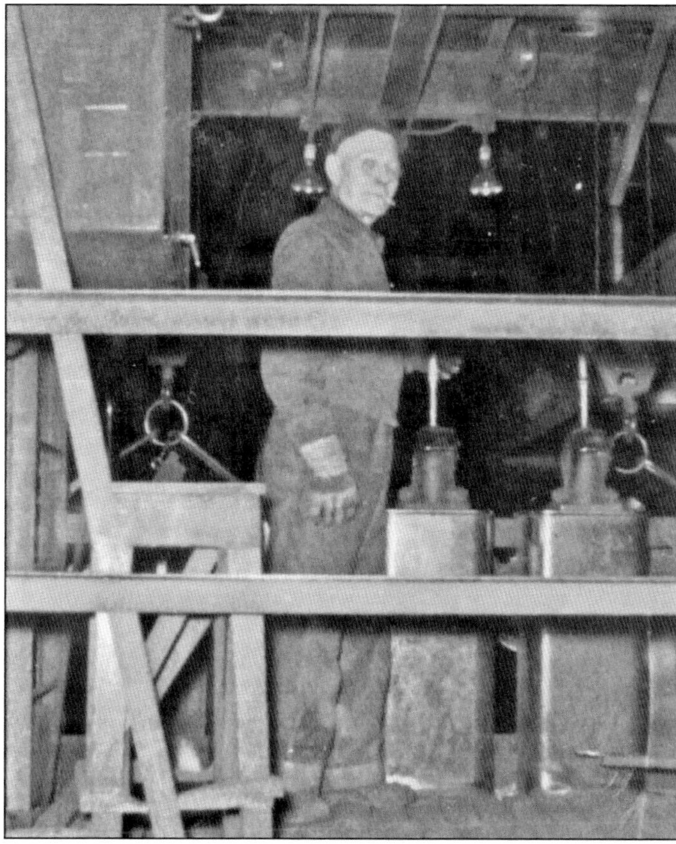

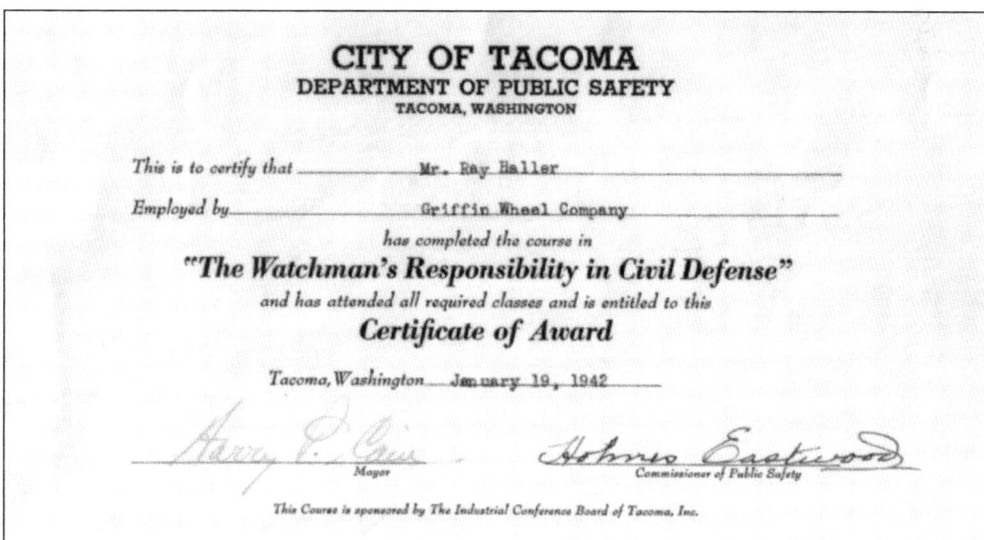

CITY OF TACOMA
DEPARTMENT OF PUBLIC SAFETY
TACOMA, WASHINGTON

This is to certify that Mr. Ray Haller

Employed by Griffin Wheel Company

has completed the course in

"The Watchman's Responsibility in Civil Defense"

and has attended all required classes and is entitled to this

Certificate of Award

Tacoma, Washington January 19, 1942

Harry P. Cain
Mayor

Holmes Eastwood
Commissioner of Public Safety

This Course is sponsored by The Industrial Conference Board of Tacoma, Inc.

In 1942, identifying airplanes for civil defense was an important contribution to United States' safety. Ray Haller, employed by Griffin Wheel, completed the necessary course offered by the city to watch for enemy airplanes that may fly over the city during World War II. The certificate is signed by Harry P. Cain, mayor of Tacoma, and Holmes Eastwood, commissioner of public safety. (Max and Amelia Haller.)

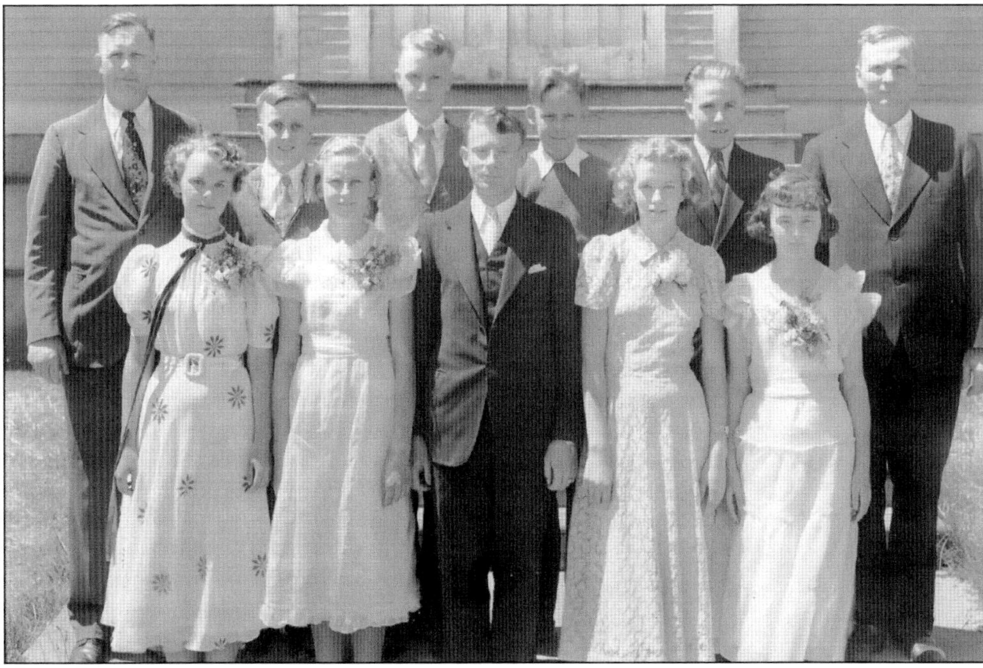

Although Hope Lutheran Church officially became a congregation in 1906, the predominantly Norwegian group began meeting two years earlier as First Lutheran Church. This 1937 confirmation class includes, from left to right, (first row) Ruth Jorgenson, Margaret Jorgenson, student pastor Earl Lund, Leona Sayre, and Marian Stewart; (second row) Rev. T. O. Svare, Lyle Kyllo, Norman Kyllo, Melvin Jorgenson, Marvin Kosemeir, and Rev. A. W. Ramstad. (Hope Lutheran Church.)

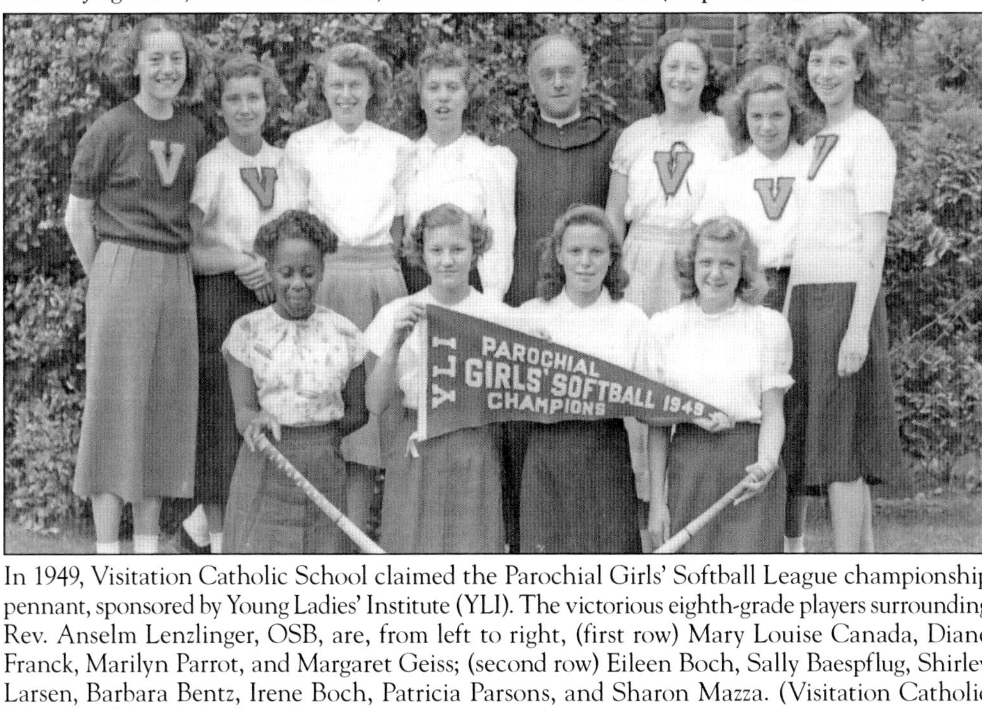

In 1949, Visitation Catholic School claimed the Parochial Girls' Softball League championship pennant, sponsored by Young Ladies' Institute (YLI). The victorious eighth-grade players surrounding Rev. Anselm Lenzlinger, OSB, are, from left to right, (first row) Mary Louise Canada, Diane Franck, Marilyn Parrot, and Margaret Geiss; (second row) Eileen Boch, Sally Baespflug, Shirley Larsen, Barbara Bentz, Irene Boch, Patricia Parsons, and Sharon Mazza. (Visitation Catholic School and Parish Archives.)

Neatly attired in matching dresses, these five women bowlers joined thousands of others in this popular sport in 1940. Representing the Atlas Foundry Pattern Shop are, from left to right, bowlers captain Bessie Walker Trowbridge, Erma Mussleman Utz, Nell Bowman, Helen Blattler Levenhagen, and Mary Becker posing behind a bowling ball for a Lee Merrill photographer. (Atlas Castings and Technology.)

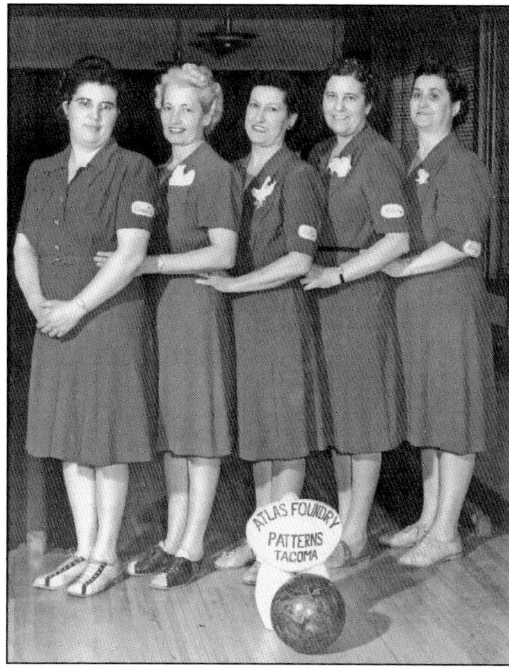

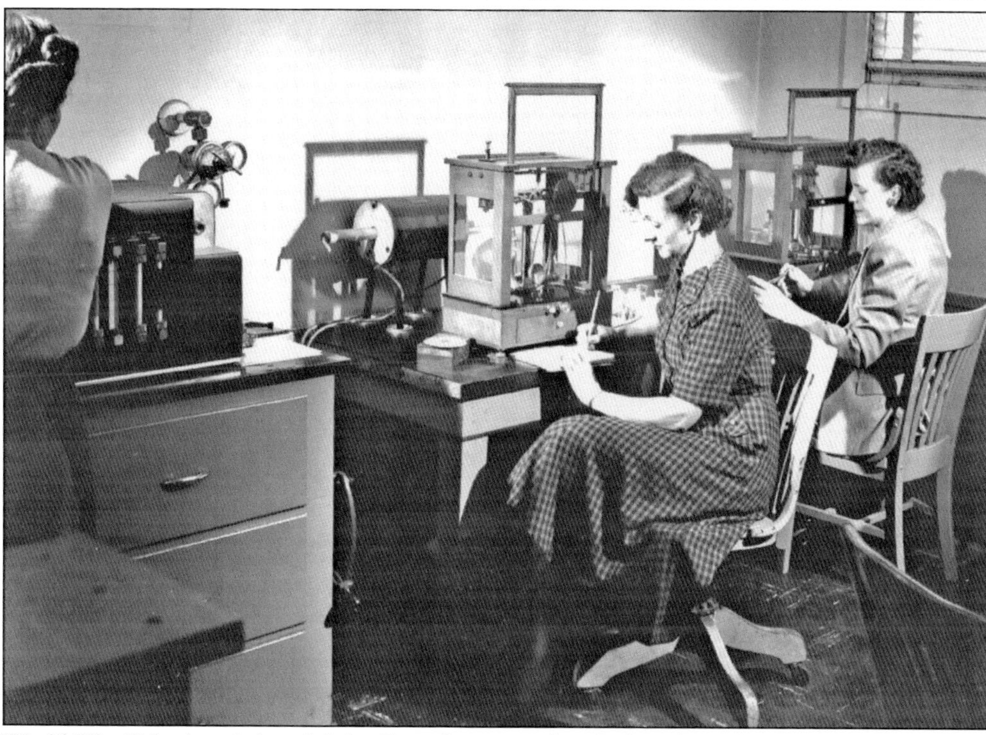

World War II had ended and Atlas Foundry, in its fourth decade at the Nalley Valley facility, had added the first electric arc furnace to increase steel production. Working in the chemistry lab around 1948, Doris Fuller (left) watches lab technician Velma Cope record sample weights on the balance beam scale as accountant Pearl Cronander (right) performs an analytical quality control procedure. (Atlas Casting and Technology.)

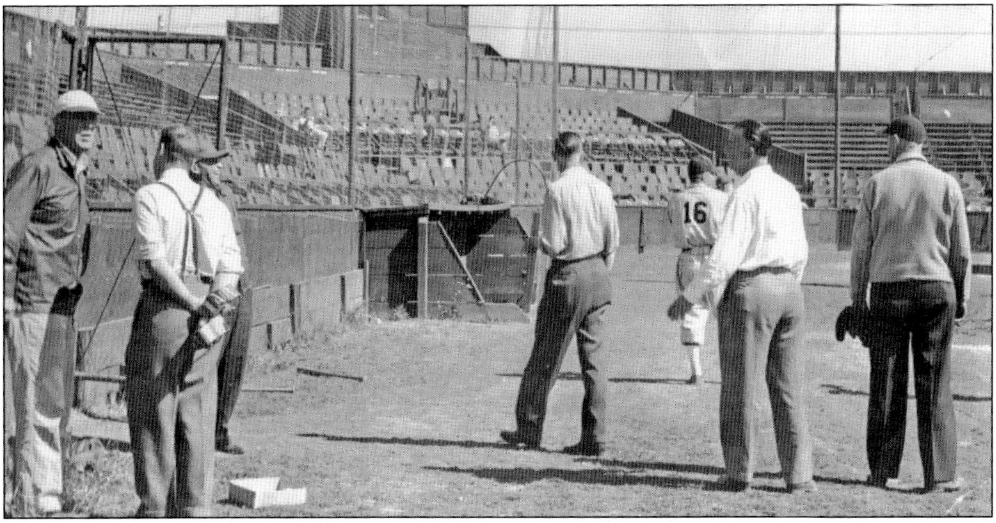

Players, coaches, and other team personnel gather at the South Tacoma Tiger Ball Park to warm up for a large crowd, much like the 1949 opening-day crowd (below). The baseball field, built in 1946 at Thirty-eighth Street near South Tacoma Way, was home to the Tacoma Tigers, who played in the Western International League until 1951, when the team was sold to San Diego of the Pacific Coast League. Jordan's Bread, "The Bread that Broadcasts Baseball," was the radio broadcast sponsor as well as a well-known South Tacoma bakery. The field was purchased by Ben Cheney in 1951, renamed Cheney Field, and hosted games through the remaining 1950s for local semi-pro games played in the area. The field was later demolished, and today the area is home to Puget Sound Energy. (Marc H. Blau collection.)

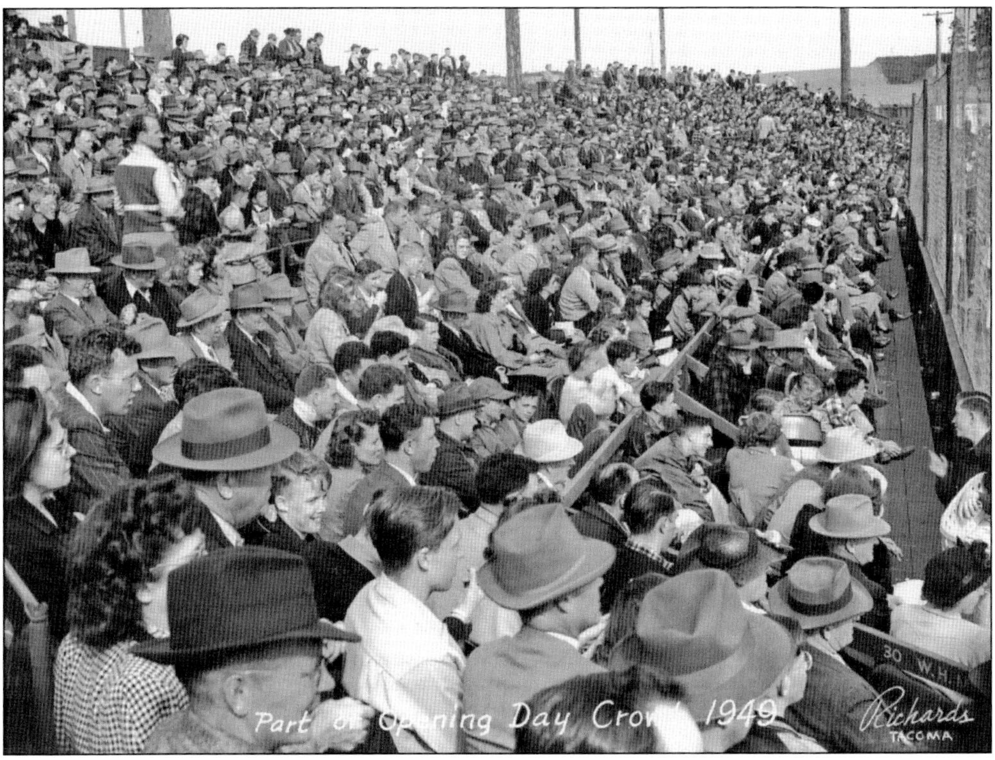

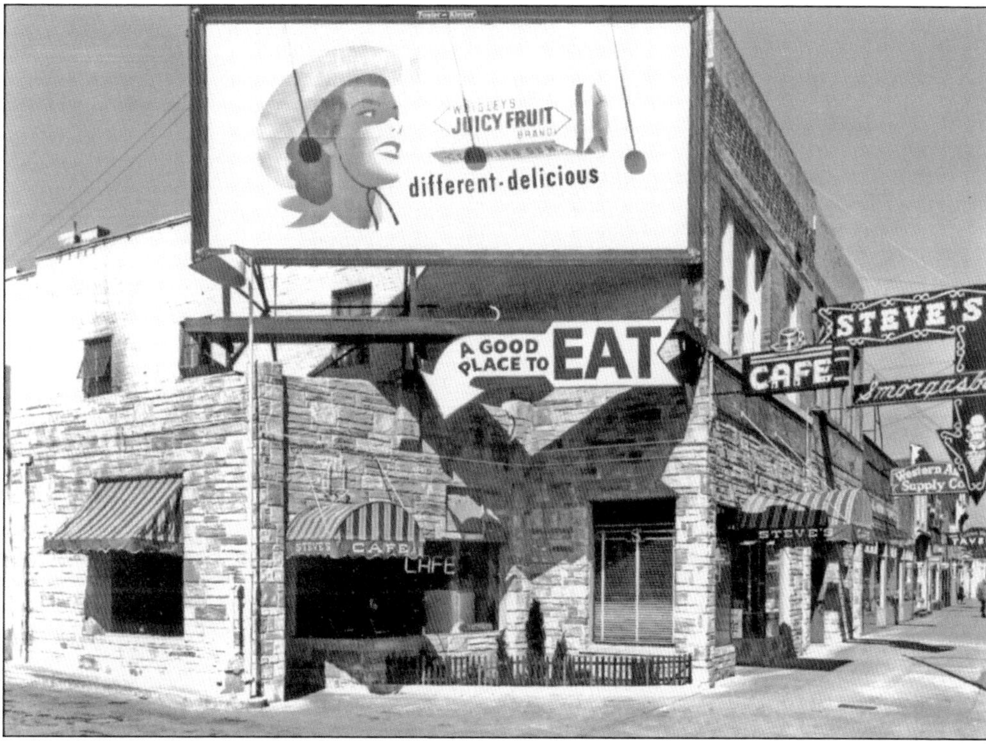

In 1951, Steve's Café, later known as Steve's Gay Nineties, was "A Good Place to Eat." South Tacoman Steve Pease and John Stanley, a Montana native, each owned adjoining buildings on South Tacoma Way, which they merged, and they obtained one of the first cocktail licenses in Tacoma. The Gay Nineties–themed restaurant was a popular South Tacoma nightspot for 27 years. (Stuart Simon and TPL.)

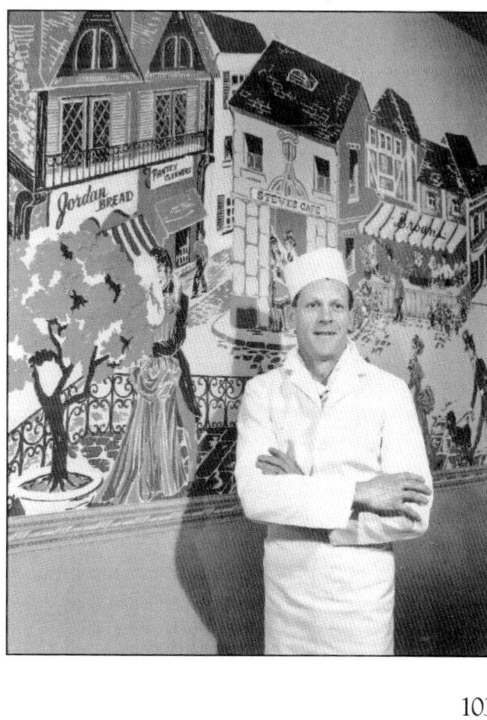

John Stanley poses in a 1951 publicity photograph for the opening celebration of the Gay Nineties Room of Steve's Gay Nineties Café at 5238–5240 South Tacoma Way. The mural on the wall behind Stanley depicts area businesses such as Jordan Bakery, Pantex Cleaners, and Brown's Flowers in the Gay Nineties. (TPL.)

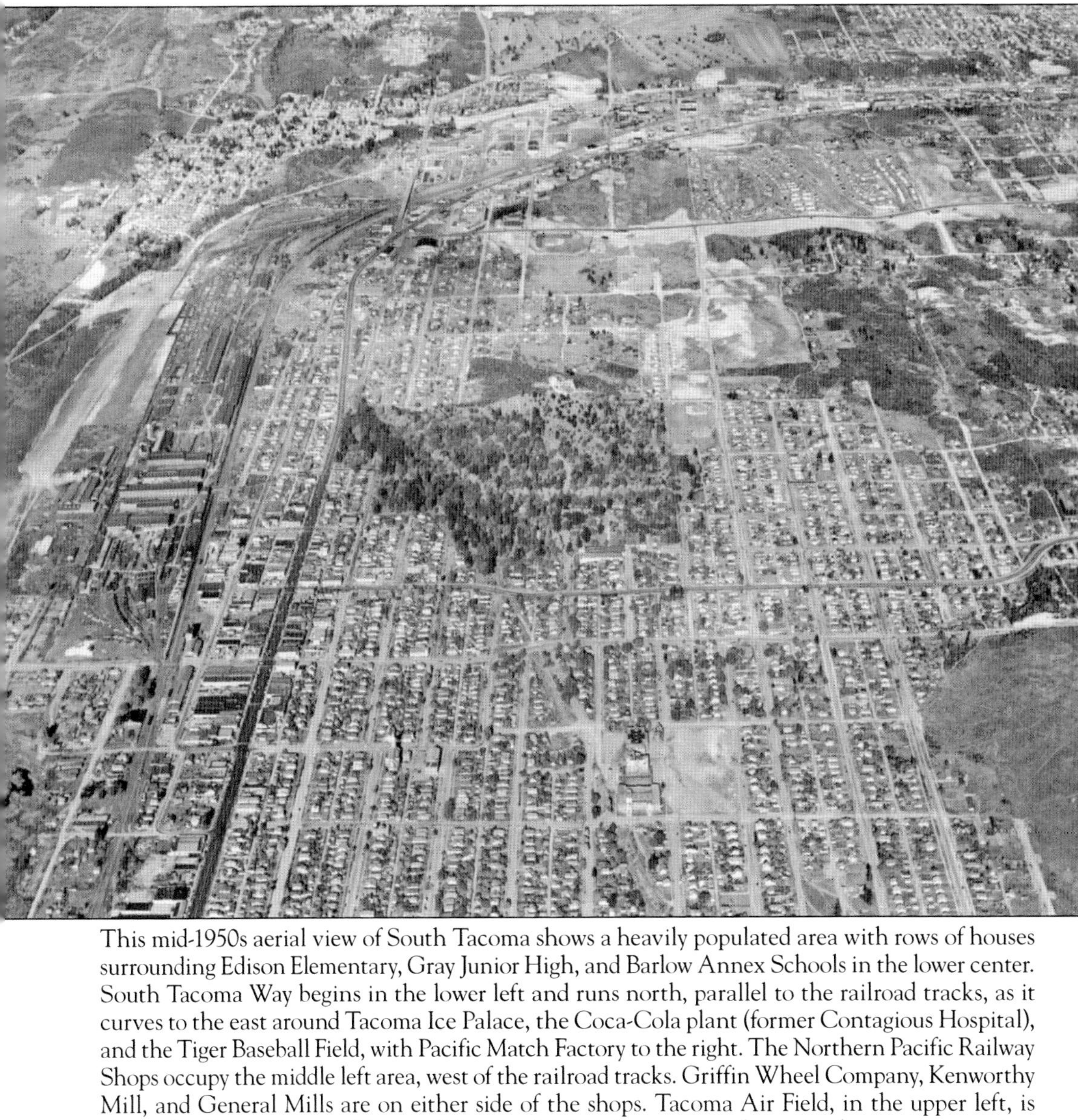

This mid-1950s aerial view of South Tacoma shows a heavily populated area with rows of houses surrounding Edison Elementary, Gray Junior High, and Barlow Annex Schools in the lower center. South Tacoma Way begins in the lower left and runs north, parallel to the railroad tracks, as it curves to the east around Tacoma Ice Palace, the Coca-Cola plant (former Contagious Hospital), and the Tiger Baseball Field, with Pacific Match Factory to the right. The Northern Pacific Railway Shops occupy the middle left area, west of the railroad tracks. Griffin Wheel Company, Kenworthy Mill, and General Mills are on either side of the shops. Tacoma Air Field, in the upper left, is above the South Tacoma "Swamps" (wetlands). The large grove of trees in the center comprises Oakwood Hills and Old Tacoma cemeteries. The South End Boys Club ball field is seen to the right of the trees, directly south of the future Tacoma Mall site. Wapato Hills is the group of trees seen in the lower right. Interstate 5 was not yet constructed. (Jim Fredrickson collection.)

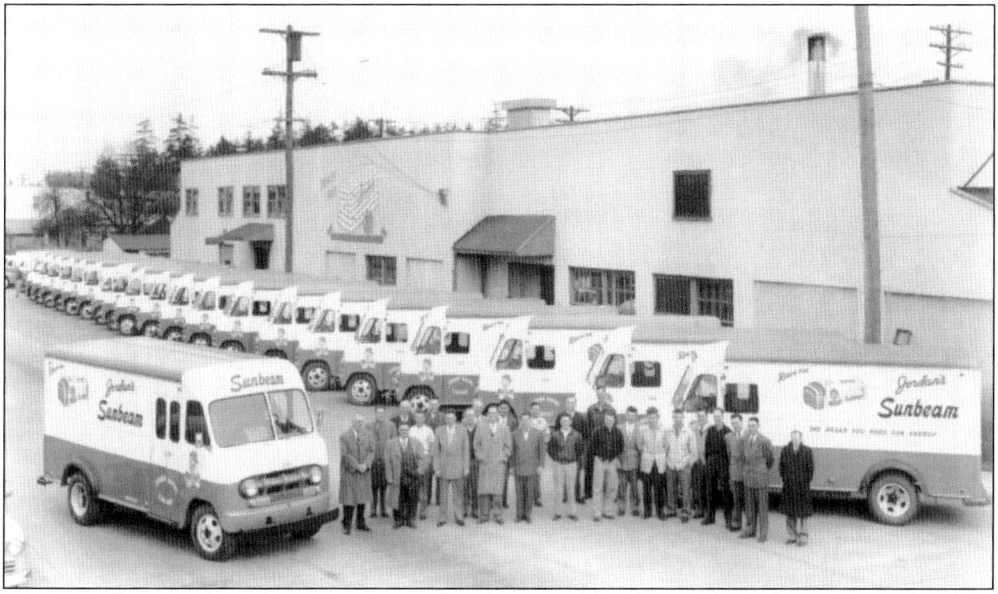

Arthur K. Jordan began his company in 1937 with six employees in Old Tacoma. The bakery quickly outgrew this location and opened at 5233 South Washington Street in 1939. Within 10 years, the company employed 131 people in Tacoma. More than 20 new Ford trucks for Jordan Baking Company are lined up in front of the bakery in 1951. Jordan stands on the far left. (TPL.)

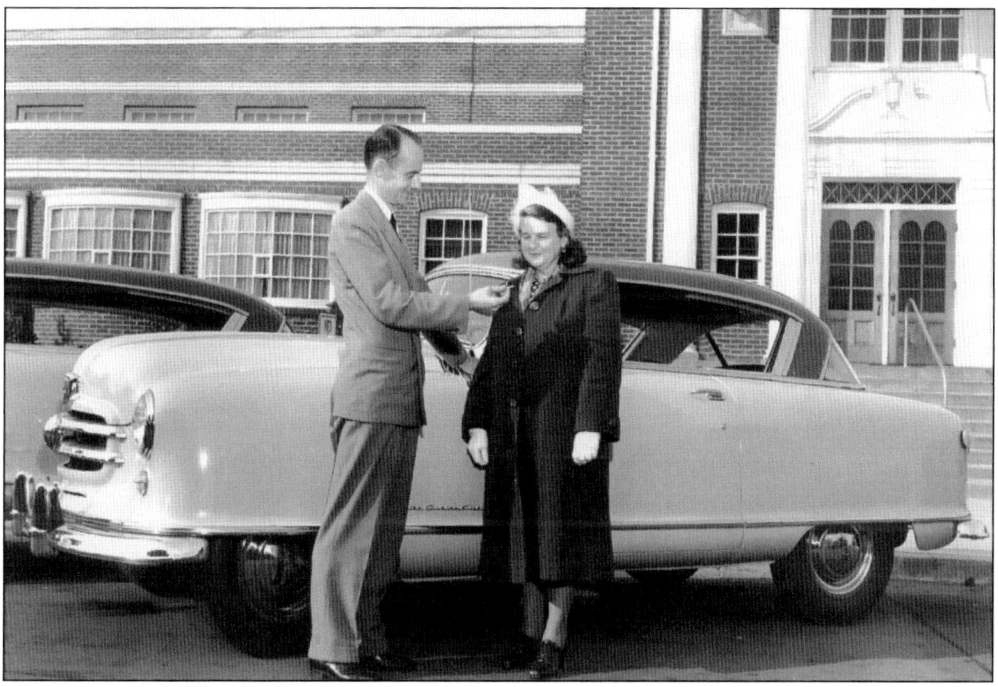

In 1951, Harkness Rug and Furniture Company promoted a contest sponsored by the Nash-Kelvinator Corporation. Jim Harkness presents Carol (Mrs. W. C.) Allen the key to a Nash Rambler Country Club Sedan for her winning entry in the "I like the Kelvinator refrigerator because" contest. Lloyd Wynans also received a Nash Rambler as the Harkness salesman who demonstrated the Kelvinator to Allen. (Dorothy Harkness personal collection.)

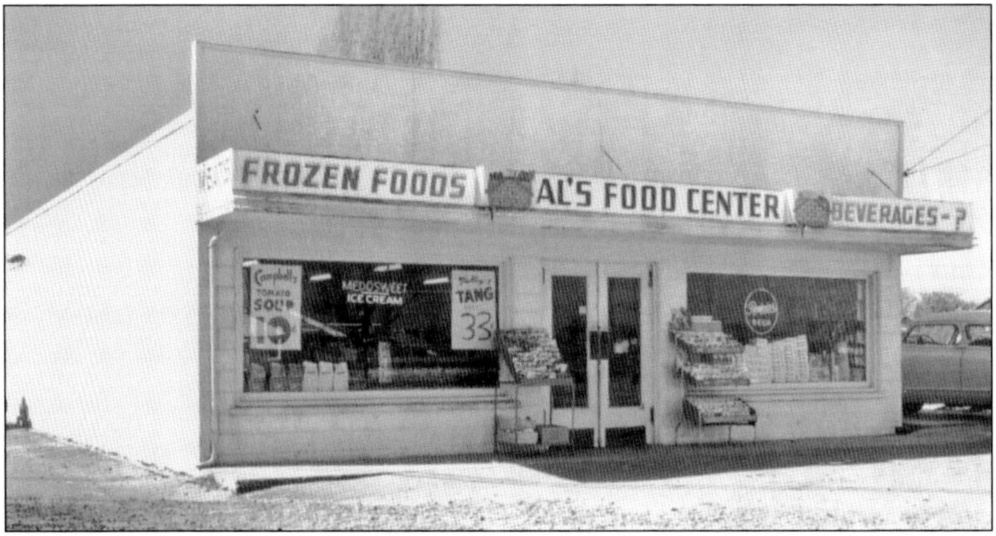

Typical mom-and-pop stores, such as Al's Food Center, were once found throughout South Tacoma. Built in 1928, Al's was a favorite neighborhood grocery for years at 7401 South Tacoma Way. In 1958, the windows display Medosweet Ice Cream and Rainier Beer neon signs. Campbell's Tomato Soup is 10¢ a can, and Nalley's Tang sells for 33¢. (TPL.)

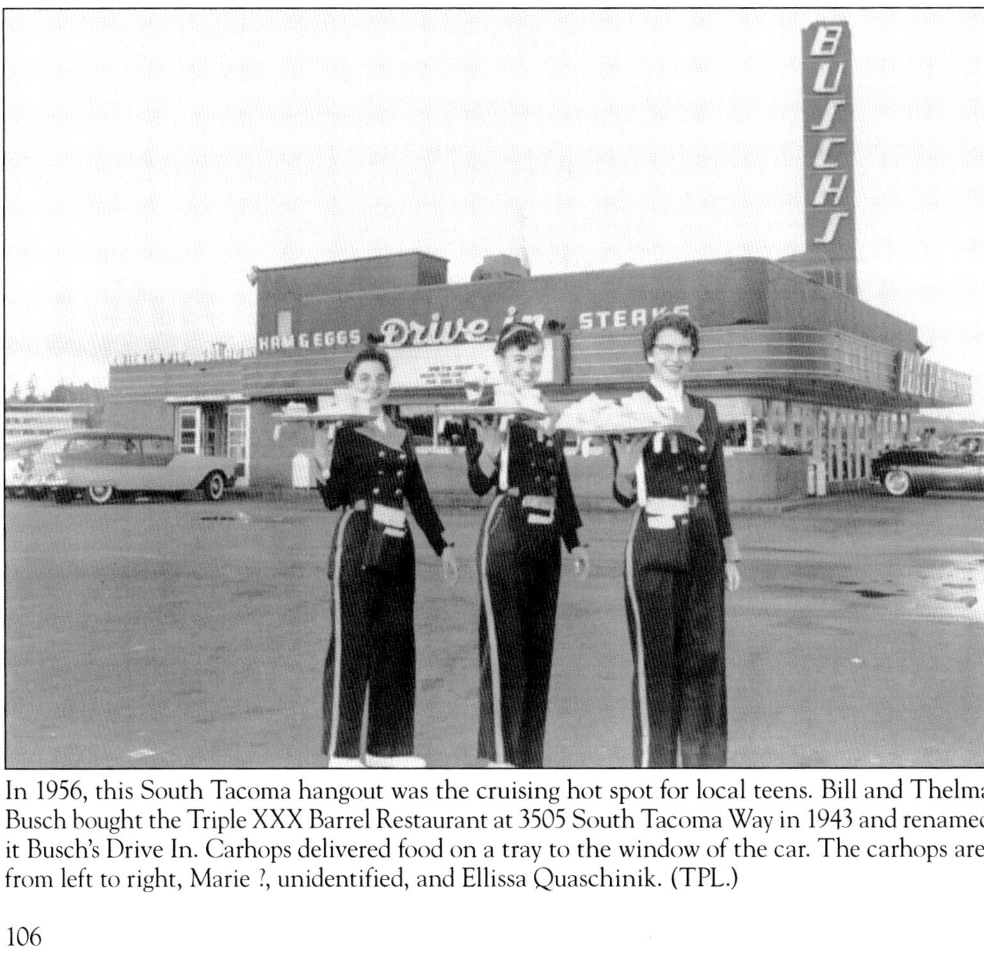

In 1956, this South Tacoma hangout was the cruising hot spot for local teens. Bill and Thelma Busch bought the Triple XXX Barrel Restaurant at 3505 South Tacoma Way in 1943 and renamed it Busch's Drive In. Carhops delivered food on a tray to the window of the car. The carhops are, from left to right, Marie ?, unidentified, and Ellissa Quaschinik. (TPL.)

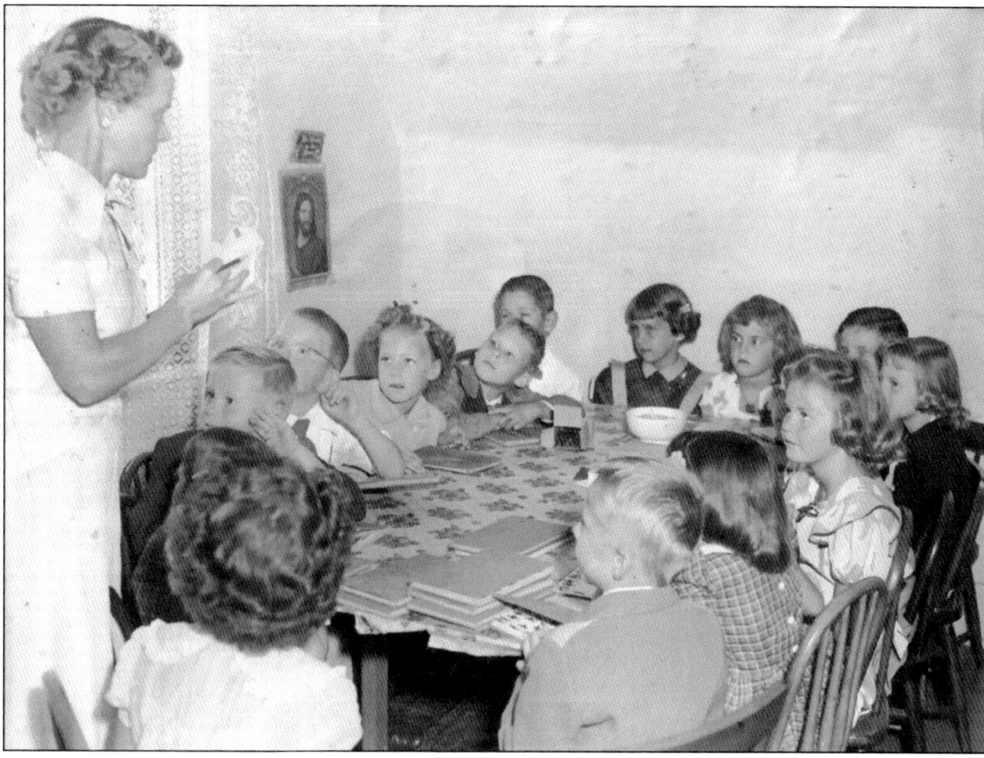

Twenty-six inquisitive little eyes watch with curiosity as their teacher shows them how to make a new craft. This Sunday school class gathered in the house next door to Hope Lutheran Church in 1953, prior to moving to their new, larger location. These unidentified children met each week while their parents participated in opening music before a service. (Hope Lutheran Church.)

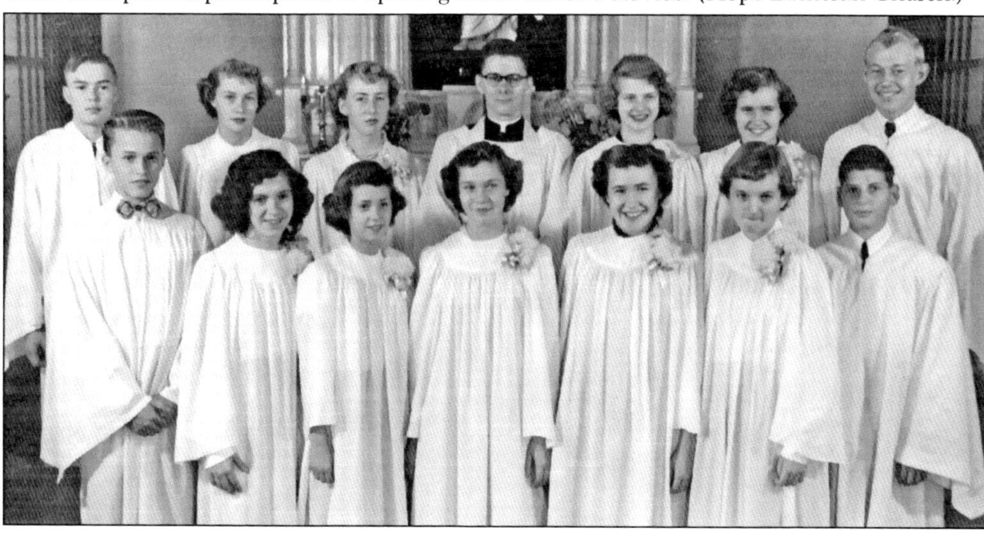

Hope Lutheran Church's congregation was just two years from celebrating its 50th anniversary when this group was confirmed. The parishioners had grown from the small group who started at Sixty-second and South Warner Streets and were soon moving to a new church at a new site. Pastor R. W. Lutness, second row, middle, poses with unidentified youths in front of the church's altar. (Hope Lutheran Church.)

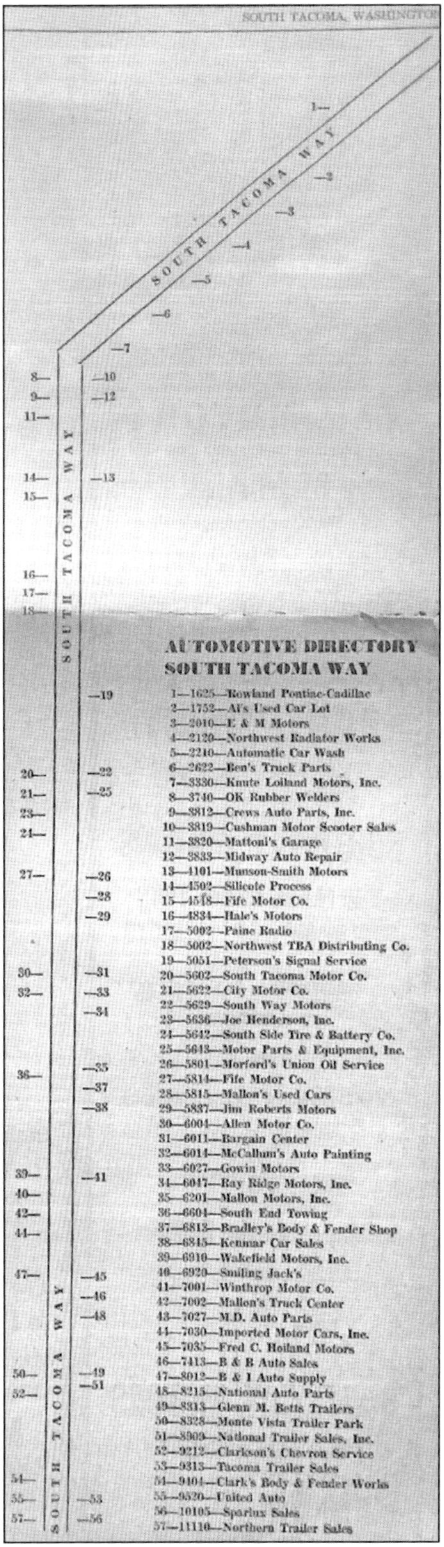

In 1956, the *Tacoma Star* presents South Tacoma Way as a haven for automotive dealerships. The hand-drawn graphic (left) shows 57 businesses from north to south that dealt in the automotive field. The dealers attracted thousands of people to South Tacoma and added millions of dollars to the economy. According to the newspaper, it was labeled the "Automotive Main Street of the Pacific Northwest." (Larry Kilen Barber Shop.)

In 1956, South Tacoma celebrated the golden anniversary of the first used car sold in America. The *Tacoma Star* advertisement below mentions a Henry Ford legacy when he sold his first used car in 1906 and commemorates South Tacoma's perpetual "Auto Show" along South Tacoma Way. Once known as "Auto Row," South Tacoma Way is still home to many new and used automotive dealerships. (Larry Kilen Barber Shop.)

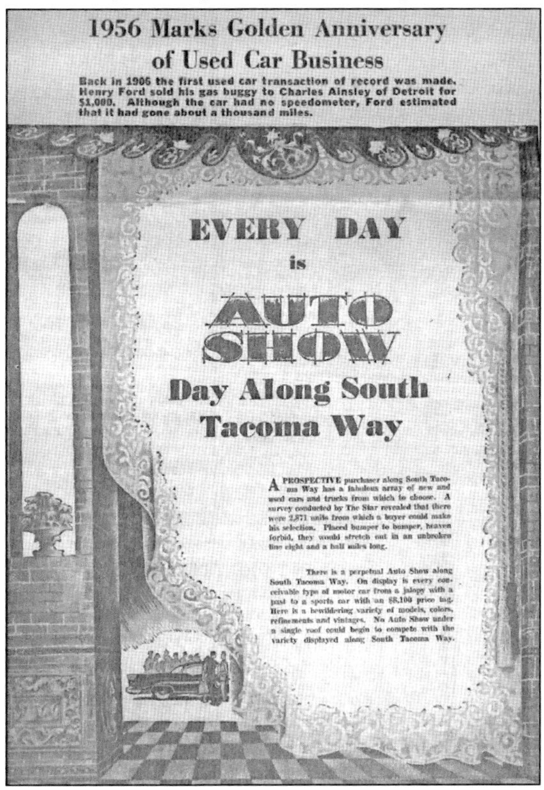

Edison Elementary opened 20 years before Girl Scouts of America was founded. While the Korean Conflict and the cold war with the Soviet Union reminded Americans that peace was not to be taken for granted, Pam Haller's Girl Scout group met weekly at Edison. Pam, nine years old in 1955, is dressed in her scout uniform as she salutes the U.S. flag. (Max and Amelia Haller.)

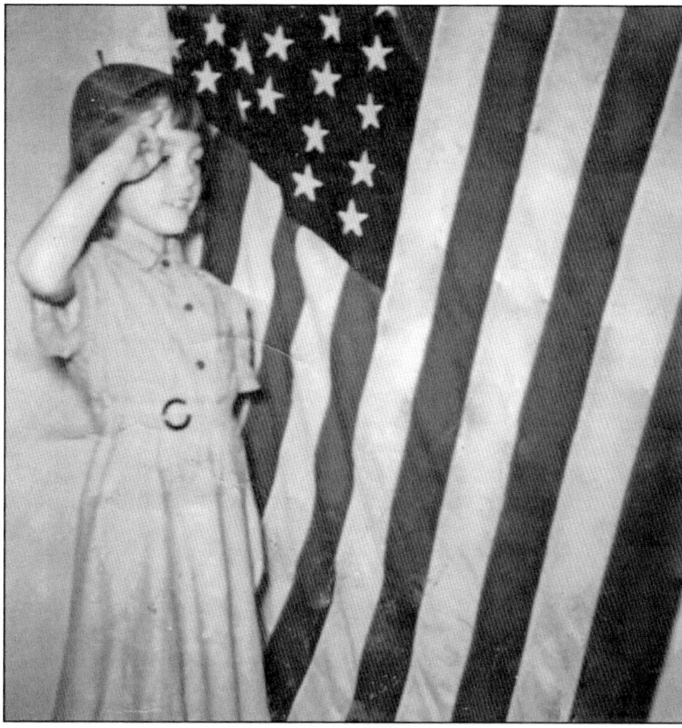

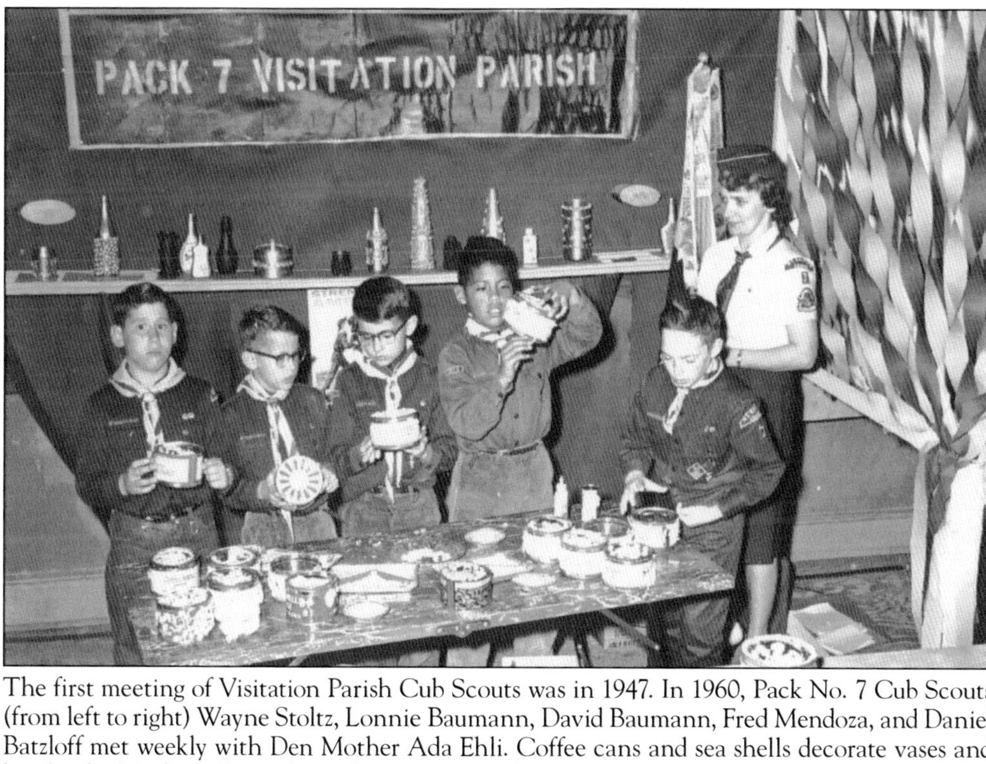

The first meeting of Visitation Parish Cub Scouts was in 1947. In 1960, Pack No. 7 Cub Scouts (from left to right) Wayne Stoltz, Lonnie Baumann, David Baumann, Fred Mendoza, and Daniel Batzloff met weekly with Den Mother Ada Ehli. Coffee cans and sea shells decorate vases and bottles for Mother's Day gifts and as entries in the University of Puget Sound Scout-A-Rama. (Al and Ada Ehli.)

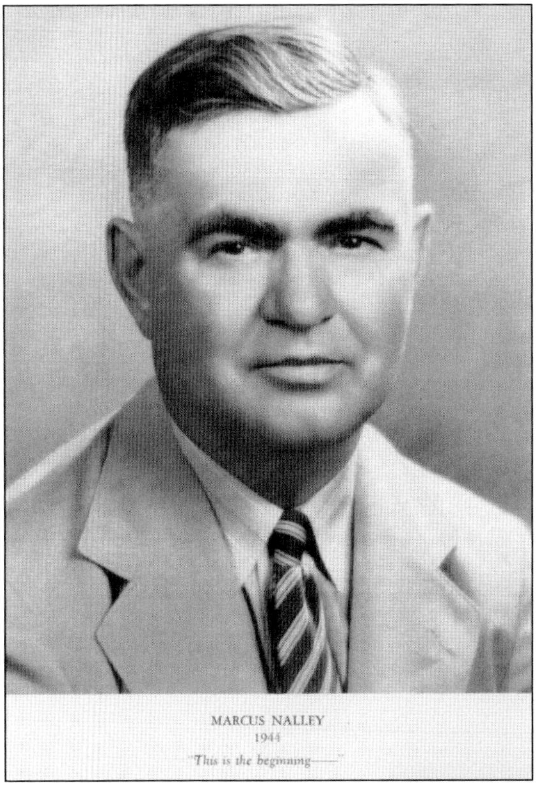

By 1944, Marcus Nalley's dream of starting his own business was well established. Nalley sincerely believed employees were part of the company's success. In a booklet for employees, he wrote, "I may be the only one in the place who has the name 'Nalley,' but 'Nalley's' is the incorporation of the hard work of many people, and everyone should receive due credit." (Birds Eye Foods, Inc.)

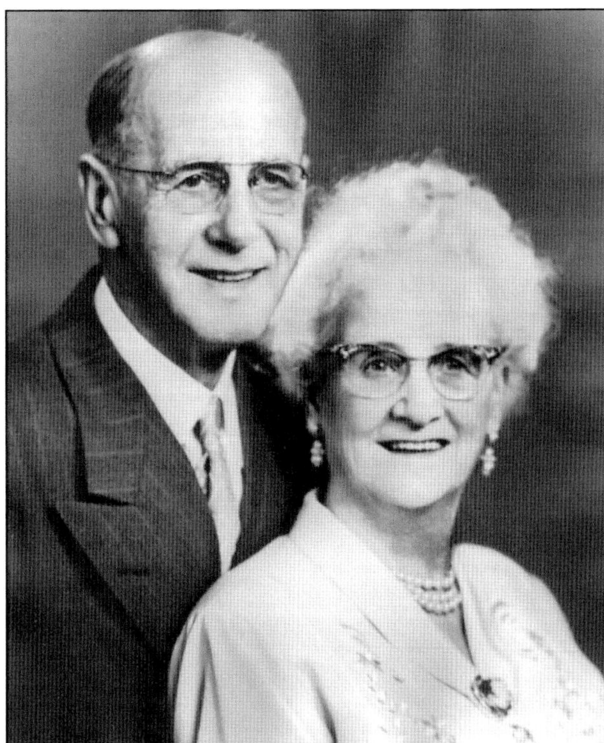

Fate intervened when Herbert Brown, an English gardener, and a girl named Rose married in 1912. Rose's mother dreamed about a tragedy and forbade the newlyweds to sail to America on the *Titanic*. Growing flowers was Brown's passion, and in 1934, they opened Brown's Flowers. In 1962, Mr. and Mrs. Brown celebrated 50 years of a gardener being married to a Rose. (Brown's Flowers, Inc.)

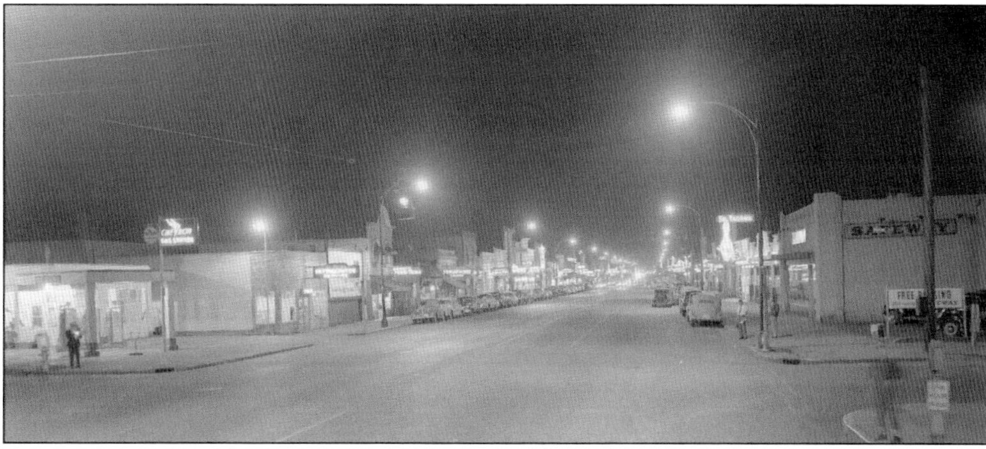

Recognizing a need for better street lighting, public utilities installed mercury vapor lights along South Tacoma Way. Looking south from Fifty-fourth Street in 1950, businesses identified are, from left to right, Chevron, South Tacoma Refrigerator Service, Sandy's Fishing Tackle, Semaphore Tavern, Oasis Tavern, Main Yon Café, Retreat Tavern, and more. Across the street identified shops include Opal Bar, a café, South Tacoma Bowl, King Café, and Safeway. (Tacoma Public Utilities.)

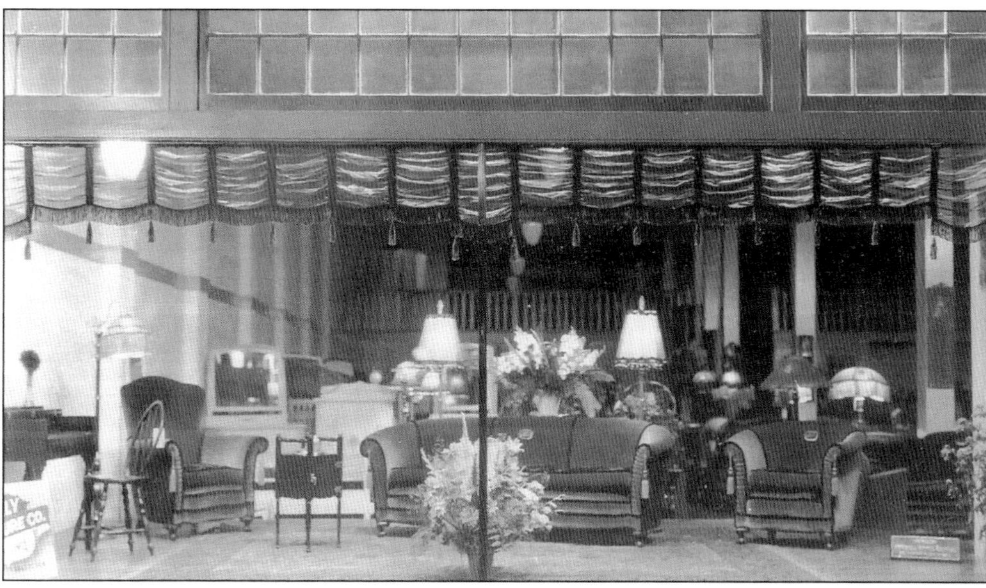

This living-room furniture display is typical of household items sold by Kelly Furniture at 5428 South Tacoma Way. "Kelly's Kolumn" in the *Tacoma Star* January 8, 1951, stated they had been in business for 32 years and "No matter what happens, war or rationing or whatever, there is not much that we can do about it. Credit will be extended unless further government regulations interfere." (Kelly Furniture.)

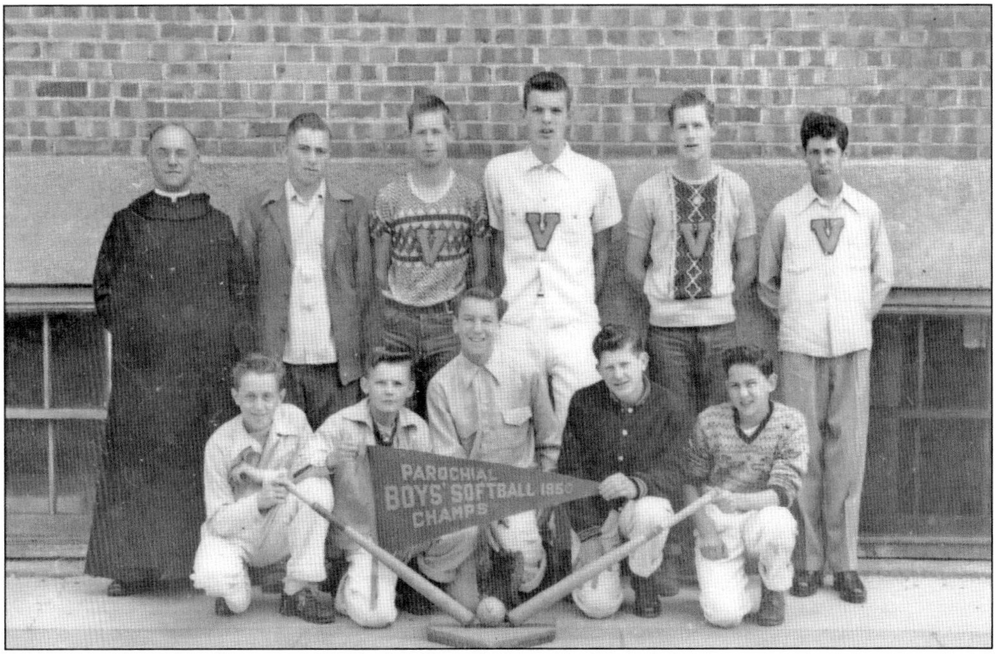

With a record of nine wins and one defeat, the boys from Visitation Catholic School took the Tacoma Parochial School Softball League championship in 1950. The players, with Fr. Anselm Lenzlinger, OSB (coach), are, from left to right, (first row) George Schwartz, Julius Schatz, Mike Conant, Dennis O'Brien, and Steve Keller; (second row) Raymond Seeberger, Mel Burdick, Jerry Tomal, Marv Burdick, and James White. (Visitation Catholic School and Parish Archives.)

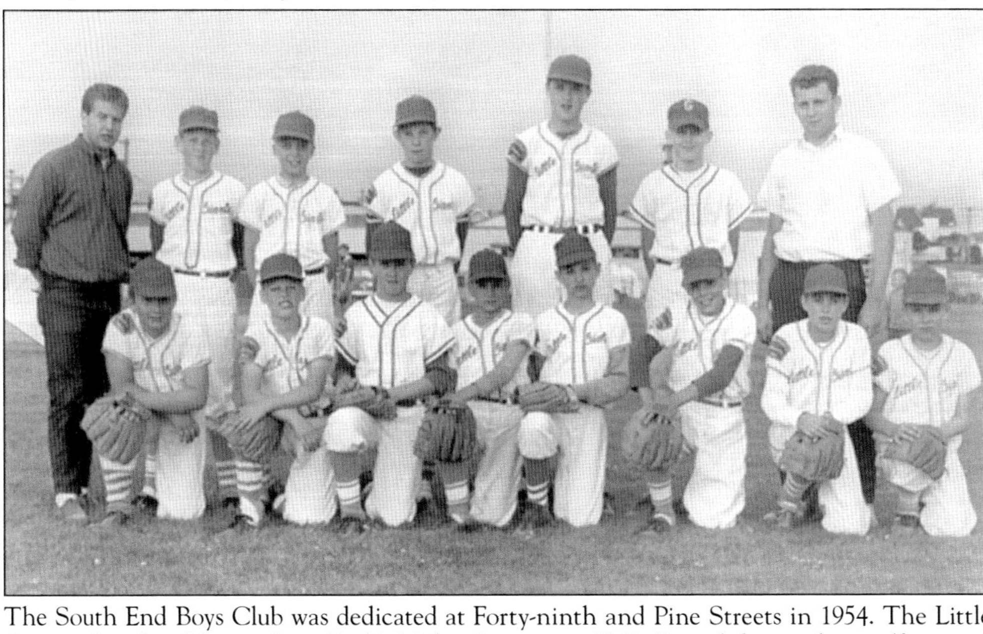

The South End Boys Club was dedicated at Forty-ninth and Pine Streets in 1954. The Little Giants played in Metropolitan Park's Midget League in 1963. From left to right are (first row) Art Kercher, Tim Burns, Hugh Lakin, Mike Halco, Bill Staab, Blayne Leingang, Ben Durance, and Gil Rouse; (second row) Fred Brown (coach), Rick Guild, Dave Wright, Gary Lakin, Dennis Hanson, Kerry Reed, and Lew Overbo (coach). (South End Boys and Girls Club.)

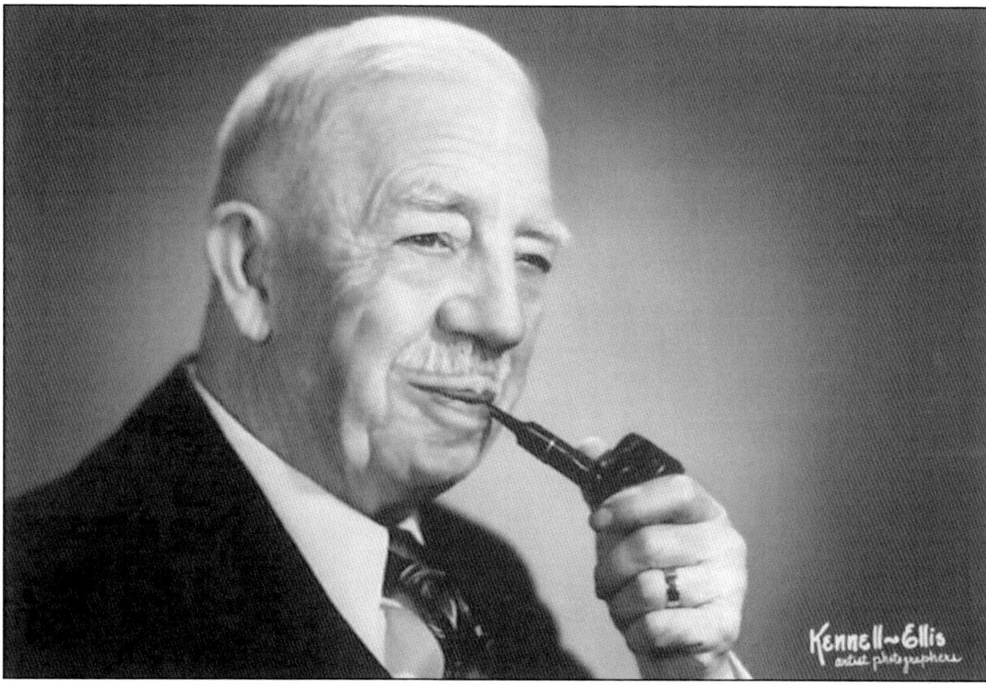

South Tacoma's Mason Clover Lodge, at 5405 South Puget Sound Avenue, began nearby in 1892—the same year, clover blossom was nominated as the official Washington State flower. It lost to the rhododendron. In 1955, Worshipful Master Killian Weiler, 1909–1910, is shown smoking a pipe. Ironically an excerpt from the lodge's January 1913 minutes states, "M.S.&C. that smoking be prohibited during sessions of the Lodge." (History of Clover Lodge No. 91, Harold O. Harris P.M., 1964.)

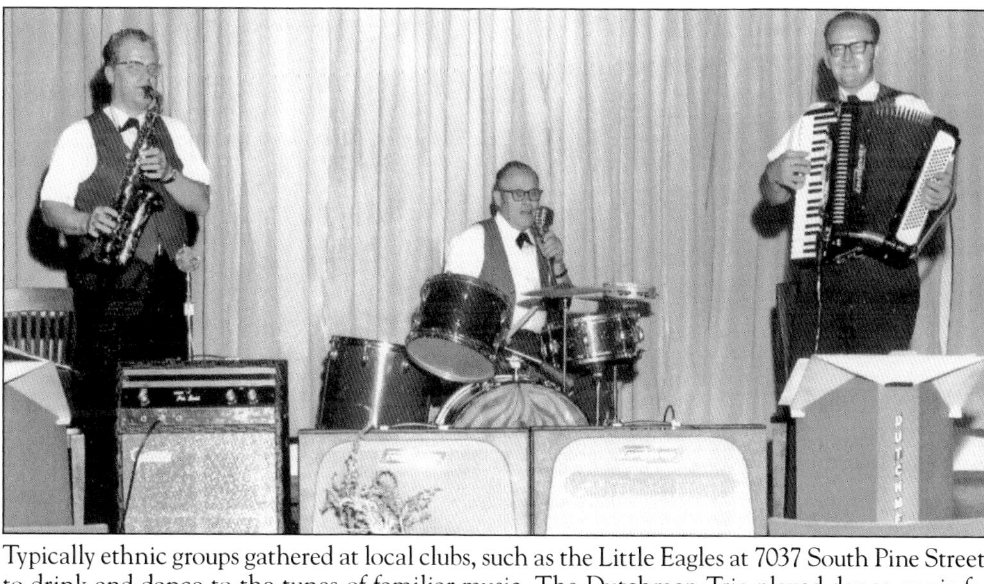

Typically ethnic groups gathered at local clubs, such as the Little Eagles at 7037 South Pine Street, to drink and dance to the tunes of familiar music. The Dutchmen Trio played dance music for Germans and Scandinavians, many from North Dakota, to socialize and celebrate weddings or birthdays. Band members are, from left to right, Sparky Leingang, John Reiter, and Luke Reis. (Luke and Patty Reis.)

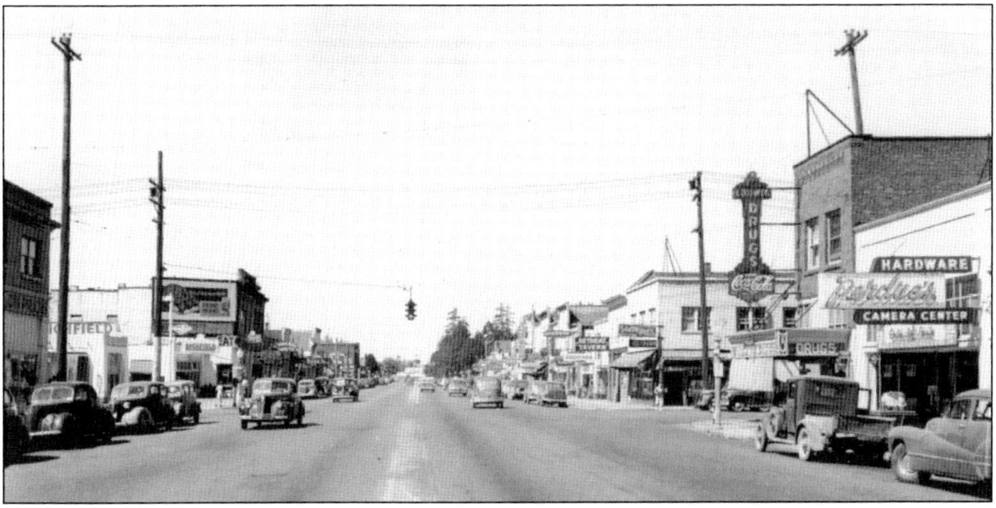

In 1953, South Tacoma Way was packed with a variety of businesses. Looking north at Fifty-fourth Street those identified are, from left to right, Richfield Gas Station, Steve's Café, and Western Auto Supply. Across the street are, from left to right, a laundry, Main Yon Restaurant (previously known as the Main Yon Café), Washington Electric, radio and furniture stores, Retreat Tavern, Savon Drugs/Ice Cream, Ludwig Drug, and Perdue's Camera Center. (Eric Swanson collection.)

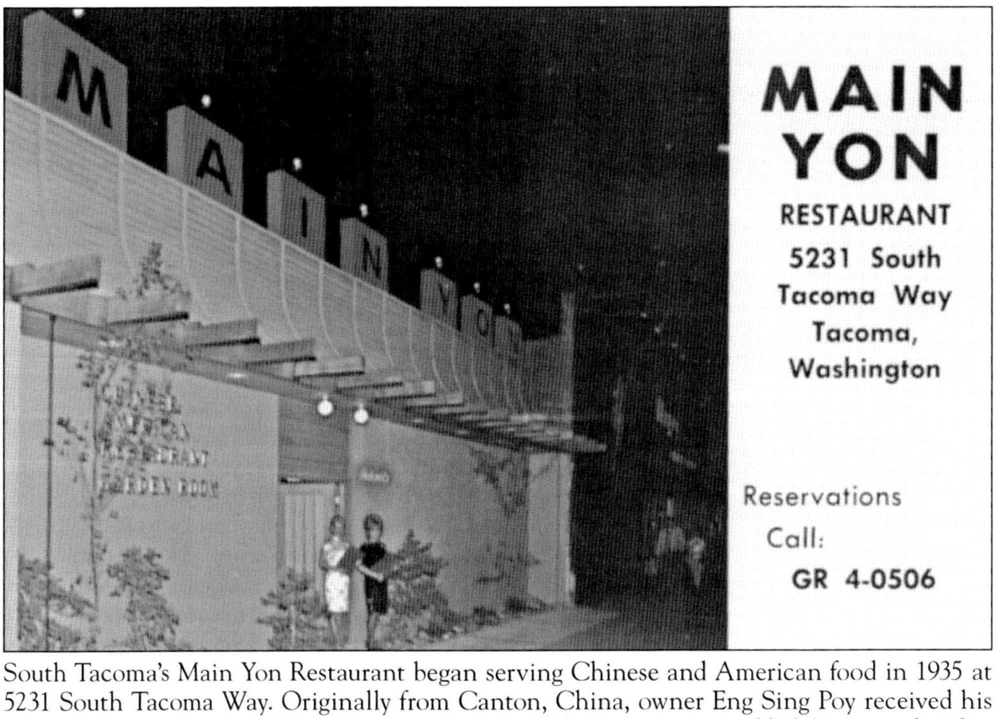

South Tacoma's Main Yon Restaurant began serving Chinese and American food in 1935 at 5231 South Tacoma Way. Originally from Canton, China, owner Eng Sing Poy received his naturalization papers in 1951 at the same time a new dining room was added. Decorated with a Chinese-themed wall mural, the addition offered booth seating and take-out food. Two employees stand out front to greet diners around 1955. (Eric Swanson collection.)

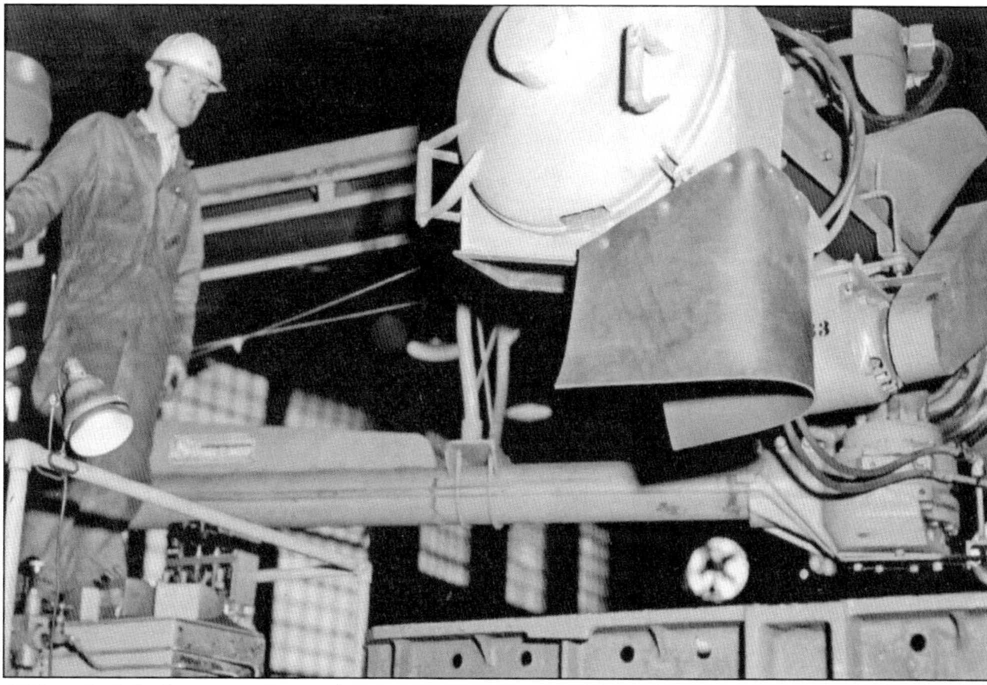

Although Atlas has moved into the computer age to control production, quality still ranks number one at the original South Tacoma location where it all began in 1899 with 20 men and a small foundry. The top image shows maintenance worker Eddie Nemchik in 1959 performing preventive maintenance on a sand slinger, which is used to blow sand into the molds. Below, in 1962, from left to right, molders Tom Kulvick, Eddie Maxfield, and Al Carver fill molds with sand from the sand slinger to ready the mold for the molder to compact the sand around a pattern—called "ramming a mold." (Atlas Castings and Technology.)

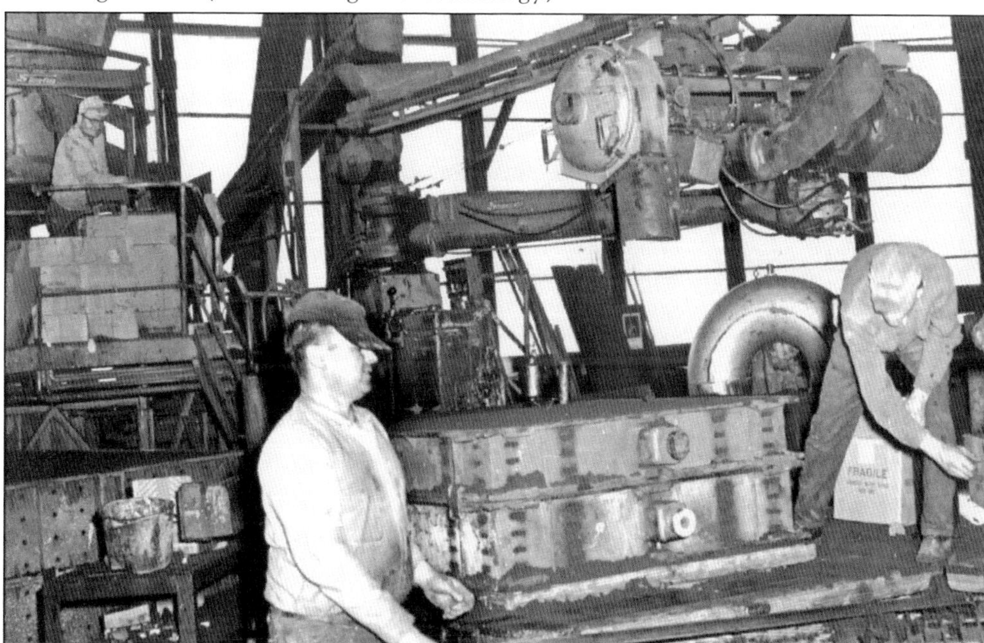

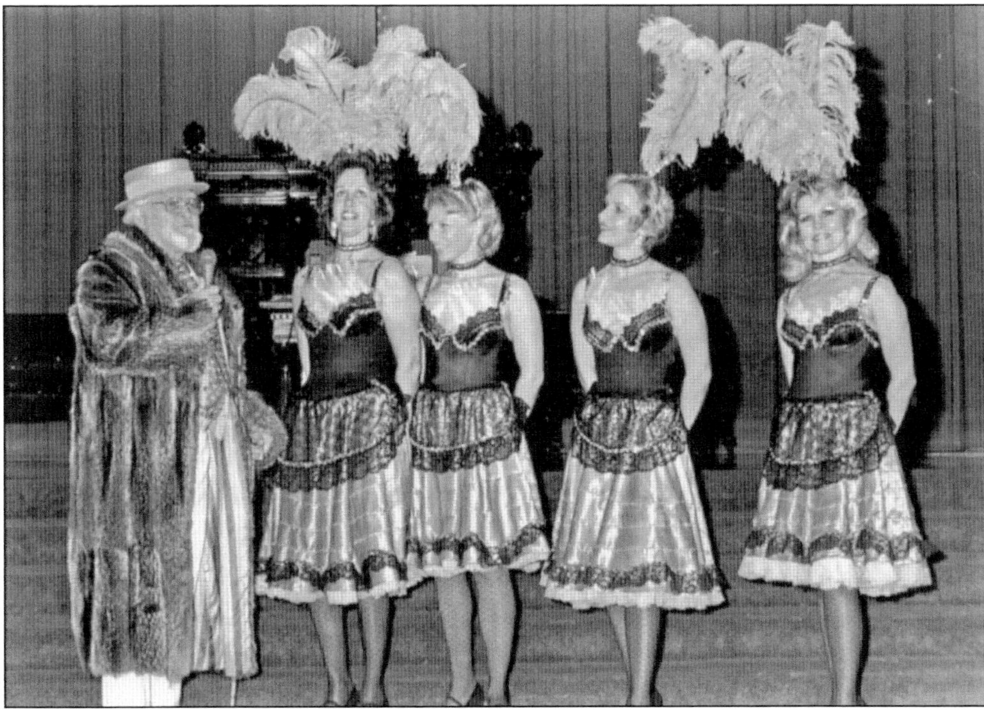

In 1955, twin sisters Connie and Callie Mernaugh went to Steve's Gay '90s for dinner. Owner Steve Pease, a born promoter, recognized the dancers, who had performed before, and asked them to return. The group who danced the can-can became regular entertainment, often teaming with other dancers. Pease, in a full-length fur coat, introduces, from left to right, Callie Mernaugh, Vicki Conner, Connie Mernaugh, and Hazelle Gjerde. (Connie, Callie, and Hazelle personal collections.)

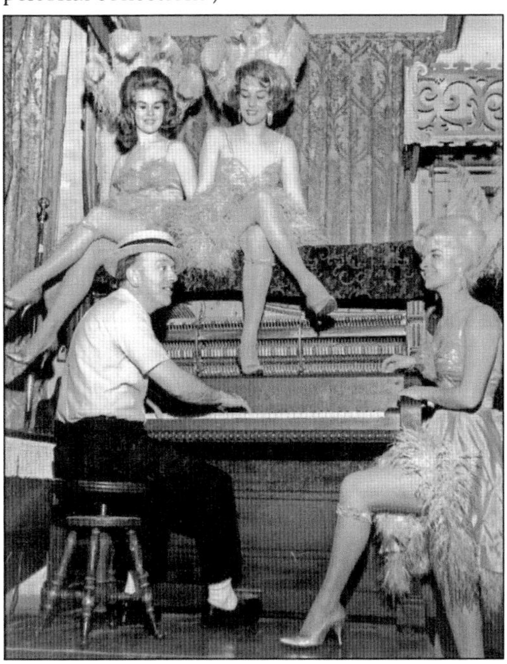

A log truck driver during the week, Bob Schonak donned a straw hat and entertained guests at Steve's Gay '90s on the weekends. The popular establishment was well known for its elaborate smorgasbord, cable-car seating, and unique entertainment. Schonak is joined at the piano bar by several dancers; from left to right are Hazelle Gjerde, Callie Mernaugh, and Connie Mernaugh in 1964. (Connie, Callie, and Hazelle personal collections.)

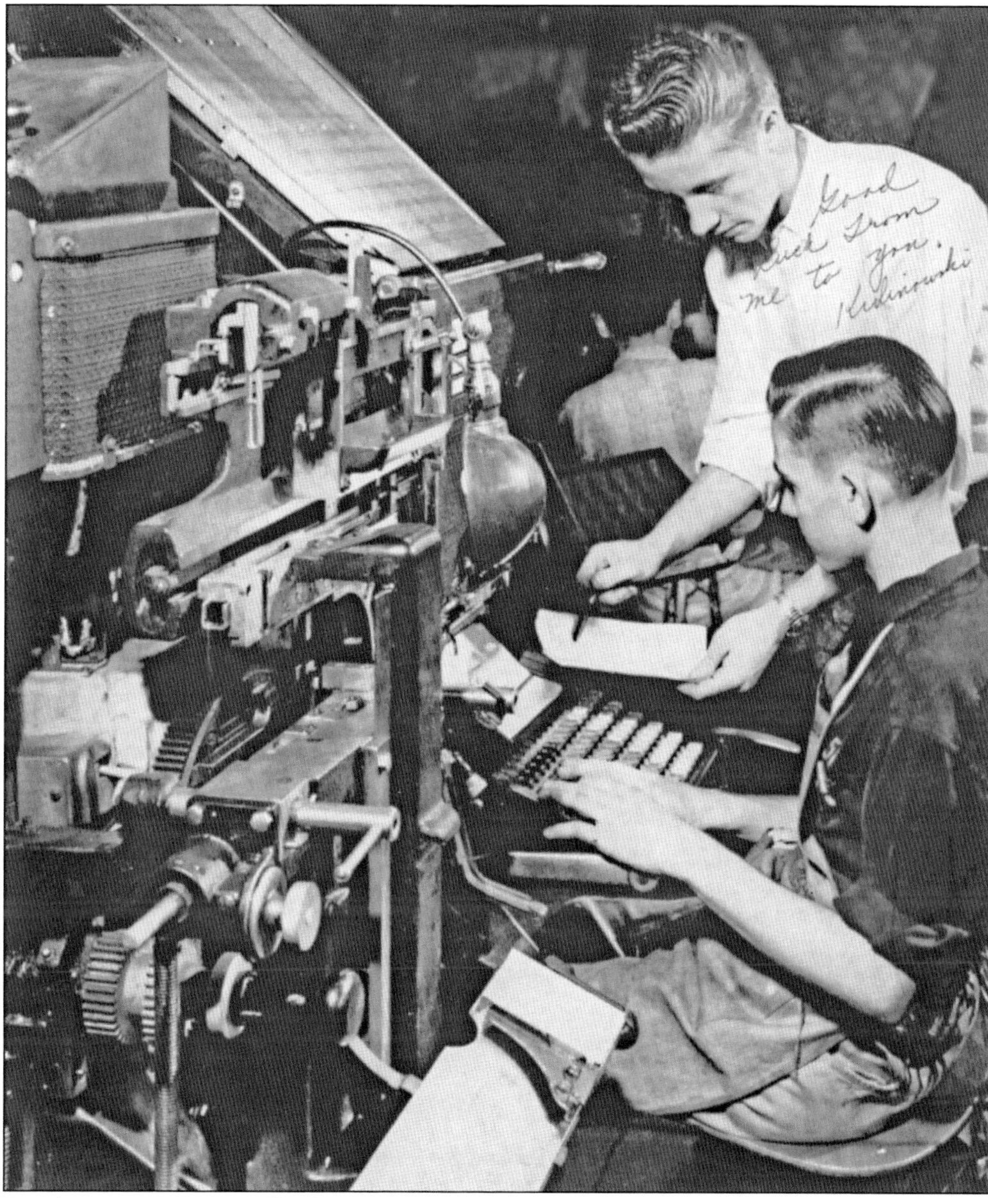

For the past 60 years, Pollard Group, from their South Tacoma plant, has provided printing services in the Puget Sound area. In 1960, Art Daniels is seated at a Linotype machine receiving instructions from an unidentified teacher. The composition system Daniels is learning sets lead type in lines as he punches the corresponding keys. The lead lines are locked in a frame to create multiple lines of type that become sentences, paragraphs, and stories—a process called casting. The frames are loaded into an offset letterpress machine, where ink is rolled over the type. The offset process occurs as ink on the type is released onto the paper through pressure. This manual process required a new piece of paper placed over the type for each copy. Linotype machines were discontinued in the 1990s, when lithography took over the industry. Art Daniels retired from the Pollard Group after an impressive 37-year career. The Pollard Group is located at 4824 South Tacoma Way, where 42 print professionals continue to serve the area. (Rob Pollard, Pollard Group, Inc.)

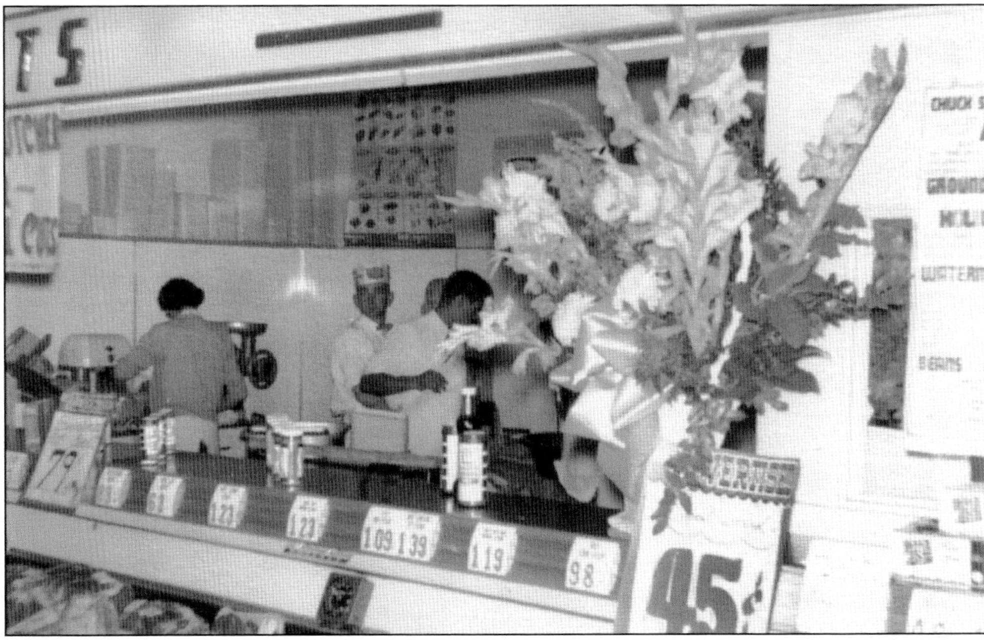

Three South Tacoma family members work at the newly opened Harry's Fine Foods at 3807 Center Street, where Harry A. Hendrixson opened a new Shop-Rite in 1958. From left to right, meat wrapper Rose Marie (Hazen) Treaton and her brother, butcher Michael Hazen, work with their nephew, meat wrapper Jimmy Hazen. (Hazen family.)

FOOD AND BEVERAGE SERVICE WORKER'S PERMIT No. 48418

Rose Treanton — Signature of Worker
Meat Wrapper — Occupation

2520 So. 41st — Home Address

THIS CERTIFIES THAT

Treanton, Rose

has satisfied the requirements of the

TACOMA - PIERCE COUNTY Health Dept.

and State Board of Health for issuance of permit

MANUAL CHAPTERS COVERED IN TEST:

1 2 3 4 5 6 7 8 9 10 11 12 13 14 15 16

SEP 7 1963 — Permit expires
C.R. Fargher, MD — Health Officer

PLEASE NOTE: This card is valid only to the employee whose signature appears on the reverse side. It must be filed at place of employment, or carried by said employee and shown upon request to sanitarian, health officer or deputy.

INSTRUCTIONS GOVERNING PERSONAL HYGIENE AND SANITATION

1. DO NOT WORK if you are ill with a "catching" sickness, such as sore throat, common cold, diarrhea or other contagious disease.
2. NOTIFY THE HEALTH DEPARTMENT if you, or any person in your home or your place of business, has a contagious disease or a disease suspected of being contagious.
3. Keep your hands and finger nails clean. Wash your hands frequently particularly every time after going to the toilet, blowing the nose or handling soiled objects.
4. Use disposable tissue for blowing the nose or spitting. Spitting can be a dangerous habit.
5. Do not pick pimples, boils or your nose. This is a dangerous source of infection. If you have sores of this kind, keep them covered with a dressing.
6. Handle foods with your fingers as little as possible. Use utensils whenever you can, as in picking up butter, etc.
7. Avoid handling rims of glasses, cups, soup bowls and eating surfaces of silver.
8. Protect food by keeping it covered from flies, keeping perishable foods and cream-filled pastries properly refrigerated.

A Food and Beverage Worker Permit from the local health department was a means of protecting the public from illnesses transmitted from improperly handled foods. Rose Treaton covered chapters one through eight to satisfy requirements set by the State Board of Health. The certificate is signed by Dr. C. R. Fargher, health officer. (Hazen family.)

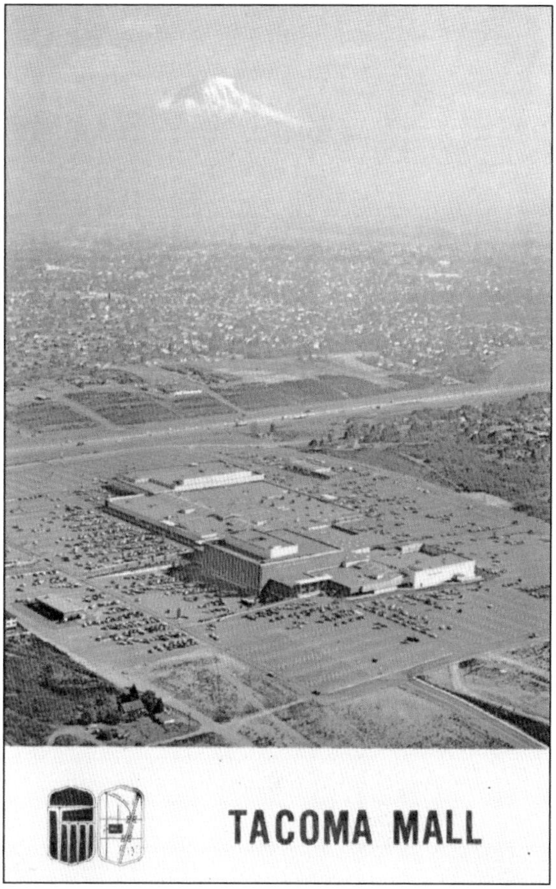

Life changed in South Tacoma with the opening of the Tacoma Mall in October 1965. Homes and farmland became the first enclosed shopping center in the Pacific Northwest. Dubbed the "most modern shopping center in the nation," the mall opened with 55 stores and gained an additional 17 stores by the end of the first year. The opening-day event enticed a multitude of people to see the new environs and experience the utmost in shopping. Tacoma Mall brought to South Tacoma stability in employment just before the railroad shops closed, which had been the major impetus for the development of South Tacoma 75 years earlier. (Right, Thomas R. Stenger collection; below, Tacoma Mall/Simon Property Group.)

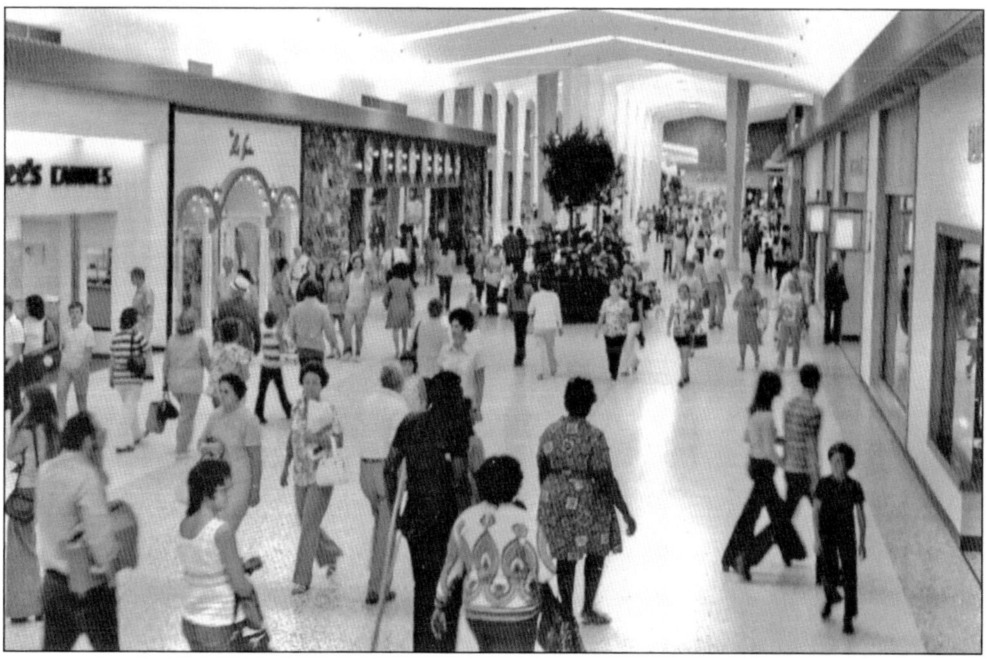

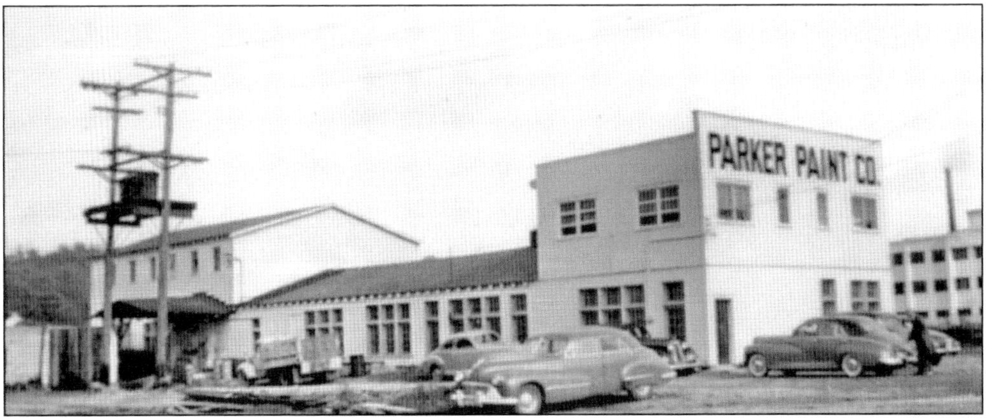

William J. and Eva Parker honeymooned while traveling from New Jersey to Tacoma in the 1920s. Mr. Parker, a painting contractor, helped paint the first Narrows Bridge in 1940 and disapproved of the paint used. Parker partnered with chemist George Martin and began manufacturing Parker Paint by 1945. Parker's paint is on the current Narrows Bridge, the Space Needle, Oregon Convention Center, and many buildings and bridges in the area. Parker's son, Bill, worked in the Nalley Valley plant at age 11, managed the business as an adult, and is shown around 1976 conferring with Martin and his mother, president of the company. The family sold the business in 1982. (Parker family.)

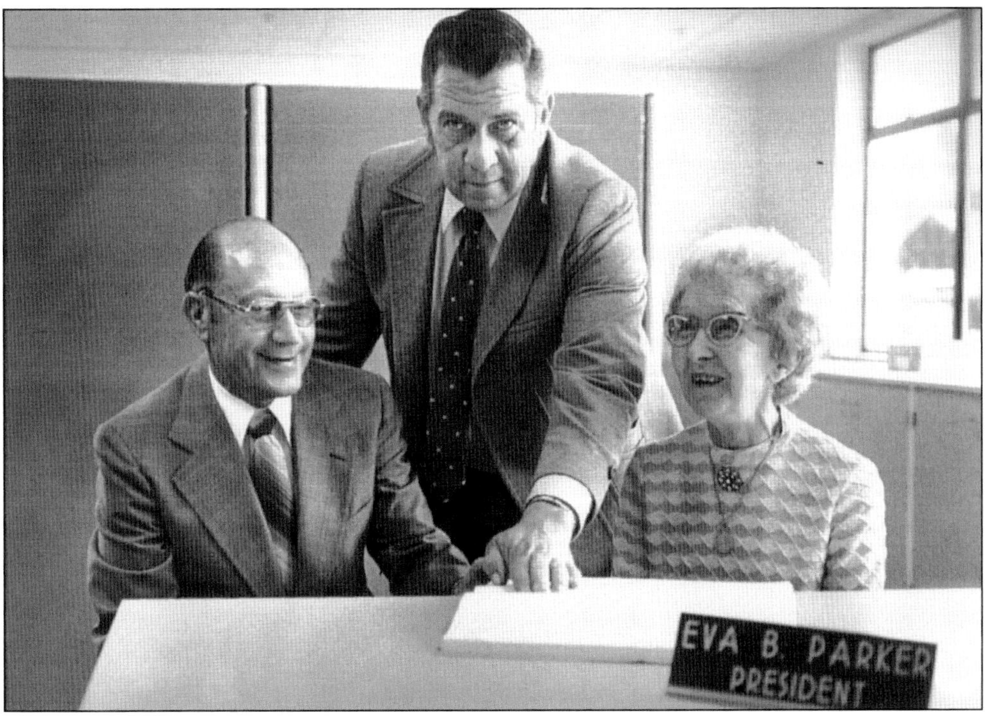

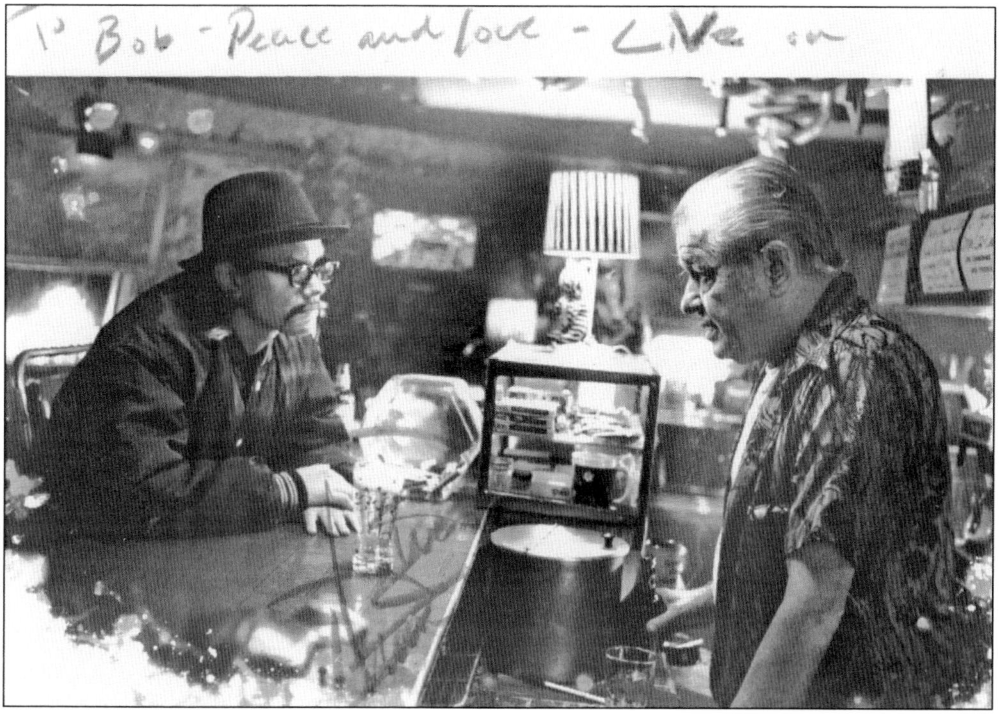

The Coffee Pot handle no longer points to the "Mom" and "Pop" outhouses, but the added Jungle Room houses pool tables and half a century of memories. In 1989, Java Jive served as a backdrop for the movie *I Love You to Death*, and owner Bob Radonich became friends with River Phoenix, who signed this photograph of the two conversing over the bar at Bob's Java Jive. (Bob's Java Jive.)

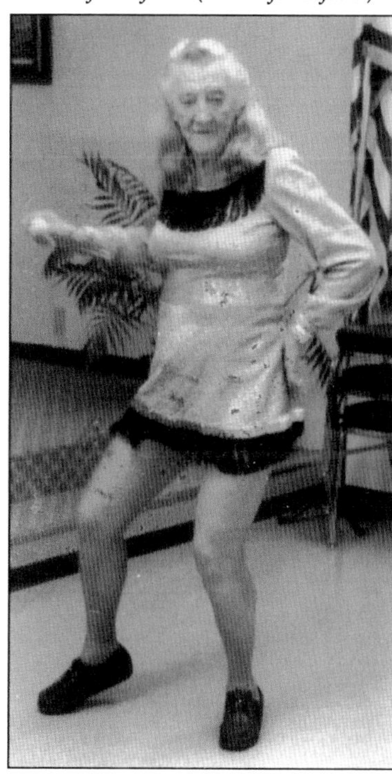

As a music club, Bob's Java Jive featured local entertainers and unique floor shows. The 1960s group the Ventures performed at the Java Jive prior to national recognition. Chimpanzees Java and Jive banged on a drum in the back room. Granny Go-Go (née Sylvia Eads) entertained at the Java Jive well into her eighth decade of life. (Darnell Porter.)

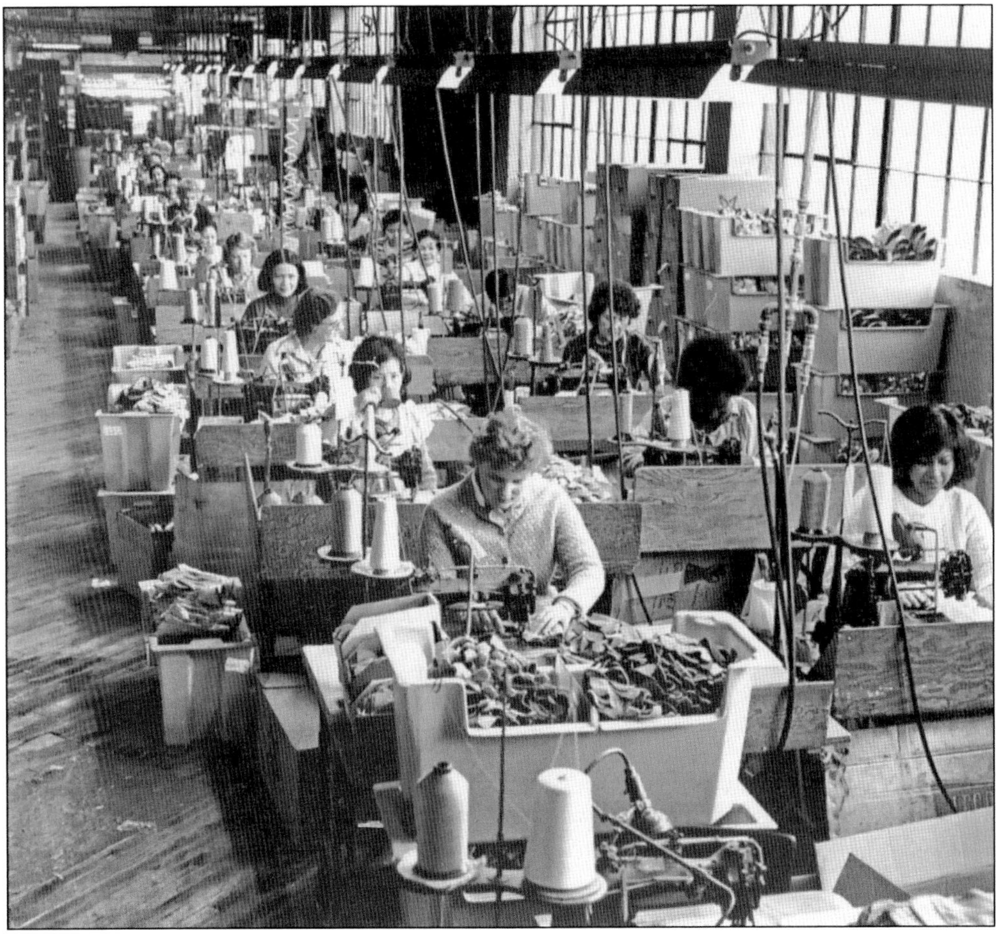

North Star Glove employees sew gloves in 1983 on machines made specifically for the product's heavy—stamped and cut—canvas material. Identified from front to back are (left row) Jane Wekell, Kil Sun, Bunnie Rose, Hahn Diep, Diane Andrews, unidentified, Jo White, Theresa Frasl, Lillian Noel, Pat Ferriera, and Doris North; (right row) Mariann Cumber, Mattie Williams, Florence Piper, unidentified, Mary Hieu Le, unidentified, and Chong Shelton. (North Star Glove Company.)

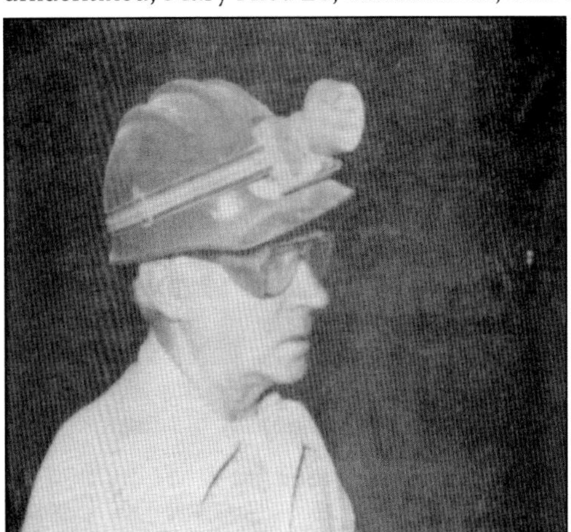

During his 30-year career at Atlas Foundry, Erwin Werner spent many hours inside a dark ladle. Determined there must be a better way to provide light than holding a flashlight in one hand while working the chipping gun with the other, Werner took initiative. In 1987, the light literally went on in Werner's head when he strapped a miner's light onto a hard hat. (Lorraine Werner.)

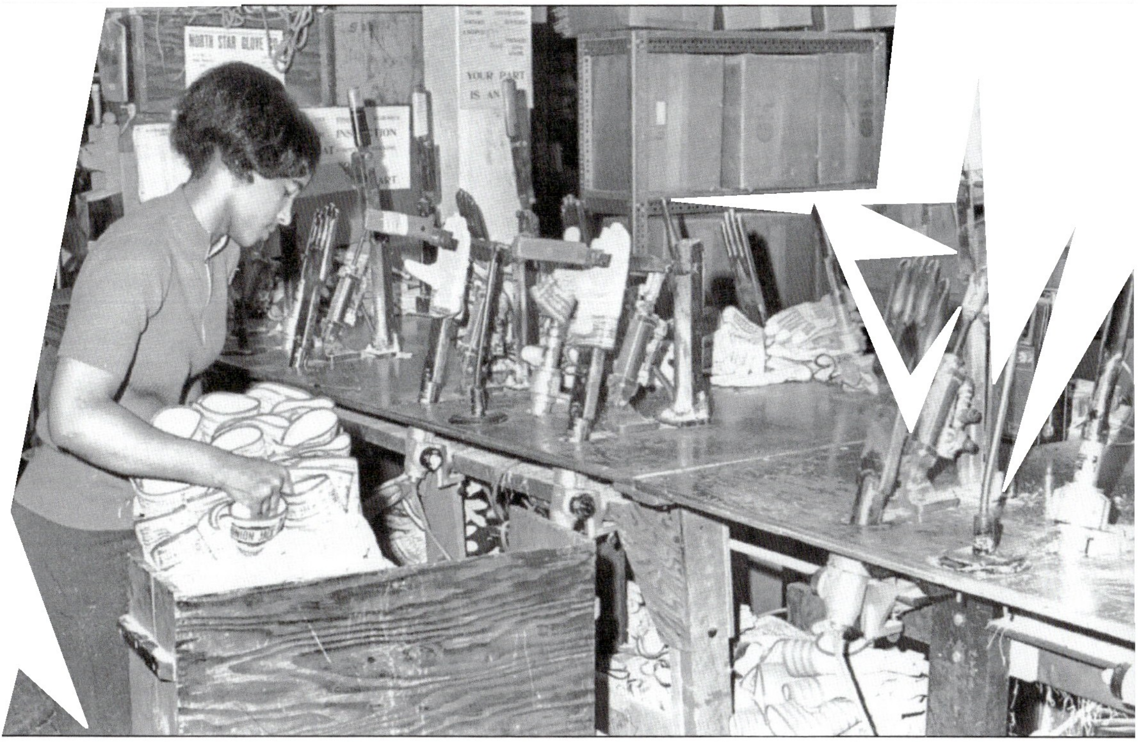

In 1910, Albert Wekell gave birth to North Star Manufacturing Company, making "100% USA made" canvas gloves in Tacoma, Washington, for the local working man. In 1963, the downtown operation combined with the Orting production line, and the company moved to Nalley Valley. Stella Eason (Lymas) works on the hot forms in 1973 to iron out leather gloves that have been turned right side out after being sewn. Stella left North Star Glove for a few years and returned to work in the leather-cutting department. In the shadowy background on the left, wearing a white smock and using a hand truck, former shipping clerk Elwood Edwards moves boxes of gloves ready for shipment from the finishing area to the warehouse. Edwards worked for North Star from 1947 through 1974. North Star Glove continues to make gloves in the United States. (North Star Glove Company.)

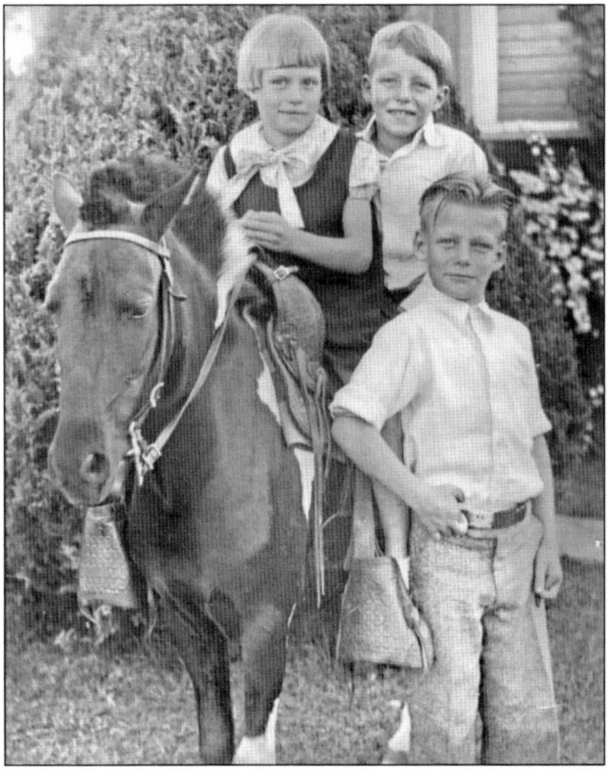

Horses and cowboys have played a role in the South Tacoma Haller family for multiple generations. As the Great Depression spread, itinerant photographers traveled to towns across America with camera and pony in tow looking for a family able to pay for a picture of their children with the photographer's pony. In 1936, Ray and Alice Haller paid $1 for a photograph of Darlene, George, and Max, (standing) by the family home at 4704 Sixty-second Street. Ray and Max built their home, which still stands today in the Manitou neighborhood. (Max and Amelia Haller.)

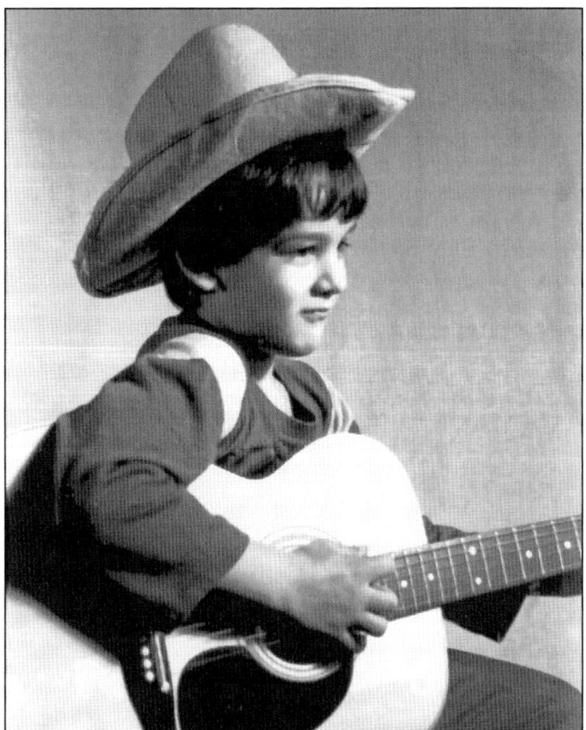

Years later, Max Haller's grandson Jason Jacobson wears a cowboy hat and strums the guitar. (Max and Amelia Haller.)

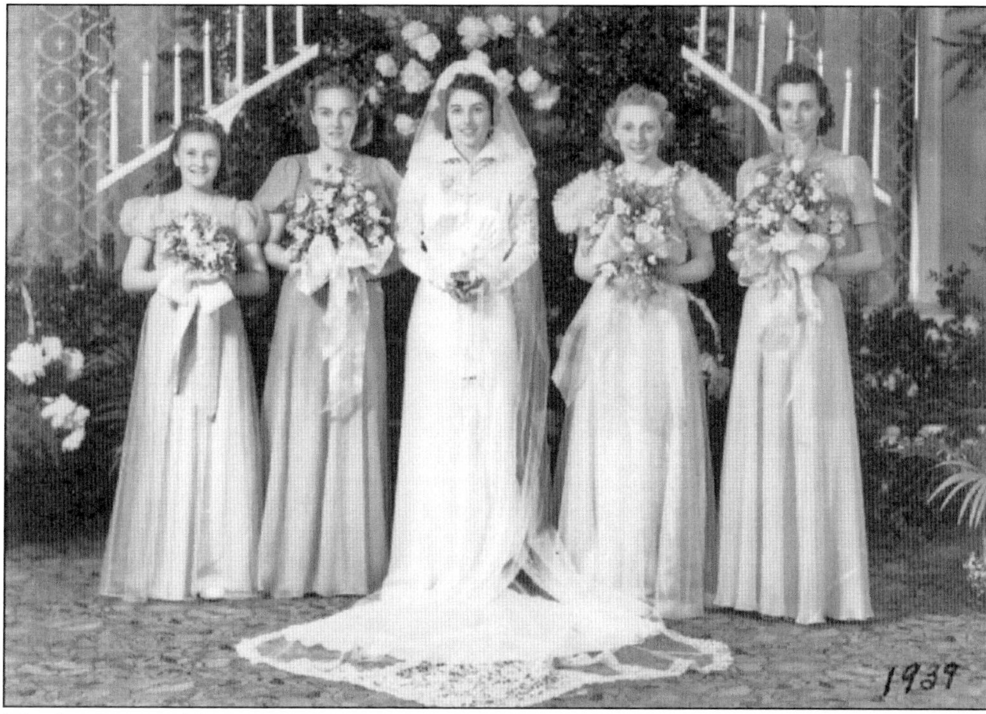

The family resemblance is obvious in two photographs taken 21 years apart. South Tacoma Harkness family and business owners celebrate two generations in two events. In 1939, Dorothy Mitchell married Jim Harkness, son of the Harkness Rug Company founders, James Sr. and Margaret Harkness. Amid generous bouquets of flowers from Cliff's Flowers, Dorothy is attended by, from left to right, Jeanne Mellish, Doris Aigner, Delores Grigal, and Marion Harkness. At right, Jim and Dorothy's daughter, Diane, grew up at 7022 South Puget Sound Avenue and attended Arlington Elementary, Gray Junior High, and Lincoln High Schools. Diane, representing Lincoln, was selected as Daffodil Festival Queen in 1960 and crowned by Gov. Albert D. Rosellini. (Above, Dorothy Harkness personal collection; right, Diane Harkness Conner, Lee Merrill photograph.)

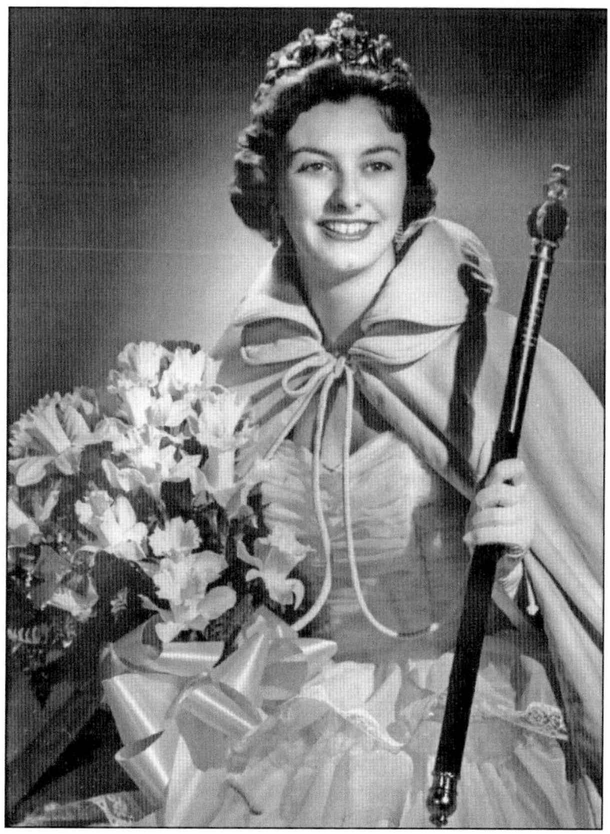

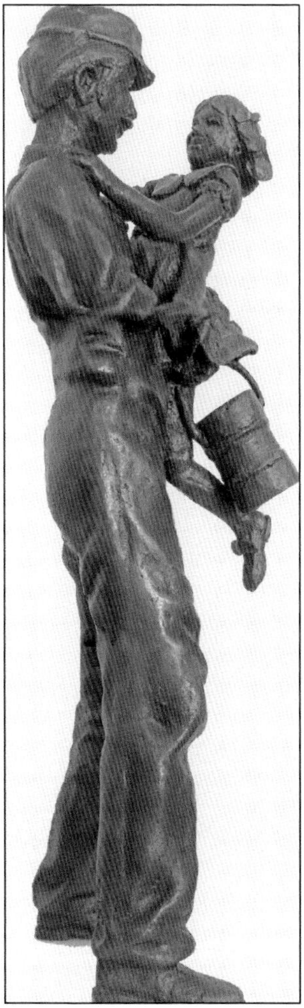

Public art abounds in South Tacoma. Larry Anderson's bronze sculpture (left) depicts a railroad worker greeted by his daughter as he returns home from work at the railroad shops. It was installed in 1984 at 5446 South Tacoma Way. In 1987, to honor North Pacific Bank's early relationship with Northern Pacific Railway, Paul Cislo was commissioned to paint a 114-foot mural (below) on the site of the bank's parking lot at 5423 South Washington Street. The weather took its toll, and it was replaced in 1998 with a similar-themed mural by Mary Mann. Additional public art is found throughout the neighborhoods. (Peter K. Wallerich.)

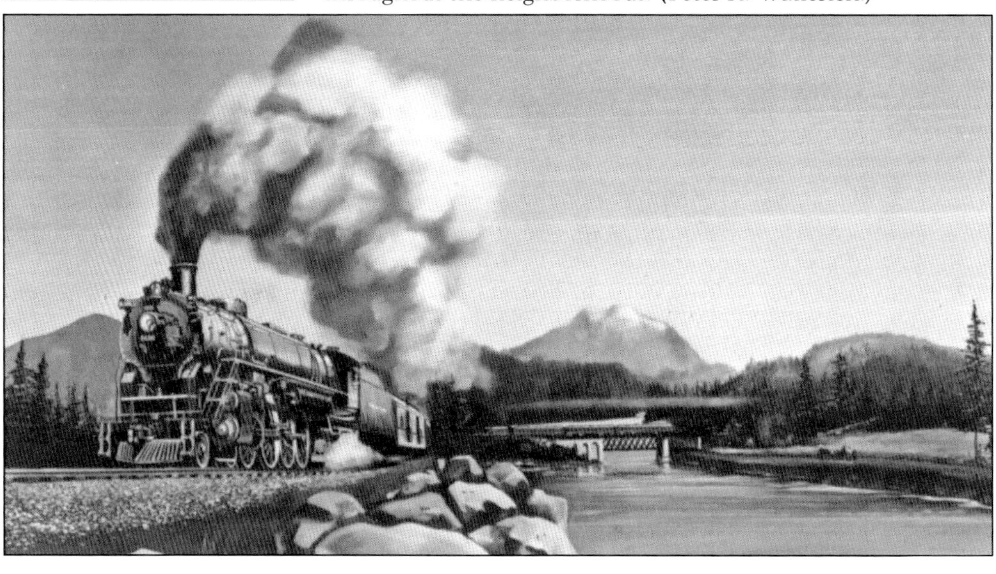

Consistent with our mission to preserve history on a local level, this book was printed in South Carolina on American-made paper and manufactured entirely in the United States. Products carrying the accredited Forest Stewardship Council (FSC) label are printed on 100 percent FSC-certified paper.

MADE IN THE USA

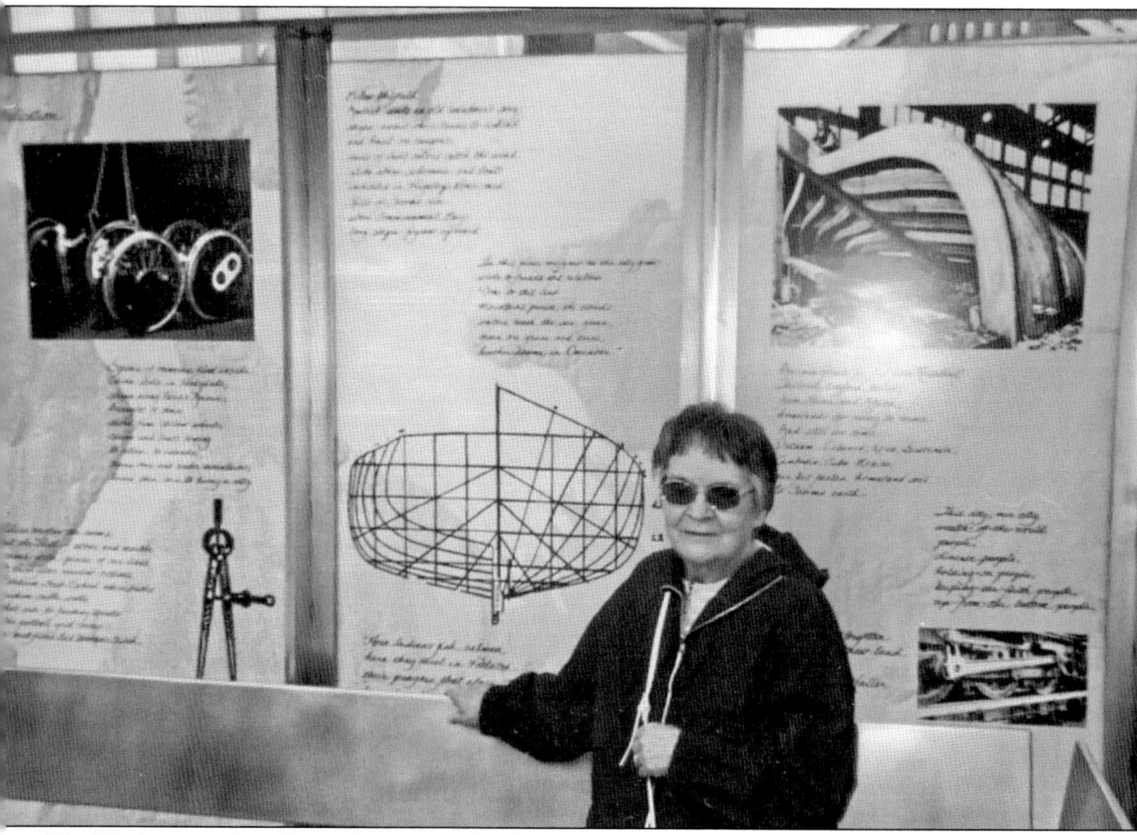

The Washington State Poets Association holds an annual contest for members only. In 1984, the theme was "Washington History." Amelia Haller, president of the association, won first prize for her poem "Even the Hills Wait." The Hallers are a true South Tacoma family: Amelia's husband, Max, a second-generation South Tacoma resident, grew up in the Manitou neighborhood and attended South Tacoma schools. The Hallers' children attended Edison Elementary and Gray Junior High. In their home at 6002 South Fife Street, Amelia Haller has written and published eight books of poetry. Amelia's 51-line poem "Dedication" is part of a public art display at the Tacoma Link Union Station platform. As South Tacoma moves forward in the 21st century, the community connects with its past with a new Sounder train station, soon to open between South Fifty-sixth and Sixtieth Streets. Eighteen trains a day will stop there, within a few blocks of the original South Tacoma station that closed in 1965. (Max and Amelia Haller.)